The Power of

Sex

The Irresistible Force

The Sex & Marriage Manual

Waltere Asili Koti

Copyrights

ISBN: 978-1-959251-13-2

Library of Congress Control Number: 2023904852

Front cover image by Expert Book Publishing
Book cover design by Expert Book Publishing
Proofreading, Editing and Formatting by Expert Book Publishing
Printed in the United States of America
First printing edition 2023.
Author : Waltere Asili Koti

Publisher: KOTIBOOKS

Visit us online: www.walterekoti.com

Other books by this author: Fending Off Suicidal Thoughts; You are Elected; Understanding Your Emotions; Handling Changing Emotions

Table of Content

Dedication

The proceeds from this book and other books that I have written will be used to advance the building of God's kingdom on Earth. To that end, we dedicate the pages of this book to widows and orphans across the world but particularly, those in Cameroon. We are currently sponsoring several orphans in Cameroon by providing food, shelter, tuition, and accommodation.We are in the planning stages to increase our support and care for more orphans. The plight of orphans is a desperate one. Children as young as six years old are abandoned to fend for themselves.

No food to eat, nowhere to sleep, and no one to provide guidance. At least, in the western world, a support network exists to provide care but in most other countries, such support falls on the shoulders of the family. We provide support to several families but this one stands out: A young single mother suddenly died and left three kids and no father or extended family to provide care and support. Another mother died and left four kids, and we arranged for a family to take in one of the kids while the other three stayed with their biological father. This one was a true orphan, no mother or father. Join the fight as the task is huge. As Edmund Burke once said, "The only thing necessary for the triumph of evil is for good men to do nothing."

If you are moved by this quote, then do something -,anything. According to a U.N. report, as of about 2019, Cameroon has about 900,000 displaced persons,of which 51 percent are children. Without family, children as young as six are on their own. Proceeds from this work will be used to support such orphan children.. The issue of orphans is not unique to Cameroon, It is a global issue. The most dire example is the current situation in Ukraine, which has left children homeless and abandoned. Other heart breaking similar situations of this, is what is happening in Haiti and many other countries around the world.

Introduction

Sex is an irresistible force and very few ever possess the ability to withstand its wrath. Its power is pleasurable, but it can also destroy each and everything in its path when misused. Sex is both enjoyable and destructive. Sex brings fulfillment and displeasure. This is the most joyous act on earth, but can also be the most destructive. Kings, presidents, and queens have enjoyed sex or have been humbled and humiliated through the power of sex. Sex can be used for good or for ill. The most powerful men,and sometimes women,in the world are easily humbled and humiliated by a very beautiful young woman or man through the power of sex. The rational thinking of the powerful and well-connected are easily disabled through the power of sex.

This is an innate and unstoppable force that disables the bravest of men, and sometimes, women. Sex is on the minds of just about every human being but few dare to openly talk about it. Sex permeates our entire existence, such that all we do centers around sex. No one wants to admit it but we constantly think about sex and that is why, even though our dressing and clothing are primarily to cover our bodies, they have steadily become a means to impress and attract the opposite sex, with sex in mind.

Sex is the apex of pleasure and for a majority of the people on the planet, there is nothing that even comes close to sex. The force that draws or attracts two people of opposite sexes to be drawn to each other is an unstoppable force. This force of attraction is beyond explanation and reason. People who are drawn by these forces lose any semblance of rational thinking;all logical reason is overcome by this irresistible force. People do really wild and crazy stuff in the

7

name of sex. People travel across the globe in search for sex and love. People run off to an unknown destination with someone that they just met, and know very little or nothing about them, all in the name of sex and love. Any sense or logic or reason is completely eradicated through the drawing power of sexual attraction.

Sex has the ability to be constructive or destructive, and that is why there is a lot of confusion in society today about the role of sex. This is the most important activity in anyone's life; and yet, very little is known about it. Parents seldom talk with their teenage children,who are about to enter into the world and go to college, about the most important activity in their lives. Truth be told, parents can only pass on what they themselves know, and so it is no surprise that children know absolutely nothing about sex because parents, most likely, know nothing or very little about sex themselves. As it is often said, "An apple does not fall far from the tree." Children are suddenly thrown into the world to figure things out for themselves. And the results of the society at large is very evident. Society is dealing with sexual chaos and confusion. Everyone is doing whatever is right in their own eyes.

The advent of technological advances, like the internet and cell phones, has exponentially exposed the problems of sexual promiscuity. These advances did not cause these promiscuous activities but only magnified or exposed what was already there. And here is a quote on this: *A major reason for the increased incidence of sex addiction is the rise of the internet, and therefore, cybersex. Today, anyone can access sexually graphic material with a few clicks. Sex chat rooms and dating and hookup apps enable people to quickly and easily locate others looking for sexual encounters. This instant gratification can feed into addictive habits.*[1]

The human desire for promiscuity in sex is a larger societal problem than most are willing to admit. Those that are on the receiving end of a promiscuous partner are wounded emotionally and otherwise; sometimes, they are wounded permanently. And here is a quote on that: *Sex addiction can cause many problems within relationships, particularly for married or long-term monogamous couples. Often, someone with sex addiction will seek multiple partners outside their relationship. They may also frequently end up with financial problems from sexual gratification, which can cause significant tension with their spouse.* [2]

These desires for more and more sex wreak havoc in the lives of those on the receiving end of such behaviors. And the effects go far beyond physical problems, like financial and the likes; they also lead to severe emotional disruption: *Romantic partners, especially women, often suffer emotionally when they discover that their partner has a sex addiction or has committed infidelity. As many as 80% develop depression, while 60% develop eating disorders. Partners or people with sex addictions are also more likely to contract STIs, such as HIV or HPV.*[3]

[1]

https://www.therecoveryvillage.com/process-addiction/sex-addiction/sexual-addiction-statistics/

[2]

https://www.therecoveryvillage.com/process-addiction/sex-addiction/sexual-addiction-statistics/

[3]

https://www.therecoveryvillage.com/process-addiction/sex-addiction/sexual-addiction-statistics/

The destructive nature of sexual promiscuity is more rampant than this report suggests. Here is one more facts sheet: The number of people in the United States living with sex addiction is currently estimated at 12-30 million. Both men and women can be affected, though little research exists on female sex addiction. Men with sex addiction have an average of 32 sexual partners, while females have an average of 22 sexual partners. Sex and porn addiction often go hand-in-hand. Many people with sex addiction turn to porn to satisfy their desires. Many people with sex addiction say that they are dependent on porn and become distressed when they go for long periods without viewing it.[4]

These statistics are modest at best and it may not be an overstatement to conclude that lacking control over our sexual desires and thoughts is an innately human problem.

A new law just went into effect in the state of Louisiana, requiring its residence to verify their age before using an app or visiting and any porn website, and here is the quote: A new state law (PDF, courtesy of Motherboard) went into effect on January 1st, requiring websites containing "a substantial portion" of "material harmful to minors" to ask users to prove that they're 18 or older. "Substantial portion," according to the new law, is more than 33.3 percent of a website's content. As major porn sites have already started asking visitors to verify their age.[5] We are in a sad state of affairs as the world is sinking and sinking fast.

4

https://www.therecoveryvillage.com/process-addiction/sex-addiction/sexual-addiction-statistics/

5

https://www.aol.com/news/louisiana-government-id-to-access-porn-online-015313277.html

The case of sexual addiction is where the person simply lacks any restraints or controls over their sexual thoughts and impulses. Someone having 32 sexual partners for males and 22 sexual partners for females are clearly cases of out-of-control sexual desires. The baffling issue is to figure out the driving force behind these out-of-control sexual desires. These forces are so powerful, they overwhelm any human ability to restrain, and even the bravest of men or women are rendered impotent in the face of such an overwhelming power of sex. Kings, queens and presidents are simply rendered powerless over the onslaught of sexual impulses and desires.

This is not merely an American problem, but a global problem. This is clearly a problem with the human race. This issue is so huge that truly speaking, everyone born of a woman struggles to control themselves sexually. Anyone and everyone who is sincere and honest with themselves can admit that they struggle with impure thoughts concerning sex. The big difference is acting on those thoughts.

 Even those who are not addicts would admit that their thoughts about sex are not where they would like them to be. Yes, some may never act on those thoughts, but thoughts are always there towards that person in the office, at church, online, a neighbor, at a grocery store line, and so on. Over time, these thoughts have become normalized by the society at large. This book will seek to untangle the mystery of the power behind this irresistible force, and how this has shaped mankind from time immemorial. The million dollar question is how did it all happen?

Chapter 1

The Origin of Sex

The origin of sex is an intriguing and somewhat perplexing subject. We are talking about the origin of sex in the specific sense that refers to human beings as opposed to the general sense that refers to all beings. The simple and plain truth of the matter is that sex, as it relates to humans, has been around for as long as humans have existed. And by "sex," I am not talking about male or female gender issues, which of course is part of the discussion; I am mainly talking about sexual intercourse in the context of human beings.

Here is what Holly Dunsworth, associate professor of Anthropology at the University of Rhode Island had to say about the origin and evolution of sex: *But after the origins of sex, it took another 1.5 billion years for sexual intercourse -as we vertebrates know it- to come about. I'm talking about the kind of reproductive sex that humans and other mammals, as well as some birds, reptiles, amphibians, and fish, have- with an external male penetrating organ and an internal female reception area.*[6]

This professor from this prestigious university concluded two things: (1) sex occurred and then (2) sexual intercourse occurred 1.5 billion years after the occurrence of sex. But here is her response to the origin of sex: *There are multiple answers to the question of where we came from: early hominins, monkeys, primordial goo, or the Big Bang, to name a few. How in the evolutionary world did sex begin?*

---

[6]

https://www.sapiens.org/column/origins/sexual-evolution-pleasure/

Algae, the green gunk that runs amok in our fish tanks, as well as the seaweed that stinks up our summer beaches, include some of the simplest sexually reproducing organisms on earth. These lineages go back nearly 2 billion years. Algae do it. Plants do it. Insects do it. Even fungi do it. Much of this sex involves releasing sperm into the wind or the water so they can be carried to nearby eggs (as in mosses), relying on a different species to carry male gametes to female ones (many flowers or maneuvering two bodies so that the openings to the internal reproductive organs are close enough together for fluid exchange (most insects and most birds)). [7]

And in the context of this book, by intercourse, I am talking about humans, male and female. For sexual intercourse to exist, there must, out of necessity, be male and female components as parties to the act of intercourse. The professor above did not answer the question of the origin of intercourse but was explaining sex in the context of evolution. She is explaining sex to mean the process by which bacteria and other organisms mutate. The professor did not really explain the origin of intercourse but was only quoted as saying that intercourse occurred 1.5 billion years after sex.

This understanding about sex and intercourse is influenced by evolutionary thinkers. According to their understanding, bacteria were on the earth before any mammals were ever present. Believing in evolution leaves the reader with many unanswered questions:(1) Where did the bacteria originate from? (2) How and where did mammals, including man (meaning mankind), suddenly

---

[7]

https://www.sapiens.org/column/origins/sexual-evolution-pleasure/

appear? The origin of sexual intercourse cannot be fully understood in a vacuum; it has to be understood in the context of the origin of man. The question of where man came from is central to sex and sexual intercourse.

The Origin of Man

Where are we from and how did we get here? This is the foundational question on which all others rest. The origin of sex and intercourse in particular cannot be properly grasped without a firm understanding of man's origin. The answer to this question rests on many other answers to the human quest. Without truly understanding man's origin, we may end up with an erroneous understanding of why we are here, on Earth, and where we go from here after our time has expired. Many views have been advanced for the origin of man but because of the limited space allotted to us, we will place our attention on two views, namely: evolutionist and creationist views.

The Evolutionist View of the Origin of Man

The view that man evolved from some other creature into a human being is quite perplexing. This idea, supposedly called "the theory of evolution," raises an infinite number of questions instead of providing real answers. If man evolved from some other creature, then where did the original creature that began the process of evolution come from? The original creature did not just appear from nowhere! How did the sexes, male and female, evolve? How is it that the male and female bone structure is uniquely different? How do male and females procreate based on evolutionary theory? Can you imagine that your brand new vehicle that is parked in front of your house just happened to be there? No one really made it, but it just evolved over time and appeared in your driveway! Really? And if humans evolved, then according to evolutionists, sex must also have evolved?

Here is a quote by evolutionists on human evolution: The process by which human beings developed on Earth from now-extinct primates. Viewed zoologically, we humans are Homo sapiens, a culture-bearing upright-walking species that live on the ground and very likely first evolved in Africa about 315,000 years ago. We are now the only living members of what many zoologists refer to as the human tribe, Hominini, but there is abundant fossil evidence to indicate that we were preceded for millions of years by other hominins, such as Ardipithecus, Australopithecus, and other species of Homo, and that our species also lived for a time contemporaneously with at least one other member of our genus, H. [8]

This entry on human evolution began using carefully crafted words to describe what they call "human evolution," namely a process by which human beings on Earth developed from now-extinct primates. The word, "process," is used here to lay the groundwork for the argument that it was not instantaneous, but happened over time. And time is a valuable and indispensable component in the evolutionary argument for the origin of man. A lot of time must have evolved for species to mutate. There is little or no consensus for the amount of time needed for species to mutate into another species form. Some will throw out numbers like millions of years, and others even go into billions of years. There is no evidence of species mutating into a completely unrelated species and yet this hypothesis is widely believed,

---

[8]
https://www.britannica.com/science/human-evolution/Background-and-beginnings-in-the-Miocene

embraced, and even taught in our public schools as fact. Another word that is used in this article is,,"developed." This word is used in the context of " human beings developed on Earth from now-extinct primates."This word implies a progression, and it sits well with the evolutionary narrative, that humans achieved their being from some non-human being.

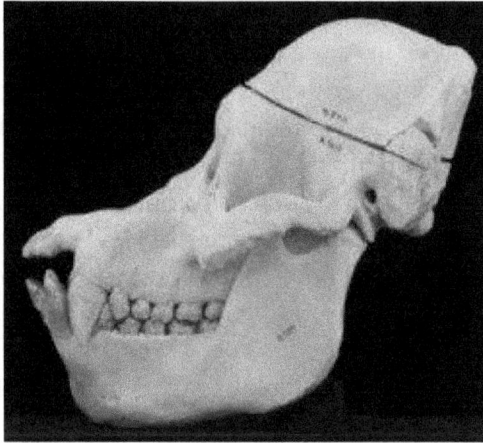

Orangutan Skull[9]

[9]

https://answersingenesis.org/human-evolution/ape-man/did-humans-really-evolve-from-apelike-creatures/

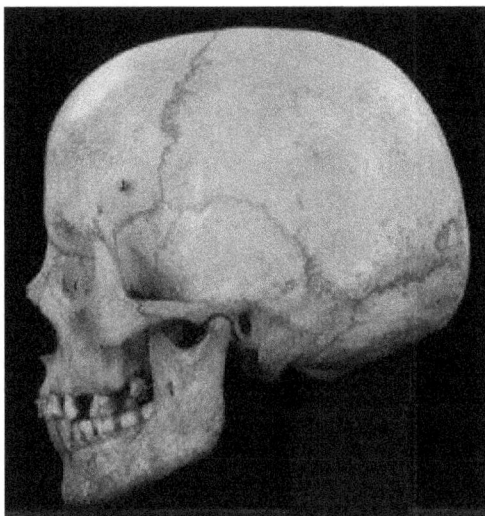

Human brain skull

The skull images above clearly demonstrate a differentiation between the human and the ape skull. The evidence is pretty clear that there is close to zero possibility that an ape skull could mutate into a human skull. Here is some commentary on that: *Perhaps the best way to distinguish an ape skull from a human skull is to examine it from a side view. From this perspective, the face of the human is vertical, while that of the ape, slopes forward from its upper face to its chin.* [10]

There is no evidence of a skull bone structure and design mutation. And here is what the author of this entry said: In addition, we and our predecessors have always shared Earth with other apelike primates, from the modern-day gorilla to the long-extinct Dryopithecus. That we and the extinct

---

[10]

https://answersingenesis.org/human-evolution/ape-man/did-humans-really-evolve-from-apelike-creatures/

17

hominins are somehow related and that we and the apes, both living and extinct, are somehow related is accepted by anthropologists and biologists everywhere. Yet the exact nature of our evolutionary relationships has been the subject of debate and investigation since the great British naturalist Charles Darwin published his monumental books, On the Origin of Species (1859) and The Descent of Man (1871). Darwin never claimed, as some of his contemporaries insisted he had said, that "man was descended from the apes."Just as they would dismiss any popular notion that a certain extinct species is the "missing link" between humans and apes.[11]

This entry is making the point that we humans and our predecessors (not sure who they are) have always shared the Earth with other apelike primates.The thrust of the argument here is that human beings evolved from some apelike being into humans over a long period of time, but no one knows for sure how long. The author of this entry is quoted above as coming to the defense of Charles Darwin by stating that Darwin never claimed that man was descended from the apes.

 This is a feeble attempt by defenders of Darwinism to backtrack on the central themes and arguments advanced by Darwin and his sympathizers. This is the central argument made in his book, "The Origin of the Species."This is what Darwinism is known for. When pressed and cornered to provide evidence for the primate that evolved into human, here is how they responded: *The ancient primate has not been identified and may never be known with certainty, because fossil relationships are unclear even within the human lineage, which is more recent. In fact, the human*

---

[11]   https://www.britannica.com/science/human-evolution

"family tree" may be better described as a "family bush," within which it is impossible to connect a full chronological series of species, leading to Homo sapiens, that experts can agree upon.

Adherents of Darwinism are desperately struggling to defend the indefensible. They are literally and figuratively speaking from both sides of their mouth.

Apelike creatures from which human supposedly evolved[12]

They are quoted above as saying that the ancient primate has not been identified and may never be known with certainty. This statement alone destroys the central arguments of Darwinism. Human beings evolved from some ancient primate, but such a primate has not – and may never – be identified. This is purely and simply a speculative hypothesis, lacking any evidentiary backing. Apes did not suddenly appear on the earth and become our ancestors. There must be some cause or origin of all things, including apes.

12

https://answersingenesis.org/human-evolution/ape-man/did-humans-really-evolve-from-apelike-creatures/

The First Cause Argument

The first cause argument argues that someone or some being is behind the cosmological created order. The heavens did not suddenly appear in the skies out of nowhere. The moon, sun, stars, sea, and the earth did not suddenly appear. The distance from the sun to the earth is precisely calculated and measured so that all created beings on the earth or sea do not freeze or scorch to extinction. Your car or house did not suddenly appear at your location.

Things do not suddenly appear out of thin air. Cause and effect are part of our daily lives. If there is an effect, then there must have been a cause. In the evolutionist's mindset, life forms evolve and mutate over time, but how did the original life forms come into existence before the genesis of the evolutionary process? In the context of the origin of sex, mankind cannot suddenly appear with its male and female sexual parts in place, for there must be a first cause. Charles Darwin and his proponents' answer to this happens to be the Big Bang theory, or some derivative of that.

Here is a report trying to explain evolution in light of the first cause arguments: A new study led by Adelaide researchers has estimated for the first time, the rates of evolution during the "Cambrian explosion" when most modern animal groups appeared between 540 and 520 million years ago. The findings, published online today in the journal "Current Biology," resolve "Darwin's dilemma," the sudden appearance of a plethora of modern animal groups in the fossil record during the early Cambrian period. [13]

---

[13]
https://www.sciencedaily.com/releases/2013/09/130912131753.htm

This report raises more questions than answers to the first cause debate. The report stated that animal groups appeared between 540 and 520 million years ago. The key word here is "appeared," and the logical question is, "appeared from where?" There was an explosion and out of the explosion, the animal groups appeared. If this was a true event, then who caused them to appear and where did they originate from? The explosion is somewhat implied here to be the first cause, but any logical person will not find that to be logically possible.

Here is what Thomas Aquinas, who was one of the most respected Catholic theologians and philosophers, had to say concerning the first cause argument: *In the world of sensible things we find that there is an order of efficient causes. There is no case known (neither, indeed, is it possible) in which a thing is found to be the efficient cause of itself; for if so it would be prior to itself, which is impossible. Now in efficient causes it is not possible to go on to infinity, because in all efficient causes following in order, the first is the cause of the intermediate cause, and the intermediate is the cause of the ultimate cause. Now to take away the cause is to take away the effect.*

Therefore, if there be no first cause among efficient causes, there will be no ultimate, nor any intermediate, cause. But if in efficient causes it is possible to go on to infinity, there will be no first efficient cause, neither will there be an ultimate effect, nor any intermediate efficient cause; all of which is plainly false. Therefore it is necessary to admit a first cause, to which everyone gives the name of God. [14]

[14]

https://www3.nd.edu/~jspeaks/courses/2020-21/10106/PDFs/2-1st-cause.pdf

Aquinas has laid out a skillfully crafted philosophical defense for the first cause argument by asserting that there is an "order of efficient causes". The implication here is probably that there are ordered causes as opposed to the Darwinian evolutionary theories of randomness. Causes are carefully orchestrated. Then he goes on to elaborate that that there is no known case for something to be the efficient cause of itself. It will be like a thing being the cause and effect to itself. It will be like a thing creating itself. Aquinas argued, "For so it would be prior to itself," to which Aquinas himself replied, "which is impossible." He proceeded to conclude,"Therefore it is necessary to admit a first cause, to which everyone gives the name of God".Aquinas made an outstanding philosophical apology for the first cause argument that leads perfectly into a theological defense for first cause and the creationist view for the origin of man.

The Creationist View for the Origin of Man

This chapter is about the origin of sex, meaning intercourse between human beings, male and female, to be precise. This subject cannot be fully understood in a vacuum, but has to be grasped in the context of a proper understanding of man and his origin. The argument here is that some being is behind the created order, and the notion of random selection or a Big Bang theory has been shown to lack support. For God to be the creator, He cannot be created, because if He is created, then He cannot be God. For a being to be the causation of the created order, such a being must stand outside of the created order.

Such a being is outside of time and is not bound by it. Such a being does not have a beginning of days nor end of life. Such a being is mentioned as the causation of all things created, visible and invisible: *In the beginning, God created the heavens and the earth,* Genesis 1:1.This verse is a summary statement of the creation order. Genesis 1:1 states what God created, and Genesis 1:2-31 details how He did it. The phrase "heaven" and "earth" is a Hebrew way of using extremities to express an all-inclusive idea. There is nothing beyond heaven and earth. And in verses 1-31, He detailed what is included in the heaven and earth expression. This includes the creation of all things, including man. The idea here is that man isn't the result of some random selection that suddenly occurred, or the evolution from some apelike primate over the span of millions or billions of years. Human beings came into being through the orderly orchestrated plan of an intelligent designer.

The human brain, and the whole body for that matter, is so complex that there is nothing like it in the universe. Here is an entry on the National Geographic website: Here's something to wrap your mind around: The human brain is more complex than any other known structure in the universe. Weighing in at three pounds, on average, this spongy mass of fat and protein is made up of two overarching types of cells called glia and neurons- and it contains many billions each.

Neurons are notable for their branch-like projections called axons and dendrites, which gather and transmit electrochemical signals. Different types of glial cells provide physical protection to neurons and help them, and the brain, stay healthy. The whole idea that man evolved from an ape-like primate is simply not supported by biology and scripture. This biological report identifies the complexity of the human brain as, "there is nothing like it in the universe".There is no similarity between the brains of apes to those of humans. God actually said: *Let us make man in our image, and our likeness, and let them have dominion over the fish of the sea, and over the fowl of the air, and over the cattle, and over all the earth, and over every creeping thing that creeps upon the earth.* Genesis 1:27.

This is the first time that the origin and creation of man is mentioned, and God identified Himself as the creator of man. This is hugely important because all attempts to pinpoint man's origin were hunting expeditions. The above text says, "Let us make man in our image, after our likeness." The word that is translated here as "man" comes from the Hebrew word "Adam" which means mankind in the general sense, or human beings in general, and does not mean "man" as in "male" in this context. This is the general word for humanity.

Then it proceeds to "making humanity in the image and likeness of God." It is very profound that humanity is made in the image and likeness of God. Man was the last of God's creation, and no other creature is made in the image and likeness of God. Man is distinct from animals in that some attributes of God have been bestowed upon man. God has graciously transferred to man some of His attributes, like: love, kindness, compassion, goodness, self-control, patience and others; these are found in man but are not found in any other created being. Man is the crown of God's created order.

Then the text says: *So God created man in his own image, in the image of God created he him; male and female created he them, Genesis* 1:27. The word, "created", has been used in this very verse three times, and that should tell us something when God uses the same word three times in a verse this short. This is the same word used in Genesis 1:1, when God created the heavens and the earth. When this word is used and God is the subject, then this word, in this context, means creating out of nothing.

Creation Ex Nihilo

Creation ex nihilo is a Latin phrase which means that God created man and the rest of creation out of nothing. This is very important information in the origin of man and sex debate. The evolutionist answer to the origin of man and the sexes is the Big Bang theory; even if there is such a thing as the Big Bang, the origin of the Big Bang was hardly addressed by Darwin or his proponents. Where did the Big Bang come from? Who caused the Big Bang (if it truly existed)? But creationists firmly and unequivocally assert that God created all things out of nothing.

Evolutionists could hardly wrap their heads around such a novel idea of something being created out of nothing. But Genesis 1:1 says," In the beginning God created the heavens and the earth." This one statement is sufficient to answer the question of the "genesis, beginnings, origins," of all things. This statement leaves no room for speculations, because if anyone questions this statement, then the bigger question is not with this statement alone but that there are bigger issues with the inerrancy and infallibility of the Scriptures.

There was nothing in existence before God created the heavens and the earth, and so the logical question that would normally arise would be something like: Where did the raw material come from? When we think of creating anything, we would normally think of assembling raw material, but this verse simply says that in the origin of time, God, out of nothing, created everything. If this statement does not move you, then I don't know what would! This statement is outside the realm of any human reasoning, understanding, and comprehension. It would require divine enablement to believe this statement. This statement is life transforming if it is truly believed.

The word "created" that is used in Genesis 1:1 in our English translations of the bible is translated from the Hebrew word, "bara" and this word is almost always used for divine activity. God is always the subject when this word is used. It is often used in the context of creating something new, astonishing.[15] It is used in Psalms 51:10 of creating a clean heart, to mean a transformed heart that is not as the previous heart. This word is almost never used when man is the subject of the action, and so when the verse says that in the beginning God created the heavens and the earth, then it must be some miraculous action taken by God. And so the brilliant and logical person may raise some objections and say, "But how did God do it and where did He get the raw material from?" That is truly a fair and logical question, but the simple answer is that God spoke the heavens and earth into existence. God decreed the heavens and earth into being.

Fiat Creationism

Fiat is an authoritative order, decree, edict, or command. This word is defined by the Merriam-Webster dictionary as :*a command or act of will that creates something without or as if without further effort.*[16] So, a government by fiat would be a government that rules by decree. Whatever it decrees becomes law, and those decrees or fiats are transformed into actions by its people.

---

[15]   https://biblehub.com/bdb/1254.htm
[16]   https://www.merriam-webster.com/dictionary/fiat

No one dares to object or oppose a fiat by the government. *The origin of the word "fiat" in English is connected to the origin of the world itself. Taken from the Latin meaning in the third person imperative, "let it be done," this word appears in the Latin translation of Genesis, the first book of the bible, when God proclaimed, "let there be light."* [17]And so the idea that the heavens and the earth were created by fiat is very pertinent to the origin of sex and mankind.

God Himself is the first cause that caused everything to come into being. This is also another concept that baffles the evolutionary mindset. How can spoken words cause things to come into being? This is an instantaneous creation of the earth that happened without any lapse of time. *God said, Let there be light: and there was light,* Genesis 1:3. Evolutionists would contend the creation of heaven and earth was a slow and gradual process but the account in Genesis is an immediate and instantaneous action by God.

The immediacy of the creationist argument is critical to the progressive creation argument advocated by evolutionists. The central argument in Darwinism is that millions or billions of years must have elapsed for man to evolve from an ape to a human being. And so, when presented with the evidence from Genesis 1, they are forced to redefine some things in the biblical account to fit their evolutionary narrative. And to make it work in their mind, they try to deny the literal interpretation of Genesis 1. For example, the word "day" used in Genesis 1:5 and throughout Genesis 1 could not really mean a literal 24-hour-day as we know it.

---

[17]

https://www.dictionary.com/e/fiat/#:-:text=The%20origin%20of%20the%20word,light%E2%80%9D%20(fiat%20lux).

They would have to redefine the word to mean a long period of time. Because, admitting that creation happened in literal 6-calendar-days would destroy the evolutionary argument since man could not have evolved in such a short time. Remember that time is a key and vital concept in the theory of evolution. The word that is translated as day in our English translations of the bible is translated from the Hebrew word "yom." We can know with a very high degree of certainty from the immediate context and its usage all over the Old Testament that "yom" means a literal, 24-hour calendar day.

What else could it possibly mean when He said: *And God called the light Day, and the darkness he called Night. And the evening and morning were the first day*, Genesis 1:5 .God Himself defined the meaning of "yom" to be "morning" and "evening." And morning and evening are two divisions of day that makes it a 24-hour-day. *The word "yom" is used over 2000 times in the Hebrew Old Testament. In over 95% of those occurrences, the word means 24-hour-day. (Most of the 5% are expressions like the "day of the Lord," So we come to each occurrence of the word "yom," with the expectation that it will probably mean a 24-hour-day.*[18] And evolutionists and others who do not hold to a literal interpretation of Genesis are in desperate search to find some way to make the creation account fit their narrative.

Some interpret Genesis as poetry or allegory as opposed to a historical narrative, which is what it is. Others go as far as making Genesis 1:1 a creation account, and Genesis 1:2-31 another creation account. They invented the so-called "gap theory" to imply that God created the heavens and the earth in Genesis 1:1, and then after millions

---

[18]

http://www.interactingwithjesus.org/resources/genesis1.pdf

or billions of years later, He began creation again in Genesis 1:2. Every effort is made to impose the idea that man evolved over millions or billions of years, and the Old Earth theory would help advance the evolutionary position that man evolved over millions or billions of years. The Old Earth theory is the view that the earth is millions or billions of years old, while the Young Earth view advocates that the earth is about 11000 to about 13000 years old based on the recorded dates in Genesis and extra biblical records.

The Creation of Man

Man is the crown of God's creation. I suppose you have probably heard the phrase, "Keep the best for last." Man was the last item on His calendar, and man was and is the best as compared to the rest of creation. There is absolutely no comparison between man and any other created being. You can love your cat or your dog, but they are still and will always remain an animal. You can sleep with your cat or dog, but they will always remain a cat or a dog. After He had made everything else, He made man. He made man on the 6th day of creation. Man could not have possibly been created on the 1st day of creation because there was no earth and water in existence.

Man is primarily composed of earth (ground) and water, and those materials were not yet in existence. But again, God is God, and He could have simply spoken man into existence on day one; but out of His divine prerogatives, He chose to create the heavens and the earth first. He knows exactly what He is doing. Man is the only created being that bears some resemblance of God in any way, shape, or form. Man is the only being that is created in the image and likeness of God. Here is what is said: *So God created man in his own image, in the image of God created he him; male*

29

and female created he them, Genesis 1:27. For the very first time the sexes, male and female, are introduced into the narrative. Out of man came a new subdivision; male and female.

The age of man when he was created is not explicitly mentioned in the text of scripture but it can be inferred that man was probably between the early twenties to early thirties. It says at the end of Genesis 2:5 that,"there was not a man to till the ground." God did not cause it to rain upon the earth because there would be no one to cut the grass. As soon as God sent rain to water the earth (Genesis 2:6), God formed man. *And the Lord God formed man of the dust of the ground, and breathed into his nostrils the breath of life, and man became a living soul,* Genesis 2:7. The source of man is the dust of the ground. Man did not evolve from an ape, but came from the dust of the earth. And once it rained, God proceeded to form man.

Man did not have to grow up but was instantly created at an adult productive age, ready for productivity. God had already created the raw material needed to form man from the dust of the earth, namely: earth and water. God creates His own raw material but evolutionists tell us the material evolved over time into something else. The law of conservation of mass states that, "matter is neither created nor destroyed." The God of all creation defies the law of conservation for He creates matter and can destroy matter at the utterance of His word. All created beings, including Man, procreate after its kind; a monkey gives birth to a monkey. An ape will never evolve into a human over time. They are innately distinct species with distinct DNA, and the possibility of mutation does not exist.

Creation of the Sexes

So this verse says that God created man in His own image and the Hebrew word that is translated here as man is from the word "Adam", to mean mankind in general; but in the next line of the verse, it said God created he him; male and female, and the English word "male" in this verse comes from the Hebrew word, "Zakar." This word is a break-out from Adam, which represents mankind in general or male in some cases, depending on the context. In this context, the word means a male human offspring from Adam. This word can also refer to male offspring from animals, Exodus 13:12, as opposed to male and female human genders as in Deuteronomy 4:16. The NIV translation of the bible translated the Hebrew word "zakar" as man and "neqebah" as woman. These Hebrew words for gender should be rightly translated as male and female, and not man and woman. They have been rightly translated in other translations of the English bible.

So, the genders were created by God so that the species would multiply and not go into extinction. We see that gender is not limited to humankind, but every other created living being has the male and female gender for the primary purpose of procreation. If God created the genders according to Genesis 1:27, then is there any possibility that genders can be uncreated by some other created being? How could a being that is created un-create what it did not create? The male and female genders are innately distinct with very complex DNA codes which are embedded in each and kept by the creator. I am talking here about genders in the general sense; whether humankind or beast, they are uniquely distinct.

The word that is translated as female in Genesis 1:27, in most of our English translations, comes from the Hebrew word, "neqebah," and this word carries with it the generic meaning for female of humankind or beast. It is used of a female child, Jeremiah 31:22, and Leviticus 15:33. It is also used in reference to a female animal in Genesis 6:19, Genesis 7:3; and in Leviticus 4:28, in reference to a female goat without blemish. The word is used to distinguish the genders. Genders are distinctly different in physical appearance, biological structure, and emotional structure. The creator purposely designed the genders to be distinct and different to accomplish His divine purposes. So a woman is a female, but a female may not necessarily be a woman; she could be a female from some other created being, like beasts and others.

The Creation of Woman

The creation of woman did not arise out of a vacuum, but arose out of a need. The creation of man was good, but it also raised other problems for the newly created man. If man were to be left alone on the earth, what would have happened?After God created the sexes in Genesis 1:27,He gave the command: *And God blessed them, and God said unto them, Be fruitful, and multiply, and replenish the earth, and subdue it: and have dominion over the fish of the sea, and over fowl of the air, and over every living thing that moves upon the earth,* Genesis 1:28.This verse is commanding them to be fruitful,multiply, and replenish the earth. It is implied here that this command is for sexes to be fruitful and multiply,and was immediately after the creation of sexes but before the creation of man in Genesis 2:7.

So, there arose a need for the woman to be created to fulfill the command to be fruitful, multiply, and replenish the earth. How would man be fruitful and multiply if he was alone? Man was unable to fulfill God's commands without the help of a woman, which poses another problem. The text says: *And the Lord God said, "It is not good that the man should be alone; I will make him an "help meet," for him."* Genesis 2: 18. Everything up to this point was declared by God to be very good but when it came to man being alone, God declared that it was not good. So the second reason a woman needed to be created was as a man's companion.

So, procreation and companionship are the two main reasons that God gave for creating woman. But the text says the man needed a "help meet" for him, but what is that? The NIV and NASB translated this as "a helper suitable for him," but there are other translations that differ. The basic idea here is someone that comes alongside man, and complements and completes him. Wherever man was deficient the woman would fill in the gap. God could have simply provided a cat, dog, snake, or some other created being to be man's help meet, but that would simply not work because they were not like man and could not be man's companion.

Man needed someone that was like man and that was also created in God's image. Animals simply do not fit that description. And the text says, *And Adam gave names to all cattle, and to the fowl of the air, and to every beast of the field; but for there was not found an "help meet," for him,* Genesis 2:20. Man (Adam) was already busy naming the other created beings as he was commanded by God, but other beings could not be his companion. Love your dog and cat as much as you would like but remember this profound and simple truth! They cannot and will never take the place of human companions.

Then God got to work to find a solution for man: *And the LORD God caused a deep sleep to fall upon Adam, and he slept and He took one of his ribs, and closed up the flesh instead thereof; And the rib, which the LORD God had taken from man, made he a woman, and brought her unto the man,* Genesis 2:21-22. This is the first recorded case of surgery in the bible. Anyone who says that medicine is not in the bible is kidding themself. This is a complete surgical operation with full anesthesia. God causes a deep sleep to fall upon Adam, (anesthesia) and God performed a successful surgery by taking out one of Adam's ribs and closing the cut. This rib was transformed into a woman and the text at end of verse 22 says, "made he a woman," and when Adam got out of the surgery room and was brought into the waiting area, God showed up with someone looking just like Adam, and the text at the end of verse 22 says, "and brought her unto the man."

And when he saw her, his countenance lit up and this is how he responded at the sight of her; This is now bone of my bones, and flesh of my flesh: she shall be called Woman, because she was taken out of Man, Genesis 2:23. Adam shouted that finally someone who looked like him had been found. His "help meet," was finally there and his solitude was over. He finally had a companion and co-laborer. God just introduced the concept of woman into the creation narrative, but whom and what is really a Woman? In Genesis 2:22, the phrase, "made he woman," is used as a woman is introduced for the very first time. The word woman in our English translations is translated from the Hebrew word, "ishshah," which carries the idea of the female form of man and distinct from the female form of beasts or other created beings, namely "neqebah."

It is also interesting that the word "ishshah" is the feminine form of the Hebrew word "ish," which carries the idea of a male form of Adam. Adam mostly means man or mankind, but "ish" refers to male and "ishah" or " ishshah" refers to female, which is woman. And the word "ishah," means from "ish," since "isha" is the female form of "ish." The reason God gave for calling her woman is" because she was taken out of Man." And this woman, created by God, was not a young child that needed time to grow up. She was created as a fully grown adult in her late teens or early twenties. Adam had no time to be nursing a baby. Just as Man was created from the dust of the earth as an adult, the woman was also created as an adult, ready for marriage and intercourse.

The Origin of Sexual Intercourse

Now that we have labored to establish the creation of Man and Woman, we can dive into the long awaited and anticipated subject of sexual intercourse. This is the subject that is on everyone's mind since Adam was created. Anyone who says that romance is not in the bible is also kidding themselves. Adam referred to this woman that was presented to him as "now bone of my bones, and flesh of my flesh." This is no doubt a profound theological statement of fact, but I will also say that it is also a romantic statement from Adam.

The statement, bone of my bones, carries the idea that I can't wait to be with you, I admire you very much, I want to be with you, and can you be part of my life forever? Or, even more profound, dropping on your knees and popping the ultimate question! Will you marry me? This is a statement of intimacy and closeness. Adam and the Women were presented with an irresistible situation. The power of sex is irresistible when two people with the right chemistry are placed in front of each other naked; after that, the rest is history. There is no self control in the Man or Woman to resist such a force. You are suddenly face to face with your dream wife or husband and the chemistry is intense, and I mean very intense.

Sexual intercourse is a powerful force that even the bravest of Man or Woman succumbs to. And the text says,,*Therefore shall a man leave his father and mother; and shall cleave unto his wife*, Genesis 2:24. The Hebrew word "ish," is a male gender in almost all of its usage in the Old Testament, and it is man in the sense of a male gender as opposed to a female. This is a masculine noun that always refers to the male gender. And this is a God-given gender identity. This Hebrew word translated as man appears about hundreds of times in the Old Testament and is always translated as a man with a male, God-given identity. And the Hebrew word used in the verse above for woman is "isha" or "ishshah," which is translated as woman, to mean a God-given female identity. This word specifically carries a God-given human female gender identity. Interesting to note that the

Hebrew word "Adam," meaning man, is often used to mean mankind in general, and is also frequently used to mean man in the male sense. So in Genesis 2:25, the word "Adam" is used to refer to male. So Adam and "ish" may be used interchangeably depending on the context. But in verse 25, "isha" is used alongside Adam to refer to the man and wife relationship. The point here is that this intercourse happened between persons of opposite sex and gender. Verse 24 says that the Man cleaved to his wife, and the result was that they should be one flesh. This sexual intercourse happened in the context of a marital union between a man and a woman. But what is really the purpose of sex?

Chapter 2

The Purpose of Sex

This is the most perplexing and intriguing question that is hunting the human race. Trying to understand all the nuances about sex and the purpose for which it was created is daunting to say the least. This is the most important activity in the life of any human being and yet there is chaos in understanding its true purpose. This is also the least understood and the most abused human activity. Millions, if not billions, of lives have been wrecked, cut short, and even destroyed over the abuse and misuse of sex.

Anything can be used for good or for ill. A knife is a good cooking tool that can be used to help prepare food in the kitchen, but it can also be used to harm someone; sex is the same. It has an intended purpose, established by its designer, and any misuse will result in dire consequences. And before we dive deep into the purpose of sex, we will spend some time looking at the meaning of sex.

In the most general sense, sex is intercourse. Then the logical question to ask is intercourse between who and who? That is an interesting and fair question! Several Hebrew words have been translated in our English bibles as sex. Among them is the Hebrew word, "yada," and it literally means 'to know'. The knowledge that is in view in the meaning of this word is both relational and cognitive. It says in Genesis 4:1 that Adam knew Eve, his wife. Adam had been married at this point for some time, and so the text is not saying that Adam had a cognitive knowledge of Eve.

And here is the text:

And Adam knew Eve his wife; and she conceived, and bare Cain, and said, I have gotten a man from the LORD, Genesis 4:1.

Some English translations translated this verse as, "Adam had sex with Eve," but the Hebrew word literally means 'to know'.In this context, a relational knowledge, meaning sexual intercourse, is clearly intended. Because the result of that knowledge was conception and a child was born. The word know is also used in a relational aspect in reference to the relationship that God has with His elect, in terms of the elect being saved. *This is eternal life: that they may know you, the only true God, and Jesus Christ, whom you have sent,* John 17:3. The word that is used here for 'know' is the Greek word, "ginosko," which is the same Hebrew word for "know" in the Old Testament.

And this word describes a relational aspect of knowledge between God and the elect. But this Hebrew word, "yada," for 'know' also carries a cognitive aspect also, like knowing someone's name. I know Joe Biden cognitively, but I do not know him personally or relationally. So the word "know," in Genesis 4:1 means sexual intercourse. There are several Hebrew words that are translated as sex or sexual, to mean intercourse in the Old Testament. Here are a few: 'nagash' is translated in Exodus 19:15 as 'come near,' and some other translators translate this word as sexual relationship. 'Shakab' is used very often in Leviticus 15:18,24,33 and all over Leviticus 18, to mean 'lie with or sleep with'.

Another Hebrew word that is used over 13 times in Leviticus 18 is 'galah,'and it is translated into English as 'sexual relations' but this word also carries the idea, 'to uncover one's nakedness.' And so, sexual intercourse is spoken using several metaphors to describe the action that is taking place. Whether it is uncovering the nakedness of a close relative, human beings having intercourse with animals, human beings of the same gender having intercourse with another human being of the same gender, these are all sexual perversions and not God's design for sexual intimacy. Sexual intercourse is never to occur among blood family relatives and non-blood family relatives. Intercourse is only to occur in heterosexual and not in a homosexual union or relationship.

All these sexual perversions would arouse a man to stick his penis anywhere that he finds a hole, whether woman, another man, or beast. It would also move a woman to lie down with another woman, man, or open her legs for some animal, dog, or beast, to thrust its penis into her vagina. This is a perversion of sexual intercourse outside the purpose for which it was intended.The human race is in desperate search for sexual satisfaction but without the proper use of sex, millions are bound to plunge to their destruction. Let's look at the intended purposes of sexual intercourse, beginning with procreation.

In an article published on psychology today.com, titled "The *Purpose of Sex*," the author said, *"Sex is one of those words that everyone uses and surprisingly few understand. Sex is much more than physical and concerning procreation. It is important to recognize and identify the breadth of sexuality. Sex serves several of life's basic purposes: from pleasure, stress reduction, and formation of our identity, to our intimate connection and (of course) procreation. The goal of sex can be defined in one word: fulfillment! (Finally, you might be thinking, one word and not a list!).*

True sexual fulfillment is when physical pleasure occurs within the context of an intimate and loving relationship. In this way, fulfilling sex transforms what could be a pleasurable and merely mechanical event into an expression of intimacy and love. Therefore, we distinguish that sex engages us in different ways emotionally, relationally, socially, spiritually, and also physically.[19] The author of this article, John Chirban, PhD, ThD, is an instructor of clinical psychology at Harvard Medical School. He asserts that the purpose of sex is pleasure, stress reduction, and formation of our identity.

Pleasure, according to him, is one of the purposes of sex. Pleasure in the general sense being the purpose of sex is debatable. Pleasure is a by-product of sex when experienced in a God-ordained heterosexual marital union. There is no pleasure in an adulterous sexual relationship.

----

[19]

https://www.psychologytoday.com/us/blog/age-un-innocence/201307/purposes-sex

There is no pleasure in prostitution and the resulting sex from it. There is no pleasure in sex with a close relative and the resulting wrath of God's judgment from it. There is no pleasure in sex with an animal. There is no pleasure in a fornicating sexual relationship. Yes there may be a momentary experience of orgasm and ejaculation, but nothing to write home about. Orgasm is defined as: *intense or paroxysmal excitement, especially: the rapid pleasurable release of neuromuscular tensions at the height of sexual arousal that is usually accompanied by the ejaculation of semen in the male and vaginal contractions in the female.*[20]

This is more likely the meaning of pleasure in sex intended by John Chirban. This is most likely the meaning of pleasure in sex as understood by a vast majority of Americans and the global population. Men and women are in desperate search of momentary excitement and pleasure. This is the driving force behind the need for more, and more, and more sex. Sex is a product and it is in very high demand, and it seems that there is a supply chain disruption. Demand is outpacing supply.Men are in desperate search for ways to release semen, and women are looking for ways to get vaginal stimulation and arousal. Why would a man pay a prostitute?

Why would a man or woman mate or have sexual intercourse with an animal? Why would a woman seek vaginal stimulation from another woman? Why would a man stick his penis into the anus of another man?Reflect and ponder on these questions! But true pleasure is long lasting in a God-ordained monogamous, heterosexual marital union. This is where there is true intimacy and pleasure. Things work very well when used as intended, including

---

[20]   https://www.merriam-webster.com/dictionary/orgasm

using sexual intercourse as it was intended by its designer. Then John Chirban moved from pleasure as the purpose of sex to stress reduction. If stress reduction is the purpose of sex, then it is no surprise that sex is being used as some sort of medication to bring relaxation to the body. Sex used in this way will be like a mood or mind altering medication to alter and control feelings.

Here are some comments about sex as a stress reliever posted on a prominent website verywellmind.com/sex: *Sexual activity and orgasm can relax your body and release many hormones that are supportive of overall health and wellbeing. Similarly, sex can boost dopamine, a neurotransmitter sometimes called the "feel-good chemical" because it reinforces feelings of pleasure.* Oxytocin *is known as the "love hormone" because it is released during physical touch, as in affectionate touching and sex between adult partners, as well as during pregnancy, birth, and breastfeeding. Sexual activity seems to be one way to release stress by reducing cortisol. One study looked at women's heart rate and cortisol levels as a measure after "positive physical contact" with a partner. These findings suggest that having sex can lead to less of a stress response during challenging situations, which is a good thing.*[21]

Relieving stress may, and certainly does, occur during sexual intercourse, but this cannot be the purpose of sex. Relieving stress may act as a by-product of sex but it cannot act as its underlying purpose. It would be like saying drinking beer or smoking cigarettes relieves stress and so an activity, so important in the life of human beings, is lumped

---

[21]

https://www.verywellmind.com/sex-as-a-stress-management-technique-3144601

into the category of a stress reliever. Really? Seeking pleasure and relieving stress has been widely understood as the primary purpose of sexual intercourse. And finally, the author of this article also identified "formation of our identity," as a purpose of sex, meaning, sexual intercourse.

The author did not elaborate on what he meant by the formation of our identity being one of the purposes of sex and I would not speculate. And procreation is mentioned as a purpose of sex but the author seems to imply that it is not as important a purpose. He asserted, "The goal of sex can be defined in one word: fulfillment!"[22] If sex is all about fulfillment, then that may imply that the more sex that someone gets, then the more fulfilled they will be. That would imply that sex addicts and prostitutes are the most fulfilled persons on the face of the earth simply because they get more sex. Is that really the case? What is the intended purpose of sexual intercourse?

Procreation as a Purpose for Sexual Intercourse

Some have argued that procreation was and is no longer the primary purpose for sex. Any species that does not procreate will soon go into extinction. One of the reasons man is still around is because the birth rate exceeds the death rate, and that results in a net gain in the human population. If the global population were to experience a prolonged net loss, then it would not be long before humans become extinct. And how would the global population be kept from becoming extinct if procreation is not the primary purpose for sexual intercourse? You may often hear things like the economy is experiencing labor shortages.

---

[22]
https://www.psychologytoday.com/us/blog/age-un-innocence/2
01307/purposes-sex

If there was no sexual intercourse then the global economy as we know it would eventually come to a sudden halt and all the bustling cities would suddenly become vacant. So how would any one come up with some other purpose for sex other than procreation? Some have identified pleasure as the purpose for sex but how does anyone get pleasure if there were no people on the earth? And how did the people get here?People do not suddenly appear on the earth, do they? Sexual intercourse must first occur for people to be on the earth and then pleasure follows as a by-product of sex.

The word "procreate" is assuming that we are talking about "beings" in general, or any being but particularly,humans. To procreate means to beget or bring forth (offspring).[23]The idea here is to propagate a species out of extinction. To propagate means, "to cause (an organism to multiply by any process of natural reproduction from the parent stock, to reproduce itself, its kind etc., as an organism does."[24]The word "being" means to exist, or existence. This word has the idea of vibrancy and life, and for any being to propagate, it must originate from a stock of its kind. Humans came from humans and monkeys came from monkeys and no cross-breeding exits. So, in Genesis 1:27, God created man and out of the creation of man, He created the sexes, male and female.

After God created them, He did not say,"Go have fun and enjoy yourselves" as the purpose for creating the sexes, did He? This is what He said: *And God blessed them, and God said unto them, Be fruitful, and multiply, and replenish the earth, and subdue it: and have dominion over the fish of*

---

[23]   https://www.merriam-webster.com/dictionary/procreate
[24]   https://www.dictionary.com/browse/propagate

the sea, and over the fowl of the air, and over every living thing that moves upon the earth, Genesis 1:28. God gave the newly created genders three basic commands that have everything to with propagating the species of man. He said unto them, "Be fruitful, multiply, and replenish the earth."

The newly created human beings were also instructed in this verse to have dominion over every other non-human created being. But there was one problem! How could they have dominion if they were the only two people on the earth? They needed a labor force in order to have dominion. The Hebrew word that is used in this verse and translated into most of our English translations as "fruitful," is the word "Parah," which carries the idea of bearing fruit or to increase. This word is used of men and animals as in Exodus 23:30, and Genesis 26:22, and the idea behind its usage is to increase the population of the species, whether man or beast.

This word is used of vines with the idea of bearing fruit as in Isaiah 32:12, and bringing forth new fruits and increasing the quantity of vines. And this word is used of living beings but also of plants and agriculture. And it is no surprise that the text moved from being fruitful to "multiply" the species. The Hebrew word that is translated in Genesis 1:28 into English as "multiply," is the word, "rabah," and this word carries the idea, "to become much, many, great."[25]

This word is used of people, in Exodus 1:10, 1:20, and of animals in Deuteronomy 7:22, 8:13. I noticed the word "multiply" is used in the text and not "add," meaning a rapidness or rapidity in the propagation of the species, whether man or beast. So, we have clearly shown that in order to preserve the species, there must be a process to

---

[25]   https://biblehub.com/bdb/7235.htm

propagate or they will become extinct. So, God created this act whereby a male and a female will have sexual intercourse and this act may result in the conception and birth of a new being, whether human or some other being.

So, in Genesis 1:27, God created man and the male and female gender but in Chapter 2 of Genesis, beginning from verse 7,God detailed how He created man and in verse 21, He created the woman from the man and brought the woman to the man in verse 22. The man was elated at the sight of the woman, in verse 23; and what naturally happens when a very beautiful woman is presented to a man and there is reciprocal love, chemistry and attraction? This is the power of sex and the irresistible force of sex.

Man and the newly created woman were the only family on the earth and they had no father and or mother and not even to talk of extended families which were non-existent. Genesis 2:24 talks about a man leaving or abandoning his natural family, dad and mom and attaching himself to a complete stranger and outsider who was an alien to his natural family, and the purpose for that attachment was to form a new family that would be separate and distinct from the former family. This is the method that God intends to use to fulfill the command in Genesis 1:28. One family at a time.This first man and woman had no father and mother and so they could not possibly know what all these meant. They were looking forward and not backward for guidance.

The man had to leave and cleave. Some men left their father and mother and never cleaved to their wife. Others cleaved but never left their father and mother. But text clearly said that there must be a leaving and cleaving for the species to propagate. The phrase 'to leave father and mother' may not be clearly apparent to the average reader, but what does it really mean? The next phrase, "and shall cleave unto his wife," leaves many readers baffled as to its meaning. The Hebrew word that has been translated here to English as "cleave" is "dabaq," and the word also means "to cling," as in Ruth 1:14. This word could also mean cling, keep close. This word has been translated in the NIV as "united," NLT as "is joined," NKJV as "be joined," NASB as "be joined," KJV as "shall cleave," CEV as "marries," and I have reviewed over 15 other translations of the bible and they all, for the most part, translated this Hebrew word using one of these English words.

I found out that only the NKJV and NASB translated this word as "be joined."This is a very significant difference from the other translations and why would these two translations choose to place the little word "be," before the word"joined"? This difference has profound theological implications for the understanding of sex and marriage going forward. The word"be" placed before the word "joined" means that the verb "joined" is in the passive voice, meaning that someone other than "man," is doing the joining of man and woman.

The other translations omitted the word "be," making "joined," to be in the active voice, which means that man becomes the subject of the verb but man cannot be the subject because no subject is listed in the immediate context that precedes the verb. In biblical Hebrew grammar, when a verb is in the passive voice and that verb is missing a subject, then it is assumed God Himself is the subject of that verb, hence the term, "divine passive." But how did these two translations determine that this was a divine passive and all the other translations missed it? This is a fair question!

The Hebrew word "dabaq," was translated in the Septuagint as "proskollethesetai." The Septuagint is the Greek

48

translation of the Hebrew Old Testament scriptures that was translated into Greek about 3 B.C. This Greek translation of the Hebrew shed more light into the understanding and parsing of this Hebrew word. The word, "proskollethesetai," is grammatically in the Greek passive voice and this grammatical classification renders the NKJV and NASB as the most precise translation Hebrew, "dabaq," in Genesis 2:24. The bigger question to answer is how does the meaning of this word relate to sexual intercourse?

The idea of a man joining to his wife has to mean sexual intercourse because the result of that joining is that they become one flesh. Here is an exposition of Genesis 2:24 from the apostle Paul: *Do you not know that your bodies are the members of Christ? Shall I then take the members of Christ and make them members of a harlot? Certainly not? Or do you not know that the one who joins himself to a prostitute is one body with her? For He says that; the two shall become one flesh,* I Corinthians 6:15-16. Paul used the phrase, "one who joins himself to a prostitute," and it cannot mean anything else but being glued or cemented with a prostitute and forming a sexual union with her.

Interestingly, the Greek word that is translated here as "joined," is "kollomenos," and this Greek word translated as, "joined" in Genesis 2:24, is "proskollethesetai," and both have their origin from the root word, "kollao," meaning to glue or cement together. Paul is explaining the meaning of the word "joined," as used in Genesis 2:24. This word means sexual intercourse in both texts. You might be saying to yourself that it does not apply to you, because you do not join yourself to a prostitute. People often think of a prostitute as someone who is paid to provide sex as a service.

The biblical definition is much broader than that. The Greek word "porne," has been translated here as prostitute

49

or harlot. This word is defined as "a woman who sells her body for sexual uses. Any woman indulging in unlawful sexual intercourse, whether for gain or for lust."[26]Any sexual intercourse outside of what God has joined together is unlawful sexual intercourse and it does not matter whether it is for gain or for lust. Sexual intercourse is pleasurable and enjoyable in a God-ordained, monogamous, heterosexual marital union.

Marital Union as a Purpose for Sex

There is still ongoing debate on the question of marriage as a purpose for sex. Is marital union a purpose for the creation of sex? Before getting deep into this question, what really is a marriage? Does signing a piece of paper at the courthouse make two people married? Here is one definition:*The legally or formally recognized union of two people as partners in a personal relationship (historically and in some jurisdictions, specifically, a union between a man and a woman).*[27]According to this definition, someone or some being,decides and determines what constitutes a marriage. The definition says, "The legally and formally recognized union of two people as partners in a personal relationship." And who determines its legality and formality? The US has 50 states and I suppose that there may be 50 definitions of what constitutes a marriage.

Unless congress intervenes and sets a federal standard of what constitutes a marriage then the definition is up for grabs. There are about 190 countries in the world and

---

[26]   https://biblehub.com/thayers/4204.htm

[27]

https://www.google.com/search?q=define+marriage&oq=define+marriage&aqs=chrome..69i57j0i512l3j0i457i512j0i512l5.7170j1j4&sourceid=chrome&ie=UTF-8

each one may have its definition of what constitutes a marriage. If you have a piece of paper that declares you as legally and formally married to another person, then that legality and formality may become null and void if you were to catch a flight and find yourself in another country. How can a piece of paper declare you as married in one jurisdiction, and suddenly nullifies your marriage in another jurisdiction

Laws are enacted based on the values and beliefs of the lawmakers in a given jurisdiction. Whether they are the congress of the United States of America, parliaments in other countries, and kings or presidents in others; laws are enacted based on prevailing values of the governing and those being governed. It is therefore no surprise that different jurisdictions arrive at diabolically opposing definitions of what constitutes a marriage.

A much larger question is who defines a marriage? Man or God? Can a created being narrate its own creation? And if such a being could narrate its own creation, then that being was not created and must exist prior to its creation. Can man say anything about his creation and origin? And if he could, then he was not

created. Why would something as intricately linked to the creation of man, as marriage and sex, be defined by man? When he was not in existence when it all happened?

The word marriage, marry or other derivatives is somewhat nuanced to fully get a handle on. This word is expressly referenced in the bible. The Hebrew word, "baal," is translated as "marry," as its first meaning in most of our English translations.[28] This word means "to own, possess, especially a wife," and in Aramaic, "to take possession of a wife or concubine."[29] This word is translated as marry in several old testament passages, including: Genesis 20:3, Deuteronomy 21:13, 22:22, 24:1, Isaiah 54:5, 62:4-5, Malachi 2:11 and Jeremiah 31:32. This word also has a second meaning. It could also mean "to rule over" as in 1 Chronicles 4:22, Isaiah 26:13, Proverb 30:23, Isaiah 62:4.[30] So, the basic meaning of this word that is translated as marry in most of

---

[28]   https://biblehub.com/bdb/1166.htm
[29]   https://biblehub.com/bdb/1166.htm
[30]   https://biblehub.com/bdb/1166.htm

our English translations is to own, take possession of a wife, or to rule over.

In the New Testament, there are about 28 occurrences of the word marry, marriage, or some derivative of it. The Greek word "gameo" has been translated into English as "marry" several times in Paul's letters, especially in 1 Corinthians 7:9,11,28,32,33,38, and 39. It is also used in Matthew 5:32, Luke 17:27 and in several other instances. This Greek word carries a meaning similar to "baal" in the Old Testament, that is, to take possession and ownership of a woman as wife; to make all the customary, cultural, legal and formal rites requires for a girl or woman to transfer her allegiance from her natural family to a new family under the umbrella of her husband.

This definition may imply and include sexual intercourse later, but the idea of transfer of allegiance is key to the meaning of this word. Joseph was betrothed to Mary and to betroth is a promise and agreement to get married and this agreement is as good as getting married, because only divorce can nullify the agreement. And here is where Joseph betrothed Mary: *Now the birth of Jesus the Messiah was as follows: when His mother Mary had been betrothed to Joseph, before they came together she was found to be pregnant by the HolySpirit. And her husband Joseph, since he was a righteous man and did not want to disgrace her, planned to send her away secretly.* Matthew 1:18-19.

A few observations to ponder: Joseph is identified as her "husband," yet they had no intercourse and the phrase "send her away secretly" means to divorce her. They were considered formally and legally married even though sexual intercourse had not happened. Here is some history about the betrothal period in the Old Testament: *Several Biblical passages refer to the negotiations requisite for the*

53

arranging of a marriage (Gen. xxiv.; Song of songs viii. 8; Judges xiv. 2-7), which were conducted by members of the two families involved, or their deputies, and required usually the consent of the prospective bride (if of age); but when the agreement had been entered into, it is definite and binding upon both groom and bride, who were considered as man and wife in all legal and religious aspects, except that of actual cohabitation.

The root of the word ("to betroth"), from which the Talmudic abstract ("betrothal") is derived, must be taken in this sense; i.e., to contract an actual though incomplete marriage. In two of the passages in which it occurs, the betrothed woman is directly designated as "wife" (II Sam. iii. 14, "my wife whom I have betrothed" ("erasti"), and Deut. xxii. 24, where the betrothed is designated as "the wife of his neighbor"). In strict accordance with this sense, the rabbinical law declares that the betrothal is equivalent to actual marriage and only to be dissolved by a formal divorce. [31] The point is well made that to marry may imply sexual intercourse but does not immediately mean intercourse.

The renowned or "go to" passage on marriage in all of scripture does not even have the word "marriage" mentioned in the text. This passage talks about both marriage and intercourse, but the word marriage is not even mentioned. We have been thought to think that marriage, as we know it, means intercourse but yes and no. The passage in question is referred by The LORD Jesus Himself and the apostle Paul on several occasions: *Therefore shall a man leave his father and his mother, and shall cleave unto his wife and they shall be one flesh,* Genesis 2:24.

31

https://www.jewishencyclopedia.com/articles/3229-betrothal

Sexual Intercourse is Marriage

And by sexual intercourse, I am primarily talking about a heterosexual intercourse relationship. What is the purpose of two people of opposite sexes, undressing themselves in front of each other and engaging in intercourse? Why did God design this activity? Sex is pleasurable but is that why it was created? Sex relieves stress but is that why it was created? Sex can be used for gain or lust but is that why it was created? Sex can be commercialized but is that why it was created?

The most sacred activity in the life of any human being, undressing themselves in front of another human being of a different sex with the purpose of engaging in intercourse. This act of intercourse permanently joins any such two persons together. Sex therapists have coined a term "fluid bonding," and by this they mean: *Couples who choose to stop practicing safer sex with each other are said to be fluid bonding. This is because they share bodily fluids with each other.*[32] I am thinking to myself, why would sex therapists use the term "bonding" to describe the exchange of bodily fluids through sexual intercourse?

Most people happen to believe that the man emits sperm or semen into the female vagina during sexual intercourse and it is only a one way transaction. The female is considered to be the receiver only, and nothing could be further from the truth. These fluids mix and bond these sexual partners together. If there was no mixture, then the male could never contract a sexually transmitted disease from the woman. When the male fluids come into contact with the vaginal fluids of the woman, there is a mixing and

---

[32]   https://www.verywellhealth.com/fluid-bonding-3132610

linking that occurs, and the mixed fluids remain in the female body and some return or are connected through the sperm and back through the penis into the male body.

A man could not contract any sexually transmitted disease from a woman if there were no transmission lines between the point of infection in the woman to the body and blood of the man and vice versa. There is clear evidence that these fluids bind the male and female through the act of sexual intercourse. This is not a game, for lives are at stake. Sexual intercourse is an action not to be entered into lightly without thoughtfully and carefully pondering all its ramifications. Sexual intercourse binds you to that person forever. Here is a quote on the two-way transmissibility: *Exchange of bodily fluids and infection work both ways in vaginal intercourse.*

Sexually transmitted infections are carried in ejaculate, pre-ejaculate, and vaginal secretions. So any tact between the penis and vagina is a risk for transmission for both partners.[33] Also, in an article published on the Center for Disease Control's website titled, "What body fluids transmit HIV?" The article says: *Only certain body fluids from a person who has HIV can transmit HIV. These include: blood, semen (cum), pre-semen fluid (pre-cum), rectal fluids, vaginal fluids and breast milk.*[34] This article is about the transmission of HIV but the common denominator here is that all fluids in the body are linked to the blood. It is only

---

33

https://www.plannedparenthood.org/learn/ask-experts/during-vaginal-intercourse-how-long-does-it-take-to-exchange-bodily-fluids#:~:text=Exchange%20of%20bodily%20fluids%20and,of%20infection%20%E2%80%94%20for%20both%20partners.

34

https://www.cdc.gov/hiv/basics/hiv-transmission/body-fluids.html

when an infection from a fluid reaches the blood and the blood becomes infected, and destroys other vital organs that death comes.

The article continues to say that: *These fluids come in contact with a mucous membrane or damaged tissue or are directly injected into the bloodstream (from a needle or syringe) for transmission to occur. Mucous membranes are found inside the rectum, vagina, penis and mouth.*[35]The point here is that even if sexual intercourse does not lead to HIV or other sexually transmitted diseases, it does leave the sexual partners with a binding of their souls. Their fluids have been reciprocally mixed in their blood and they cannot be unmixed.

And Genesis 2:24 says, "Therefore shall a man leave his father and his mother, and shall cleave unto his wife and they shall be one flesh. And they were both naked, the man and his wife, and were not ashamed." The word "marriage and sexual intercourse,"is not expressly mentioned in this passage, but it is implied and clearly written all over the text. The word "cleaved" has been rendered in other translations as "joined," and this word carries the idea of cementing, welding two pieces of metal to metal without any possibility of separation. The text says that the man abandons his natural family and cleaves to his wife.

This word is clearly speaking of sexual intercourse because the result of that cleaving was when they became one flesh. This sexual intercourse resulted in some internal unity. Their individual identities were not completely demolished, but a new identity was formed as a result of

---

35

https://www.cdc.gov/hiv/basics/hiv-transmission/body-fluids.html

sexual intercourse. But what does it really mean that they became one flesh? There are two Hebrew words that could be translated as "one" in the Old Testament.

One is "echad," and the other is "yachid," and "yachid," is often used for numeric "ones," with the idea of singularity in view. On the other hand, the word "Echad" is often used for unified or plural ones in view. "Yachid" is seldom used of God as one, but "echad," is almost often used of God as one, meaning a plurality in ones. One of the biggest theological issues for Jews and Muslims is the idea that God is One. And they both would use Deuteronomy 6:4, which says, "Hear, O Israel, The LORD our God, The LORD is One." The meaning of the word "one" in this verse has been used by both Jews and Muslims to refute the pivotal Christian doctrine of the trinity.

They argue that God cannot be manifested in three persons when this verse, (according to them) clearly says, "God is one." The problem is understanding the meaning of the word "one" in this verse. When God is mentioned as one, the Hebrew word, "echad," is always often used, to mean a unified or a plural "one". So, the word that is used exclusively for God as one is also used in Genesis 2:24 to describe husband and wife as one. So this new union between man and wife is described as "echad". This is a mystery beyond our comprehension.

This verse is used on several occasions in the New Testament to define marriage as a sexual union between a man and a woman. Paul said, "Or do you not know that the one who joins himself to a prostitute or a harlot (these words mean sexual deviations of the marital union) is one body with her? For He says, 'They two shall become one flesh.'"Paul is making the case that sexual intercourse, which is to cleave, join, or unite, permanently binds you forever with that person. So, sexual intercourse is marriage. Paul is making an exposition of Genesis 2:24. So, sexual intercourse is not something to be entered into lightly, but we must ponder the long term ramifications because these actions can never be reversed. You are forever joined to that person and multiple sex partners means multiple unions.

Here is a very interesting interaction between Jesus and the woman at the well: Jesus said to her, "Go, call your husband, and come here." The woman answered him, "I have no husband." Jesus said to her, "You are right in saying, "I have no husband"; for you have had five husbands, and the one you now have is not your husband. What you have said is true, " John 4:16-18. The LORD Jesus clearly says that the woman had what He called, "five husbands," but He goes to nullify all five by saying that the one you now have is not your husband. She may not be considered to have been joined to all five men then she would to be one flesh with all five. Maybe she needed companionship!

Companionship as a Purpose for Sex

Procreation has been identified as the primary purpose for sex and rightly so, since our very existence depends on it. But procreation would be non-existent without someone to share life with. Living alone is a dreadful experience and yet it is exactly where billions of people find themselves. According to the Census Bureau, *There were 37 million one-person households in 2021, or 28% of all U.S. households. In 1960, single-person households represented only 13% of all households.*[36] These statistics reveal that a

---

36

https://www.census.gov/newsroom/press-releases/2021/families
-and-living-arrangements.html#:~:text=At%20the%20same%20ti
me%2C%20living,from%207%25%20to%208%25.

population about the size of California is living alone. Thousands of people die each year in their homes and it takes weeks for someone to find out that they were dead because they lived alone and don't even have someone, like a friend or family member, that would call and check on them on a regular basis.

And by the time the authorities were called, the body was already decomposed. The problem of being alone is humongous, and it is far wider than the statistics would seem to suggest. I have read about thousands of instances where someone is living with people and the person died, and it took about 7-10 days for someone to find out that they were deceased. So, millions of people live in a two-or-more person household and yet they are technically living alone. Millions of people have no-one that would call and check on them if they did not hear from or see them for more than 48 hours.

People have experienced medical emergencies during the night or day and they could not reach the phone to call for help, simply because they were living alone. Living alone does not only pose physical challenges but also poses a host of psychological problems. According to an article posted on the American Psychological Association (APA) website, writer Amy Novotney says, "*Lacking encouragement from family or friends, those who are lonely may slide into unhealthy habits. In addition, loneliness has been found to raise levels of stress, impede sleep and in turn, harm the body. Loneliness can also augment depression and anxiety. Last year, researchers at the Florida State University college of Medicine also found that loneliness is associated with a 40% increase in a person's risk of dementia. (The Journal of Gerontology: series B, online 2018)".[37]* So, companionship is critical for an improved quality of life. God created man as a social being in desperate longing and need for companionship. It is no surprise that social media sites, like Facebook, have soared in popularity as they have stepped in to fill the gap in creating companionship and connectivity; yet people are more disconnected now than at any time in history.

After God formed man from the dust of the ground, in Genesis 2:7, there immediately arose a new problem: man was alone. And here is what God said: And the LORD God said, It is not good that the man should be alone; I will make him an" help meet," for him, Genesis 2:18. Up to this point, everything that God made was declared to be very good but when it came to being alone, God said that it is not good. Being alone was and is such a dangerous thing that God declared it not good. But God had already created the animals, and so why not simply use one or any of the animals as man's companion? That may have been the most logical thing to do since that would have saved God a lot of time.

After all, creating a subset of man, called woman, would require more time, so why not just use one of the animals that were readily and already available as man's companion? That was not an option because an animal is not a man and cannot be a man's companion. A dog has been nicknamed, "man's best friend," but can a dog really be man's companion? A dog may lead the blind, rescue a child in danger, help find a lost person, and protect a home from intruders, but can anyone engage a dog in an intelligent

37

https://www.apa.org/monitor/2019/05/ce-corner-isolation#:-:text=%22Lacking%20encouragement%20from%20family%20or,also%20augment%20depression%20or%20anxiety.%22 dialogue, or expect a dog to give you a kind word when you feel down? A true companion is someone of the same essence as you. A human needed another human to be his companion. The gap of lack of companionship cannot be filled with a non-human species.

Then God said, "I will make him an "help meet ,"for him."But what is really an "help meet?" The Hebrew word "ezer" has been translated into English as" help meet," and this word carries the idea of "a helper bringing the right aid in time, to meet an urgent need." This Hebrew word is translated in the Septuagint (the Greek translation of the Hebrew Old Testament) as "boethos," and this same Greek word appears in the book of Hebrews (New Testament) and here is what it said: So we say with confidence, "The LORD is my helper; I will not be afraid. What can man do to me?" The Greek word translated here as "helper," into English is the same Greek word that is translated from the Hebrew word "ezer," in Genesis 2:18.

Man, being alone, is incomplete, and the woman comes alongside the man to help make man complete. So, sex is also for companionship and to give pleasure into the life of a man. The happiest men and women are those that have a good sex life, and they find true companionship and pleasure in their spouse. The most miserable men or women are those with multiple sex partners and sex outside the plan of God and what He has joined together. True pleasure is found in a God-ordained, monogamous, heterosexual marital union.

Pleasure as a Purpose for Sex

God created sexual intercourse primarily for procreation and companionship, but pleasure is no doubt an integral component of sex in the right context. There is hardly any lasting pleasure in any illicit sexual activity. Pleasure happens during intercourse but there is also plenty of pleasure before intercourse is ever conceived. Sometimes, true pleasure is actually what happens before sexual intercourse actually takes place. You must take pleasure and delight in your partner before intercourse can be pleasurable. And taking pleasure in your partner requires time to get to know them and take pleasure in them.

But what does pleasure really mean? Here is how sexual pleasure has been defined: *Pleasure is a feeling of enjoyment of satisfaction, often associated with a positive and enjoyable experience. Sexual pleasure has been described as a physical and/ or psychological satisfaction and enjoyment that comes from erotic experience. Things like consent, safety, privacy, and the ability to communicate are all factors that enable pleasure to contribute to sexual health. Pleasure, including sexual pleasure, is different for everyone and can be impacted by so many things, like emotions, location, weather and mental state.*[38] This definition would seem to imply that any sexual experience is pleasurable and enjoyable regardless of the partners involved. So, according to this definition, pleasure is derived from the sex act regardless of the partners involved.

If that is the case, then all sexual deviations would be considered pleasurable. So, for pleasure to take place there must be arousal, ejaculation, and orgasms. Unfortunately, a vast majority of people who engage in sexual intercourse are searching for exactly this kind of pleasure. They are in desperate search for an enjoyable experience.

There are reported cases, in the millions, where partners engage in sexual intercourse and immediately after

---

[38]   https://shq.org.au/2020/07/pleasure/

that act is completed, there is regret and animosity between them that the act was enjoyable but disappointing. Enjoyable but not pleasurable. It did not live up to expectations. Something was missing but they could not verbalize what it was. So, there was arousal, ejaculation and orgasms, but no pleasure.There is no real pleasure in sexual intercourse outside a God-ordained, heterosexual, monogamous marital sexual union.

There may be some short term pleasure but nothing real and long lasting. So, sex, in the right context, is pleasurable but it is not primarily for pleasure. Here is what the wisest man that ever lived said about pleasure in sex: *Drink water from your own cistern, And fresh water from your own well. Should your springs overflow into the street, Streams of water in the public squares? Let them be yours alone, And not for strangers with you,* Proverbs 5:15-17. This text is written in Hebrew poetry and the context clearly sheds light on the meaning of the passage. Verse 15 talks about drinking water from your own cistern and the second poetic line reinforces the first line by saying, fresh water from your own well. Water is here used symbolically, since we are dealing with poetic language. Solomon is making the point to have sexual intercourse with your God given wife and not just anybody.

And verse 16 and 17 are alluding to avoiding sexual promiscuity of any sort, including adultery, fornication and the likes of it and here is a commentary on verse 15: *In this verse, Solomon compares monogamy to a well of flowing water. He advises his son, or students to enjoy the water that flows from his own well. Part of the joy that comes from within a marriage is knowing if it is pleasure that is sanctioned and celebrated by God. The confidence of knowing something is moral, legitimate and sacred only enhances the happiness it brings.*[39] This commentary is clearly in-line with the context and meaning of the passage. And it becomes vividly clear once we read verse 18 and 19. These verses interpret what was not so clear in verse 15-17.

Let your fountain be blessed, And rejoice in the wife of your youth. As a loving hind and a graceful doe, Let her breasts satisfy you at all times; Be exhilarated always with her love, Proverbs 5:18-19. Solomon is pronouncing a blessing on his fountain. This fountain is the source of life. And the source of life is the male reproductive organ, penis. This is probably the clearest portrait of pleasure in sexual intercourse in the bible. There is nothing as vivid as this. Let her breasts (plural) satisfy at all times. This is an unending pleasure and not momentary and temporary pleasure that is achieved through various illicit sexual activities. This is real pleasure.

Then it goes on to say that, "be exhilarated always with her love." The word, "exhilarated," means to be very happy, animated or elated. And the idea of being exhilarated always and not just sometimes, but always, never ending excitement and happiness. People are in desperate search for this kind of sexual intercourse experience but it has eluded billions of people because they have kept God out of sex. Sexual intercourse is the most pleasurable act that God created but billions of people are left out of its full potential and have sought other sexual deviations. But all this pleasure begins with something called romance, and yes you heard me right, romance!

39

https://www.bibleref.com/Proverbs/5/Proverbs-5-15.html#verse

Romance that Leads to Pleasure and Sex

It is almost impossible to talk about pleasure in sex without mentioning romance, because it is the initial set of activities that will lead to pleasure. Even though romance by itself involves mystery, excitement, anticipation and the unknown, it also involves heightened levels of emotional activity in the brain and the heart. Feelings of attraction to the other person overwhelm any rational and logical thought processes of a person in the initial and ongoing stages of romance. And during this process, the rational and logical decision making faculties are superseded. People act in ways outside their normal character in the name of romance. Even the bravest of men and women succumb to this irresistible force.

This is the power of sex, the irresistible force. But what really is romance? The meaning of romance may, at the end of the day, be all subjective. Some may say that romance is physical contact made during and before sexual intercourse, others may say that romance is some caring action taken by a partner that may or may not lead to sexual intercourse. Some think that romance is words spoken by a partner that communicate care and concern. In reality, romance may mean different things to different people.

But of course, we are concerned about romance and pleasure in the context of a union sanctioned by God. Here are some definitions of romance: *(1) A romance is a relationship between two people who are in love with each other but who are not married to each other. (2) Romance refers to the actions and feelings of people who are in love, especially behavior that is very caring or affectionate. (3) You can refer to the pleasure and excitement of doing something new or exciting as romance.*[40] Of interest and concern to me is the first definition which defines romance as "a relationship between two people who are in love with each other but who are not married to each other."

This understanding of romance assumes that this is something that happens outside of marriage. Nothing could be further from the truth. Real and true romance happens mainly within a God sanctioned union. I will define romance as any communication, spoken or unspoken, verbal or non-verbal, action taken or withheld, with the known or unknown intent to communicate erotic love. This is a borderline definition between flirtation and romance. But romance is actually found in the context of marriage. Now, hear how Adam adored his wife: *Adam said, This is now bone of my bone, and flesh of my flesh, she shall be called woman, because she was taken out of man,* Genesis 2:23. The phrase, "bone of my bone, and flesh of my flesh," may not seem too romantic to today's readers but this is a profound statement of endearment and affection. During romance people often let their partners know how much they mean to them.

There is no deeper romance than letting the one you love know that you and they are one. They are your missing ribs. God took the rib from Adam to create the woman and Adam has been searching for his missing rib since then. And Adam found his missing rib, he shouted in exclamation, "This is now bone of my bone, flesh of my flesh." It is no surprise that in the next verse after the romance, the man abandoned his parents and was joined to his wife (sexual intercourse) and then they became one flesh. But it all began with romance and they became inseparable. Just in case you are

---

[40]

https://www.collinsdictionary.com/us/dictionary/english/romance

looking for romance in the bible, read the Song of Solomon! So, the idea that romance is something that happens outside the context of marriage is simply false. This kind of thinking had led to destructive sexual deviations for far too long.

Chapter 3

The Destructive Power of Sexual Deviation

At this point when I talk of sexual deviations, then it is assumed that by this time you would have known that I have been arguing that there is the standard and expectation set by the Creator, and any sexual conduct short of that standard is considered a deviation. Every sexual activity is measured against some standard and that standard will determine if there is a deviation. The question always arises as to who is qualified to set the standards? Who really defines what qualifies as a sexual deviation?

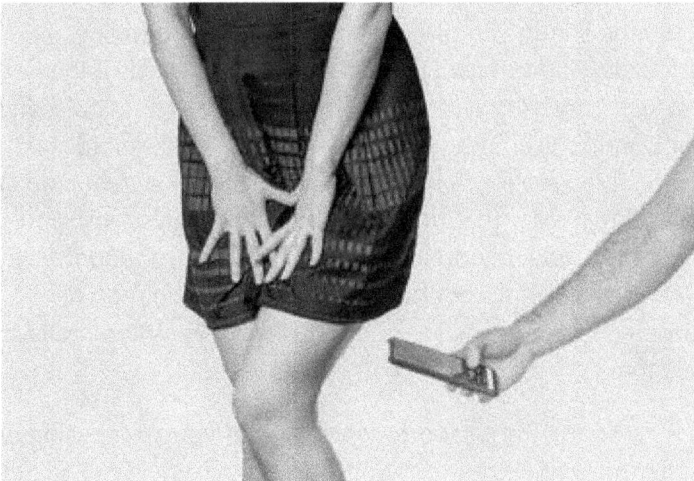

*Ima*ge of a Paraphilia in action

Here is a definition of sexual deviation from the American Psychological Association (APA): *Any sexual behavior, such as a paraphilia, that is regarded as significantly different from the standards established by culture or subculture. Deviant forms of sexual behavior may include voyeurism, fetishism, bestiality, necrophilia, transvestism, sadism, and exhibitionism. Any sexual practice that is regarded by a community or culture as an abnormal means of achieving orgasm or sexual arousal. Sexual perversion is an older term that is little used nowadays, largely having been replaced by sexual deviance or, in a psychiatric context, paraphilia.*[41] The key takeaway from this definition by the APA is that it qualifies sexual deviation as sexual behavior that is regarded as significantly different from the standards established by culture or subculture.

So, this would imply that in the case of a shifting culture, there would be a fluid or a shifting standard. A cultural shift should not necessitate a shift in standards unless the shifting culture is the sole arbiter of those standards. And how accurate are those standards if the goal post keeps moving with the shifting culture? You would often hear phrases like: "get with the times," or "you are old school," "you are stuck in your ways," and the idea behind these phrases are that the standards have shifted and you have not. You have not kept pace with shifting standards. If you say that you do not have sex with multiple men or women and some will look at you, like really? Who really does that?

So the implication would be that you are missing out on the fun, and the exhortation from them would be "to get with the program!" And the result of shifting standards is that there would be no absolutes and no right or wrong. Something that was wrong and shunned 50 years ago is

---

[41] https://dictionary.apa.org/sexual-perversion

now accepted and has become main-stream. Adultery, fornication and sex outside of marriage that was once considered a deviation, is now accepted and has become main-stream. The APA identified several sexual deviations and these are what I call hyper-sexual-deviations, meaning that these are extreme cases of deviations and outside the main-stream, and not what the average person is dealing with on a daily basis. Now, I could be completely wrong on this! Here are some of them:

Voyeurism:

Is defined as the *practice of obtaining sexual gratification from observing others.*[42]The idea behind this is that, two people are having sex in their home and someone who is not a party to the sexual activity is piping through an opening, like a hole, a window or some other opening, and that person is viewing them on the bed through some opening and the person viewing is aroused and receives gratification from illicit viewing of the sexual activity.

The action of voyeurism has actually been codified into law in some jurisdictions and here is how it is defined: *The criminal act of surreptitiously viewing a person without their consent in a place where the person has a reasonable expectation of privacy (such as a home or public bathroom) or using a device (such as a camera)for the purpose of such viewing.*[43] People have actually been criminally charged with the crime of voyeurism and here is a case in point:

A 21-year-old man has been charged with voyeurism for allegedly using his phone's camera to view

---

[42]

https://www.merriam-webster.com/dictionary/voyeurism
[43]https://www.merriam-webster.com/dictionary/voyeurism

the person using the restroom in the stall next to him in a dorm on the Notre Dame campus.[44] This is actually a bigger problem of sexual deviation than most people realize. Most people are unaware that this is a sexually deviant behavior.

Can such a sexual deviation really happen in the bible? I will let you decide! Here is a case in point: *Then it happened one evening that David arose from his bed and walked on the roof of the king's house. And from the roof, he saw a woman bathing and the woman was very beautiful to behold.* 2 Samuel 11:2. This should qualify as a clear case of voyeurism. There is no evidence that the woman knew that someone was watching, so there was no consent. She was bathing which means that she had a reasonable expectation of privacy. David was clearly aroused and possibly received some gratification by the sight of her because in the next verse, he sent someone to check her out and bring word back to him. So David moved from voyeurism to adultery.

Fetishism:

The term fetishism was actually borrowed from anthropological writings in which "fetish" (also spelled fetich) referred to a charm thought to contain magical or spiritual powers. Its influence on psychiatric usage is indicated by Sigmund Freud's reference, in his Three Contributions to the Theory of Sex, to the sexual object of the fetishist as being comparable to "the fetich in which the savage sees the embodiment of his god.[45] It is believed that fetishism involves powers that are derived from human-made objects, like carved objects. Sometimes, sex

---

[44]https://www.merriam-webster.com/dictionary/voyeurism
[45]https://www.britannica.com/science/fetishism-psychology

acts are performed by invoking the imaginary presence of another human being. Or performing sexual activity with some material object from someone from the opposite sex. This seems to involve some mystical spiritual sexual activity. This seems to be clearly a borderline demonic sexual activity and something to steer clear off and to abstain from and it clearly smells disaster for anyone involved in it.

This is clearly used as witchcraft to achieve sexual arousal and gratification. Here is what the LORD God said: *There shall not be found among you any one that makes his son or his daughter to pass through the fire, or that uses divination, or an observer of times, or an enchanter, or a witch. Or a charmer, or a consulter with familiar spirits, or a wizard, or a necromancer. For all that do these things are an abomination unto the Lord,* Deuteronomy 18:10-12. Fetishism is clearly a demonic activity that uses charm to take over the mind of another person to gain arousal and sexual gratification and it is to be abstained from.

Bestiality

It's simply defined as *a sexual relations between a human being and a lower animal.* [46] I cannot wrap my head around the reason why Merriam-Webster's dictionary would make the difference between a human being and a lower animal. The implication may be that human beings are a higher animal (strange definition).Here is revelation about prevalence of bestiality in America: *It's disgusting to hear that ASPCA officials in Rhode Island are tracking down someone who allegedly sexually assaulted a poor four-year-old Corgi-Labrador mix. What's even more repulsive is the fact that people having sex with animals are*

---

[46]https://www.merriam-webster.com/dictionary/bestiality

much more common than you think! It's been pervasive ever since the etching of our human story in rocks. Some states don't think there's anything wrong with it. It's actually legal in places like Washington DC. West Virginia, Kentucky, New Mexico and Wyoming. The famed sexual researcher Alfred Kinsey estimated that eight percent of men and 3.6 percent of women engage in some sort of sexual activity with an animal, and that study was conducted in the 1940s. The Journal of sexual Medicine found that about 34 percent of men in Brazil, mostly from rural homes, have sex with animals quite often. Do you think this is why penile cancer was so high there? [47] This is mind boggling that human beings have degraded to such a dark place, in desperate search for sexual arousal and gratification regardless of how it is achieved.*

So because governments are controlled by people, standards are shifted to adapt and fit the beliefs of the law makers. If the majority of law makers believe in bestiality, then they would naturally pass laws that are in-line with their beliefs. Sexual deviation is becoming a much bigger issue than I ever anticipated. Human beings have degraded into such a dark place and again, it is not really surprising because of human depravity. Why would a human being mate with an animal? The human being, who is created in God's image, is joined to an animal and becomes one flesh with that animal.

---

[47]https://wbsm.com/bestiality-is-much-more-widespread-than-you-think-phil-osophy/

Image of a dog having sexual intercourse with a woman

This is unbelievable conduct. This is not only happening in our day because the bible warns against this, meaning that sexually deviant human conduct has been around since the fall of man in Genesis 3. Here is what the bible actually says about bestiality: *Also you shall not have sexual intercourse with any animal to be defiled with it, nor shall any woman stand before an animal to mate with it, it is a perversion,* Leviticus 18:23. Sexual intercourse is the most sacred activity in the life of a human being and it is something to be done with great care and reflection about all its ramifications and consequences. It is not something to be entered into lightly.

Necrophilia

Also known as necrophilism is sexual attraction towards or a sexual act involving corpses. It is classified as a paraphilia by the World Health Organization (WHO) in its International Classification of Diseases (ICD) diagnostic manual, as well as by the American Psychiatric Association.[48] Unless I missed something, I do not see any explicit mention of necrophilia in the bible but the application is clearly there. Here is a verse that comes close: Nor shall he approach any dead person, nor defile himself even for his father or his mother. Leviticus 21:11. The context is clearly against a high priest coming in contact with a dead person but application can be made against coming in contact with the dead for sexual intercourse purposes. Having sexual intercourse with a dead corpse is clearly a case of severe psychological, psychiatric and spiritual disorder.

Transvestism

It is the practice of dressing in a manner traditionally associated with the opposite sex.[49] This may be clearly a case of confused identity and gender confusion. This is also different from transgender even though there is some limited association. *Transgender is a general term that describes people whose gender identity, or their internal sense of being male, female or something else, does not match the sex that they were assigned at birth. By contrast, the term cisgender describes people whose gender identity aligns with the sex that they were assigned at birth. About 1.4 million transgender people live in the United States.*[50] So, there is a distinction between transvestism and transgenderism. Here is what God says about transvestism:

---

[48]https://en.wikipedia.org/wiki/Necrophilia
[49]https://en.wikipedia.org/wiki/Transvestism
[50]https://www.webmd.com/sex-relationships/what-is-transgend er

A woman shall not wear a man's clothing, nor shall a man put on a woman's clothing, for whoever does these things is an abomination to the LORD your God, Deuteronomy 22:5.

This is a gray area and I do not see this command as an absolute prohibition against women wearing pants or trousers that are normally associated with men's clothing. The key thing to consider is intent and deception. What is the intent of the person and what is in their heart? Is there any intention to deceive others about your identity? If you are a woman and believe that your identity is a woman and you have no intention of deceiving anyone into thinking that you are a man then you may be free to dress as your conscience leads you. Remember, dress not to entice or draw people of the opposite sex to you, but dress for the glory of God.

Deuteronomy 22:5 says that whoever does cross-dressing is an abomination to the LORD. This text says the cross-dresser is an abomination and not the act of cross-dressing. The person is an abomination and not the clothing. This is serious and profound. Whether you are a male or female, dress not to entice or attract the opposite sex, but dress to the glory of God.And if you are in the word of God on a consistent basis then your conscience would guide you as to a God glorifying dress code. The key thing is to inform your conscience and bath it in God's word regularly and at the proper time, it will either accuse or excuse you as to what to wear.

Exhibitionism

Exhibitionistic disorder is a condition marked by the urge, fantasy or act of exposing one's genitals to non-consenting people, particularly, strangers.[51] This too smells and looks like a severe mental disorder as opposed to a need to get arousal and sexual gratification except in some rare instances. I was not able to find any covert or overt cases of exhibitionism in the biblical record but that does not mean that it may not exist.

These are most of what has been identified as paraphilias, by the American Psychological Association. These are what is identified and considered to be abnormal sexual activities or out of the main-stream sexual activities. Missing on this list are activities like adultery, fornication, incest, homosexuality. By inference, these may be considered normal sexual activities. Since the society is the gate-keeper, standard bearer, and the arbiter of what is considered normal sexual conduct, then these have been determined to be normal. Even things like anal and oral sex seems to be also considered normal sexual activity, so it seems. The bible has a different standard and it identifies any deviation from that standard as sexual immorality. The standard has been set by God in Genesis 2:24 and the rest of scripture.

Sexual intercourse is to take place in a God ordained marital union only. One man, one woman for life. You may want to throw this book away at this point and I understand your frustration but just keep reading! This is the standard and any sexual conduct outside of this is considered sexual immorality. This is the biblical standard of deviant sexual behavior. You may often hear things like, "He who controls the definition, controls the argument!" Mankind is bent on redefining what is considered "immoral sexual conduct," but what really is sexual immorality?

---

[51]https://www.psychologytoday.com/us/conditions/exhibitionism

Sexual Immorality

The Greek word, porneia, has been most often translated in most of our English translations as "sexual immorality." All sexual deviations in the bible fall under the major heading of sexual immorality. This is the same Greek word that has been transported into English as porn or pornography. The Hebrew word "ra" is found in Deuteronomy 22:22 and 24. That Hebrew word is translated into the Septuagint (the Greek translation of the Hebrew Old Testament) as porneia. This Hebrew word, "ra," means bad, evil, wicked, displeasing.

The Septuagint translators understood ra to mean porneia, then sexual immorality carries the idea of evil and wickedness. Here is the context in which it was translated: *If a man is found sleeping with a married woman, then both of them shall die, the man who slept with the woman, and the woman; so you shall eliminate evil from Israel. If there is a girl who is a virgin betrothed to a man, and another man finds her in the city and sleeps with her, then you shall bring them both out to the gate of that city and you shall stone them to death: the girl, because she did not cry out for help though she was in the city, and the man, because he has violated his neighbor's wife. So you shall eliminate the evil from among you*, Deuteronomy 22:21-24.

The word, "evil," in these verses is from the Hebrew word, "ra," translated as porneia into Septuagint. This is a clear case of sexual deviation. In this context, the word, "porneia," is evil. It is so bad that the death penalty is the only appropriate remedy. The goal of applying the death penalty is stated at the end of verses 22 and24. Eliminating the perpetrators would sound unreasonable in the human mind set but in God's economy, the goal is holiness and the eradication of sin.

It is better for two people to die than for the whole city, country or world to die if this sin becomes normalized and infects many more people. The death penalty is an appropriate remedy for such a fragrant and blatant infraction. The woman was in the city and could have shouted for help but she did not, implying that she consented to the act. She was not in some isolated place where no one could not hear her if she shouted; rather she was in the city and she remained silent. For the man, the text does not tell us if the man knew that she was married.

The author of the text addressed the woman as "his neighbor's wife," and the word," neighbor" could mean a next door neighbor or the wife of anyone on the street. In either case, it was illicit sexual conduct punishable by the death penalty. The phrase, "you shall eliminate the evil from Israel," is mentioned twice in the verses above and it helps to explain God's purpose for requiring the death penalty for something that we may consider as minor infraction. But in God's eyes, any form of sexual immorality is a big deal.

If someone has cancer and it is spreading, the doctors may take radical steps to stop its spread. This may include the amputation of a very vital body part or organ to stop its spread. Sexual immorality is like cancer and God must take very radical and unorthodox steps to stop it dead in its tracks before it spreads and takes with it millions of lives. This Greek word, "porneia," is translated as, " sexual immorality," in several new testament passages, including, Jude 1:7, Corinthians 6:18, 5:1, 4:3, 6:9, 10:6, 1, and Timothy 1:10.

Sexual immorality is actually a sub-category under the major heading of unrighteous or un-Godlyperson. The sexually immoral being is no worse or better than a liar, thief, cheater, idolater, for they are all under the judgment of God. Here is how it is defined: *Or do you not know that the unrighteous will not inherit the kingdom of God? Do not be deceived; neither the sexually immoral, nor idolaters, nor adulterers, nor homosexuals, nor thieves, nor the greedy, nor those habitually drunk, nor verbal abusers, nor swindlers, will inherit the kingdom of God*, 1 Corinthians 6:9-10. Sin is sin and there is hardly a ranking of greater or lesser sin. Adultery, homosexuality and stealing are of equal ranking because they are all and equally un-Godly and unrighteous deeds before a holy God. They all receive equal punishment and condemnation. It is quite interesting that the above text places adultery and homosexuality on equal footing. Society has tried to differentiate their severity and gravity, but in God's eyes, they are equally acts of the unrighteous. Let's now look at a few acts of sexual immorality.

Acts of Adultery

Adultery is a sexually immoral act that violates the covenant of marriage between a husband and his wife. It is defined by a secular dictionary as, *voluntary sexual intercourse between a married person and someone other than their lawful spouse.*[52] I am not sure why the emphatic use of the word, "voluntary," to qualify the activity. What really qualifies as voluntary? Can a party to adultery be coerced into action? These and many more are questions to ponder as you reflect on the acts of adultery.

---

[52]https://www.dictionary.com/browse/adultery

The act of adultery has been normalized to the point where it is seldom considered a sexually deviant behavior. It has gotten to the point where many think and believe that it is impossible to be dedicated to a monogamous heterosexual marital relationship in this contemporary culture. But the issue of adultery is very serious business, and so serious that God included it in the giving of law at Mount Sinai to Moses, and here is what He said: *You shall not commit adultery*, Exodus 20:14. This command carries the idea of an absolute negation and as opposed to a temporary negation. There are at least two Hebrew words used to negate a word, phrase or sentence in the bible.

The Words are "lo" and "al" and depending on the context, "lo," often carries the idea of an absolute negation, and"al" often carries the idea of temporary negation. So Exodus 20:14 should better read, "You shall never commit adultery." This is an absolute negation meaning there is never going to be a time when adultery is even momentarily permitted. Adultery is mostly considered to be a voluntary act of the human will to engage into sexual intercourse by a married person with someone other than their lawful spouse.

But if the truth is to be told, it is much bigger than that! The act of committing adultery did not just happen out of thin air. It all began with a thought that conceived and gave birth to adultery. Here is what Jesus said on this occasion: *You have heard it was said you shall not commit adultery, But I tell you that anyone who looks at a woman with lust for her has already committed adultery with her in his heart,* Matthew 5:27-28. If we are to embrace this enhanced definition by Jesus then every human being since Adam until Jesus' return are adulterers– at least, spiritually. All have looked at members of the opposite sex lustfully, no exception.

This is more than an act but it is ultimately a problem of the heart. The eyes see and thoughts are conceived in the heart and those thoughts are believed and belief turns to action in the members of our bodies. All thoughts come from the heart and once believed, they then turn to actions. Here is what Jesus said on another occasion: *For out of the heart come evil thoughts-murder, adultery, sexual immorality, theft, false testimony, slander*, Matthew 15:19. This verse states the source of sexually immoral thoughts and adultery to have come from or originate from the heart.This verse clearly links the source of thoughts to the heart.

If a city has a bad source of drinking water, the whole water supply which comes into every household would be bad and contaminated. Bad hearts are the sources of sexually immoral thoughts that are ravaging the globe. The condition of the heart will determine what kind and quality of thought originate from that heart. Jesus said again: A good tree cannot bear bad fruit and a bad tree cannot bear good fruit. In order words, a good heart cannot think evil thoughts and likewise, an evil heart cannot think good thoughts. A man or woman's thoughts and actions are a function of the condition of their heart.

So, because of bad hearts, adultery has left a trail of blood in its path. Anyone who succumbs to it will pay a hefty price. King David, King of Israel, knew it very well with his adulterous relationship with Bathsheba, the wife of Uriah, the Hittite. Why would the King risk his kingdom, the power given to him to rule, just because of a short-lived, momentary and temporary pleasure of sex? This is the irresistible force, and even the bravest of men or women have succumbed to its wrath. Sex is good and pleasurable in its proper context but all forms of sexual immorality and its after-effects have ruined more lives than anything else in the history of mankind. The after effects of sexual immorality have killed more people than all other diseases and illnesses combined. Did you know that most cancers are linked to STDs? Think about all kinds of sexually transmitted diseases, the millions of babies killed through abortion, the financial ruin to a family as the result of adultery that ultimately leads to emotional ruin for the family, including children. This is the destructive power of sexual deviation.

Think of President Bill Clinton and his adulterous relationship that is all listed in the public domain. Just as David, King of Israel, lacked any control over the sexual desires that dragged him to his destruction, so was Bill Clinton, who also lacked the power and ability to control himself. His presidency and legacy was marred by adultery for all eternity. The forces of sexual desires were so heavy and overwhelmed him that he even lacked the capacity to reflect and think of the ramifications of his actions. Sexual desires take over the rational decision making processes of a rational human being so that they are unable and unwilling to control such desires. The truth is that without the Spirit of God, any human being is capable of falling into severe sexually immoral conduct. Another act of sexual immorality is fornication.

Acts of Fornication

What really is fornication and how is it different from adultery? In the most general sense, it is sexual intercourse between people who are not married to each other. Here is how one dictionary defines the difference: Adulterare (from Latin), from where we get the English word, "adultery," means, *"to pollute, defile, commit adultery,"* a word formed ultimately from the Latin elements ad- *"to, near"* and "alter" *"other."* In legal use there is a difference between adultery

84

and fornication. Adultery is only used when at least one of the parties involved (either male or female) is married, whereas fornication may be used to describe two people who are unmarried (to each other or anyone else) engaging in consensual sexual intercourse.[53] So for adultery to have occurred, at least one of the parties must be the lawful spouse of someone else and for fornication to have occurred, none of the parties to the intercourse act is a lawful spouse to anyone else.

The society at large today may intuitively know that adultery is wrong even though many may not see it as sinful. One of the reasons for seeing it as wrong is the taking of somebody's husband or wife. So,many may simply normalize it as any other sexual activity but according to them, the only difference is that the person belongs to someone else. Now, on the other hand, fornication has received a very high level of acceptability by the culture. Telling a young person or anyone else for that matter that fornication is wrong would be like telling a human being that it is wrong to drink water.

This has become a normally accepted behavior. This is the accepted norm in today's culture and any other idea is viewed as alien and foreign. This is deeply entrenched into global thinking and culture. People live, think and breathe sex. The sex industry is booming and revenues are at an all-time high. I was recently speaking with some high school kids who are college bound and the issue of sex came up and I advised them that they should preserve their bodies for their future husbands or wives and abstain from any sexual activities until they get married and enjoy sex perpetually. They looked at me like, "He must be from

---

[53]https://www.merriam-webster.com/dictionary/adultery

another planet," and scoffed at me as I watched their body language change.

The demand for more sex is not abating. Here is a recent news report on the financial status of the global porn industry: *Globally, porn is a $97 billion industry, according to Kassia Wosick, assistant professor of sociology at New Mexico State University. At present, between $10 and $12 billion of that comes from the United States.*[54]The global porn economy is larger than the economies of many smaller nation states. Women and men, partly dressed, are featured in a lot of advertisements because that drives sales.

This is the biblical description and injunction for fornication: *Flee fornication: Every sin that a man does is outside the body, but he who commits fornication sins against his own body. Or do you not know that your body is the temple of the Holy Spirit who is in you, whom you have from God, and you are not your own? For you were bought at a price; therefore glorify God in your body and in your spirit, which are God's,*1 Corinthians 6:18-20. The Apostle Paul intended for this verse to apply to people who are already followers of Jesus Christ.

This is addressed to people whose body is the temple of the Holy Spirit and Spirit of God is living in them permanently since they are sealed with Spirit, Ephesians 4:30. The Spirit of God cannot live in anyone unless they are Christians, Romans 8:9. It is also assumed that the natural man cannot and is even subject to obey the command to "flee fornication," because the Law of God is spiritually discerned, 1 Corinthians 2:14. This command to "flee fornication," is assuming that you are already a disciple and follower of

---

[54]https://www.nbcnews.com/business/business-news/things-are-looking-americas-porn-industry-n289431

Jesus as is evident by the Holy Spirit living in you as you receive your inner witness of the presence of the Holy Spirit, Romans 8:16.

It is almost impossible to flee fornication without the ability and presence of the Holy Spirit. The Greek word "porneia "that is translated in these verses above as fornication in some of our English translations, is also translated in other translations as sexual immorality. In Deuteronomy 22:21-24, the Hebrew word, "ra," has been translated into Septuagint (Greek translation of the Hebrew Old Testament) as "porneia," and in that context, "porneia," is translated as "evil." The context there is clearly that of adultery, since a man is having sexual intercourse with his neighbor's wife.

The point is that "porneia" could mean adultery, fornication, evil and hence, any sexual deviation from the standard set by God: one man, one woman for life. Based on this analysis, there is no distinction between adultery, fornication, homosexuality, incest and any form of sexually immoral and evil conduct. The secular community has made a distinction between fornication and adultery but the bible makes no such distinction. The context will be the clearest determinant of the intended meaning of the word. Even though another Greek word, "moicheuo" is often translated as adultery in the Old and NewTestament.

There is a very interesting use of "moichiea," and "porneia" in the Old Testament. These words are used not in terms of anthropomorphic relationships but in reference to the relationship between God and human beings. The basic idea behind sexual immorality is unfaithfulness and uncleanliness. These words shed a new light in the Old Testament and here is how it reads: *Contend with your mother, contend. For she is not my wife and I am not her* husband; *And let her put away her harlotry from her face And her adultery from between her breast,* Hosea 2:2. In the context of the book of Hosea, God is the faithful husband and Israel is the unfaithful wife. In this verse above, the word translated as "harlotry," is from the Greek word, "porneia," and the word translated as "adultery" is from the Greek word "moicheia," and both words in this context are about unfaithfulness to her husband, or in other words, Israel being unfaithful to God.

But in the human context, it is unfaithful to either partner. In another context, both words are used in reference to uncleanness and here is the text:"*As for your adulteries and your lustful neighing, The lewdness of your prostitution on the hills in the field. I have seen your abominations. Woe to you, O Jerusalem! How long will you remain unclean?*"Jeremiah 13:27.Again the Greek word "moicheia" is translated here as adultery and "porneia" is translated here as "prostitution" and they are speaking of Israel's relationship with the LORD God of Israel. And Israel is unfaithful and unclean towards Yahweh.

Any unfaithfulness and uncleanness in human marital union mirrors the relationship that couples have with Yahweh. This brings us to a concept called spiritual adultery-fornication and tangible adultery-fornication. Unfaithfulness and uncleanness towards Yahweh is spiritual adultery-fornication and unfaithfulness and uncleanness in a physical sexual relationship is tangible adultery-fornication.

You might be thinking, "Where did he get this idea of spiritual adultery-fornication?" and this is a fair objection! Here is what the Lord Jesus said about this: *An evil and adulterous generation seeks after a sign, and no sign shall be given to it except the sign of the prophet Jonah, And He left them, and departed,* Matthew 16:4. The word "evil" has

88

been translated from the Greek word "porneia," and the word "adultery," has been translated from the Greek word "moicheia," and in this context, the Lord is talking about the spiritual condition of the people and not sexual intercourse, but He is using the same language to describe both. Adultery and fornication are also closely linked to idolatry.

Acts of Idolatry

At this point you may be thinking, "But what does idolatry have to do with sexually deviant behavior?" I would argue that it has everything to do with it, but what really is idolatry? That is a very fair question! *It is the worship of a cult image or "idol" as though it were God. In the Abrahamic religion, idolatry connotes the worship of something or someone other than the Abrahamic God as if it were god. In these monotheistic religions, idolatry has been considered as the worship of false gods and it is forbidden by texts such as the Ten Commandments.* [55] As you can see from this definition, idolatry is a serious violation of God's law and comes with severe consequences. Worship of other gods is a very serious matter.

It is no accident that idolatry is often placed alongside adultery and other sexually immoral acts in several passages in the bible. Here is a case in point: *Do you not know that the unrighteous will not inherit the kingdom of God? Do not be deceived, Neither fornicators, nor idolaters, nor adulterers, nor homosexuals, nor sodomites, nor thieves, nor the greedy, nor those habitually drunk, nor verbal abusers, nor swindlers, will inherit the kingdom of God,* 1 Corinthians 6:9-10. I will take the list in verse 9 as sins committed to and within the body and those in verse 10 as

---

[55]https://en.wikipedia.org/wiki/Idolatry

sins committed outside the body, according to 1 Corinthians 6:18. Idolatry is sandwiched among sexual sins and for very good reason.

As we have established earlier, unfaithfulness to God is considered as fornication and adultery in nature. This would be like a wife who is unfaithful to her husband as Israel was repeatedly unfaithful to God. This unfaithfulness takes on an adulterous and fornicating connotation as Israel was unfaithful and worshiped other gods, and so an adulterous and fornicating spouse is also idolatrous. Among those who will not inherit the kingdom of God are those who commit various sins to and within the body and sins committed outside the body, and idolatry is sandwiched in the midst of various sexual sins. Our God is jealous, and He will not share His love and devotion with anyone or any being. Any such sharing of devotion would be considered idolatry. 'All or none' loyalty and devotion is required. Another sexually deviant behavior in the text above is homosexuality.

Acts of Homosexuality

Homosexuality is no different from any other sexually immoral conduct listed above. It is not in a class of its own and is no worse than adultery, fornication, sodomy, stealing and others. It is simply a sexually deviant behavior like all the others. Society's moral compass cannot be redirected or recalibrated through the passage of laws. I understand that governments cannot sit idle and let immoral conduct get rampant. Some governments pass laws for homosexuality and others pass laws against it, but is it sinful or illegal? Who determines its legality or illegality? Here is a recent comment by the pope on this: *VATICAN CITY (AP) — Pope Francis criticized laws that criminalize homosexuality as "unjust," saying God loves all his children just as they are and called on Catholic bishops who support the laws to welcome LGBTQ people into the church.*

"Being homosexual isn't a crime," Francis said during an exclusive interview Tuesday with The Associated Press.

Francis acknowledged that Catholic bishops in some parts of the world support laws that criminalize homosexuality or discriminate against the LGBTQ community, and he himself referred to the issue in terms of "sin." But he attributed such attitudes to cultural backgrounds, and said bishops in particular need to undergo a process of change to recognize the dignity of everyone.[56]These comments by Pope Francis just happened Tuesday, January 25th 2023.

The Pope says that "God loves all His children as they are," and I guess his use of the word, "children," is referring to all human beings ever created. If that statement is true then no one will go to hell, don't you think? The idea that we are all God's children may have taken root in what is widely believed through the popular saying, "God loves the sinner but hates the sin," but is this widely believed statement supported by biblical evidence? Here is some evidence: *This idea that God hates the sin but loves the sinner is contrary to two Psalms (Pss. 5:5; 11:5) and the opening verses of the book of Malachi: "Esau have I hated, Jacob have I loved" (Mal. 1:2–3). We have to be very careful that we don't think we are somehow helping God by improving His PR. We have to be governed by the text.*[57]

---

[56]https://www.aol.com/news/ap-interview-pope-francis-homosexuality-143054742.html

[57]https://www.ligonier.org/learn/qas/is-it-true-that-god-loves-the-sinner-but-hates-the-sin

Society is not the arbiter of moral conduct. Man or mankind did not create themselves and lacks the capacity and/or authority to determine the rightness or wrongness of any moral conduct. The creator of the universe is the only arbiter of the rightness or wrongness of any moral conduct. So what does homosexuality really mean? Some advocates for homosexuality have argued that the word, "homosexual," that is used in 1 Corinthians 6:9, 1 Timothy 1:10 and other New Testament passages, is a Pauline invention.

Also others have contended that Paul may have wrongly applied Leviticus 18:22, which says, *You shall not lie with a male as with a woman, it is an abomination.* At issue here is Paul's use of the term, "homosexual, "in the New Testament and does it mean,"man who lies with man as with a woman?" The word, "homosexual," as used in 1 Corinthians 6:9 and other New Testament passages has been translated from the Greek word, "arsenokoitai," and this is a compound word, meaning that two words have been joined together to form this new word and new entity.

The two words are,"arsenos," and "koite." The Greek word, "arsenos," *is literally "masculine," from arsen, meaning, "male, strong, virile" (compare arseno-koites "lying with men" in the New Testament).*[58]The Greek word, "koite," has been translated into English as "lie," "lie down," "bed." The Latin form of "koite," is "coitus," and is translated as *Physical union of male and* female *genitalia accompanied by rhythmic movements: sexual intercourse.*[59] This Greek word "koite," is translated from the Hebrew word "shakab," and this word is always translated in the sexual context to

[58]https://www.etymonline.com/word/arsenic#:~:text=The%20for m%20of%20the%20Greek,As%20an%20element%2C%20from%2 01812.
[59]https://www.merriam-webster.com/dictionary/coitus

mean "lie,""sleep," "bed," in at least 36 Old Testament passages and here are a few: Leviticus 15:24, Genesis 30:15,16, Genesis 39:7,12,14, Exodus 22:13, Deuteronomy 22:22, just to name a few. Leviticus 18:22 should literally read: Don't bed, lie (koite,shakab,coitus) to a man (aserno) like you would a woman. I am baffled that proponents of homosexuality would argue that the words "bed or lie, man," cannot be translated to mean sexual relationship.

What is the purpose of a man lying in bed or sleeping in bed with another man or a woman lying in bed with another woman? What are they doing in bed together? Watching TV? Playing poker games? Interestingly, the Latin word, "coitus," also means *"a meeting together; sexual union," past participle of "coire" to come together, meet,"from the assimilated form of come 'together'"* Proponents of homosexuality would have to deny a fundamental hermeneutical principle and to redefine the meaning of "arsenos," and "koite," found in Leviticus 18:22. Words mean absolutely nothing without a context. Words derive their meaning from the context.

I will not entertain another debate from a proponent of homosexuality until they answer this question: What is the context of Leviticus 18? Until someone rightly answers that question, there is really no debate. The argument that the compound word, "arsenokoitai," used by Paul in 1 Corinthians 6:9 and 1 Timothy 1:10 does not mean homosexuality, is weak at best, and the interpretation of the words in the passage ignores the context and refuses to follow normal hermeneutics (the science and principles of biblical interpretation). A compound word does not alter the meaning of the individual words but explains further their singular meaning. The meaning of "arseno" and "koite," as found in Leviticus 18:22, did not come from Paul.

The context of the entire chapter of Leviticus 18 is about sexual deviation in every possible and imaginable sense and these words have to be understood in that context. The context of 1 Corinthians 6 in which the word is found is surprisingly about sexually deviant conduct and, among which, is homosexuality. "Arsenos" and "koite" are exported from Leviticus 18:22 into 1 Corinthians 6:9 and 1 Timothy 1:10 to form a new compound word "arsenokoitai."The word "homosexual" is also a compound word from "homo" and "sexual."

The word "homo" is often understood in today's culture to mean "a gay man," but that word has a Latin origin "homo," meaning "man" or "human" and a Greek origin "homos," meaning,"same." We are only concerned about its Greek meaning for now. The idea of people of the same gender and sex having intercourse is the basic thrust of the word homosexual. Support against same sex intercourse is also mentioned in Leviticus 20:13 and Romans 1:26-27. Paul did not invent anything new but only expounded on a well-established Old Testament teaching.

But at the heart of all this is the purpose of sexual intercourse. What was the purpose of creating a woman if Adam could have sexual intercourse with another Adam? Did God really design the anus for sexual intercourse? The anus was designed to discard body waste, and not for sexual intercourse. How could a man stick his penis into the anus of another man and call it sexual intercourse? How could a woman, using a sex toy, insert it into another woman's vagina, stimulate another woman, and call it sexual intercourse? A male penis is only intended to be inserted into the vagina of a female and no other location, and not even in the mouth for oral sex. That is not what the designer intended and it is a deviation and abomination.

94

A woman can only derive sexual pleasure from receiving a male inserted penis into her vagina and not having a sex toy inserted into her by another person of the same sex. Pleasure is a by-product of sexual intercourse and not its primary purpose. In Genesis 1:27, it says that God created the genders, male and female, and the primary purpose was that they should multiply and fill the earth. And in Genesis 2:24, it says that the man shall leave his father and mother and be joined to his wife and they shall become one flesh.

And the purpose of the man becoming joined (sexual intercourse) to his wife is so mankind would not become extinct from the earth. A man (male) and another man (male) having intercourse through the anus will never procreate or produce a child. A woman and another woman having intercourse using a sex toy will never bring forth children and procreate. The goal of homosexual intercourse is pleasure and not procreation, because they can never procreate. Sex is primarily about procreation. A male and another male seek a homosexual relationship to get penetration, ejaculation, arousal, orgasm, and pleasure. These are all by-products of the natural use of sex, but depraved mankind has decided to achieve these ends using unconventional means.

Sin is at the root of all sexually deviant behavior, including homosexuality. Romans chapter 1 through 3 is Paul's exposition of God's condemnation of the entire world because of human depravity. Any transgression of God's law is sin and that is how Paul concluded the long expositions of the sin of mankind in Romans 3:25 by asserting that all have sinned and come short of the glory of God. Homosexuality is on equal footing with all other sins because sin is sin. People are in desperate search for what they call freedom.

And freedom to mankind, is seeking to be loosened from the control of God. That is actually bondage, but mankind has been deceived in believing that it is the truth. Here is what God said: *Therefore God gave them up to vile impurities in the lusts of their hearts, so that their bodies would be dishonored among them. For they exchanged the truth of God for falsehood, and worshiped and served the creature rather than the creator, who is blessed forever. Amen,* Romans 1:24-25.This text above says that God "gave them up," and this is quite a terrible place to be when the restraining hand of God has been removed and mankind is left to himself.

The truth of God has now been happily exchanged as falsehood and the creature is served and worshiped rather than the creator. Man has now taken the place of God. He created man but man is now in control of the definition of sex and marriage. All kinds of sexual deviations have now been elevated as truth, and the truth is ridiculed as falsehood. And it is in this context that God said, "Do you really want to have fun? Then be my guest!" and the text says that: *For this reason God gave them over to degrading passions; for the women exchanged the natural relations for that which is contrary to nature, and likewise the men, too, abandoned the natural relations with women and burned in their desire toward one another, males with males committing shameful acts and receiving in their own persons the due penalty of their error,* Romans 1: 26-27.

According to these verses above, there is natural use for sexual intercourse and man or mankind does not determine how sex is to be performed, but God does. Sex and the parts of the body that perform sex are carefully and skillfully designed by the Creator. The vagina has been skillfully designed to provide and release lubrication at the appropriate time to reduce friction during ejaculation and intercourse. The anus is not so designed and its function is to provide an exit for waste and not to allow any object to be inserted into it and this leads us to the sexual deviation of sodomy.

Acts of Sodomy

Sodomy through lenses of the legal minds: Sodomy refers to anal or oral intercourse. As explained in Bass v. State, "Sodomy is defined as a sexual act involving the sex organs of one person and the mouth or anus of another." Traditionally, sodomy has been referred to as a "crime against nature" by various courts and statues. Under common law, sodomy mainly consisted of anal sex. However, in the U.S., the term eventually included oral sex as well as anal sex.

As recent as 1960, sodomy was considered illegal for everyone in the U.S., but the law banning sodomy was often enforced only against homosexuals. By the beginning of the 21st century, a majority of states in the U.S. had repealed all sodomy laws. In 2003, the U.S. Supreme Court in Lawrence v. Texas, struck down a Texas sodomy law as unconstitutional, and thereby, invalidated any remaining sodomy laws across the U.S. [60]

So, as the societal values change, so also will the laws change because the law makers are from the society and are a direct reflection of the values of the society. In the 60's and before, a large majority of society did not approve of sodomy, divorce, homosexuality, adultery,and a host of other sexually deviant behaviors, largely because of the influence of the church on society.But once prayer and the

---

[60]   https://www.law.cornell.edu/wex/sodomy

bible were taken out of schools and from the educational system, over time, there was gradual degradation of the society's moral compass. Now laws are being enacted to reflect that moral degradation. As we can see from the definition above, acts of sodomy are committed in heterosexual as well as homosexual relationships.

Sexual deviations like anal and oral sex happen also in heterosexual relationships. So, you will have men who will stick their penis into the vagina, anus and mouth, or men sticking their tongue into the vagina of a woman in the name of sex, and women sucking on the penis of a man to achieve pleasure. These are all sexually deviant behaviors and are outside the intended purpose of these body parts and organs by the creator. The anus and the mouth are never intended to be used to accomplish any sexual act. Mouth to mouth kissing and sucking of the tongue by partners of the opposite genders (in the context of marriage) are well within the bounds of acceptable sexual behavior. Pleasure is at the heart of all sexual deviations. But what do the words "sodomite or homosexual" mean in 1 Corinthians 6:9 and other places where it is found?

The word "sodomy," in some of our English translations as found in 1 Corinthians 6:9, has been translated from the Greek word, "malakos," and means effeminate, soft, translated in the KJV as effeminate and the NKJV as sodomites. The words, "malakos," and "arsenokoites," are the Greek words that describe homosexual behavior in the New Testament and both are found in 1 Corinthians 6:9. The word "malakos," is used to describe a passive male partner in the homosexual act. This word also carries the idea of weak, soft, passive and acting as a female in a normal homosexual relationship.

The word "malakos" is used to describe the male partner who is acting as a female and opens his anus to receive the penis from the "arsenokoites," who is taking the role of the male to insert his penis into the anus. Some translations translate and blurs these two words into one and thereby translating "malakos" and "arsenokoites" as " men who have sex with men," like the NIV, which is basically interpreting the text as opposed to translation. The meaning of the text is lost in a NIV translation. The King James translation uses the word, "effeminate," which describes a male with female-acting qualities. Some proponents of homosexuality have argued that "malakos," simply means "soft," and it is not describing a homosexual relationship.

Some have even gone as far as saying that translating "malakos," to mean homosexual is a Pauline invention. This word appears at least three times in the Septuagint, Job 41:3, Proverbs 25:15 and Proverbs 26:22. It also appears in the New Testament in Matthew 11:8 and Luke 7:25 and is mostly translated as "soft," based on the context, but in 1 Corinthians 6:9, the context is sexual deviation and so the word carries a different meaning based on the context. Thayer's lexicon defines "malakos," as soft, soft to the touch as in Matthew 11:8 and Luke 7:25, as effeminate, a male who submits his body to unnatural lewdness as in 1 Corinthians 6:9. [61]There is hardly any debate as to the meaning of "malakos," in context. So, it is evidently clear that anal and oral sex are a deviation from the intended plan and purpose of God for sex, but is the anus and the mouth really designed for sexual activity?

---

[61]   https://biblehub.com/thayers/3120.htm

Anal Sex

As has already been discoursed, anal sex is not limited to homosexual activities alone. Anal sex is the practice of inserting the penis, fingers, or a foreign object such as a vibrator into the anus for sexual pleasure.[62] It is well documented that heterosexuals also practice anal sex but is the anus really designed for sexual activities? Here is a description of the anus: The anus is the last part of the digestive tract. It's at the end of the rectum. It's where stool comes out of the body. It consists of a muscular ring (called) a sphincter, that opens during a bowel movement to allow stool (feces) to pass through, as well as flat cells that line the inside of the anus. Most anal cancers start in these flat lining cells. These are also called squamous cells. The lower part of the anus, where it meets the skin, is called the anal margin.[63]

It is quite clear from this anatomy of the anus that its function is to serve as the exit gate for stool or feces. The anus is an exit point and not an entry point and to make it an entry point will be contrary to its engineering design function and like any other engineering design, if used contrary to its design then it will ultimately lead to a malfunction sooner or later. Anal sex is a pretty dangerous activity that goes against its design function and dangerous to the health of anyone involved in such activity.

62
https://www.medicalnewstoday.com/articles/324637#bacterial-in fection
63
https://www.saintlukeskc.org/health-library/anatomy-anus#:~:tex t=The%20anus%20is%20the%20last,the%20inside%20of%20the %20anus.

Stool or feces is a factory and incubator of deadly bacteria and any contact with it can be deadly. Here is what is said about it: Parasites and viruses like hepatitis A and hepatitis E are also transmitted via poop. You can become ill by coming in contact with these through other measures, such as kissing an unwashed hand. Therefore, if you eat a larger amount of poop directly, you're at greater risk for adverse symptoms. Examples of bacteria commonly present in poop include: Campylobacter, E. coli, Salmonella, Shigella. [64]

So the idea of anyone sticking his penis into the anus of another human being (male or female) or some other animal is beyond my comprehension. The penis comes into direct contact with stool, feces or poop, a factory and incubator of deadly bacteria. What about the engineering design of the anus! Is it designed as an entry point? Here are some risks involved in anal sex: There are different potential risks that may not be present in vaginal or oral sex. For example, the anus cannot naturally lubricate itself to reduce discomfort and friction-related concerns, such as skin injuries.

The anus lacks the cells that create the natural lubricant that the vagina has. It also does not have the saliva of the mouth. The rectum's lining is also thinner than that of the vagina. Lack of lubrication and thinner tissues increases the risk of friction-related tears in the anus and the rectum. Because stool that naturally contains bacteria passes through the rectum and anus when leaving the body, the bacteria can potentially invade the skin through these tears. This

---

[64]https://www.healthline.com/health/what-happens-if-you-eat-p oop#What-happens-to-a-person-when-they-eat-poop?

increases the risk of anal abscesses, a deep skin infection that usually requires treatment with antibiotics.[65]

And here is a description of the vagina: The vaginal wall is made of muscle covered in a mucus membrane, similar to the tissue in your mouth. The wall contains layers of tissue with many elastic fibers. The surface of the wall also contains rugae, which are pleats of extra tissue that allow the vagina to expand during sex or childbirth. [66] The engineering design of the vagina is like a vehicle that is designed for rugged terrain when compared to the anus. The vagina serves a tri function: sex, childbirth, and exit for body fluids.

It is quite plain and clear that the anus was not designed for sexual activities of any kind. The material components and the engineering design of the walls of the anus is not for the entry of any object in and through it. No provision is made to reduce friction because it was not expected to have friction. Its wall material is weak and fragile as it was never intended to be robust and strong but was adequate to withstand the pushing force to release stool and for nothing else. On the other hand, the vagina is robust, and its wall is designed with robust material, equipped with a natural lubricating system, and ready to withstand any force exerted through it, like the pounding of the penis during sexual intercourse. The stated goal of anal sex by a homosexual or heterosexual is pleasure but this pleasure is being sought outside the intended use of the anus by the Creator and this is a deviation, and oral sex is also a deviation.

---

[65]https://www.medicalnewstoday.com/articles/324637#bacterial-infection
[66]https://www.healthline.com/human-body-maps/vagina#anatomy-and-function

Oral Sex

What is really oral sex? Here is a definition from Center for Disease Control (CDC): Oral sex involves using the mouth to stimulate the genitals or genital area of a sex partner. Types of oral sex include the penis (fellatio), vagina (cunnilingus), and anus (anilingus).[67] The amount of people involved in oral sex is mind-boggling and beyond my comprehension. There are more people doing oral sex than voting for President of the United States. The penis (fellatio) oral sex, is where the woman or female sucks and licks on the penis of the man or male. The vagina (cunnilingus) oral sex is where the man or another woman uses their mouth and tongue to suck and lick on the clitoris in the vagina of the woman to seek arousal and pleasure.

Here are the stats on oral sex in America: Oral sex is commonly practiced by sexually active adults. More than 85% of sexually active adults aged 18-44 years reported having oral sex at least once with a partner of the opposite sex. A separate survey conducted during 2011 to 2015 found that 41% of teenagers aged 15-19 years reported having oral sex with a partner of the opposite sex. [68] The mouth is not made and designed for any form of sexual activity and neither is the vagina designed and made to be sucked into with the tongue.

And the last form of oral sex that we were able to identify is anus (anilingus) and this is defined as: the oral and

---

[67]https://www.cdc.gov/std/healthcomm/stdfact-stdriskandoralsex
.htm#:~:text=from%20oral%20sex.-,What%20is%20Oral%20Sex
%3F,practiced%20by%20sexually%20active%20adults.
[68]https://www.cdc.gov/std/healthcomm/stdfact-stdriskandoralse
x.htm#:~:text=from%20oral%20sex.-,What%20is%20Oral%20Sex
%3F,practiced%20by%20sexually%20active

anal sex act in which a person stimulates the anus of another by using the mouth. [69]This is beyond anything that I am able to comprehend. A human being, licking and sucking the anus or shithole of another human being in the name of sexual arousal; is it any surprise that sexually transmitted diseases are through the roof? Sexually transmitted diseases are taking down lives in the millions and with no sign of abating.

---

[69]https://en.wikipedia.org/wiki/Anilingus

Chapter 4

The Destructive Power of Sexually Transmitted Diseases

Sex is pleasurable but sexually deviant activities are not, and they have left a trail of blood in their path. These activities seem pleasurable for the moment but the end product is destruction. Millions of lives have been cut short because of the destructive power of sexually transmitted diseases. Sexually deviant activities are a contributing factor to the destructive power of sexually transmitted diseases or STDs.

Here is the Center for Disease Control, (CDC's) assessment of the situation: *CDC continues to work on multiple fronts to address the nation's STD epidemic. For example, CDC provides resources to state and local health departments for STD prevention and surveillance. CDC's current funding program for health departments, Strengthening STD prevention and Control Health Departments, supports several high-priority strategies and activities, including eliminating congenital syphilis.*[70]

According to the CDC's own assessment, STDs have been identified as a public health crisis requiring a coordinated government response. The human body has three primary openings through which disease mostly goes through to invade and attack the organs; the mouth, the

---

[70]https://www.cdc.gov/nchhstp/newsroom/2019/2018-STD-surveillance-report-press-release.html

vagina, and the anus for the female and for the male, there is the penis, the mouth, and the anus. These are the major entry points for all kinds of diseases and bacteria. We can live longer and healthier lives if we guard these entry points and carefully control what goes through them, and only use them as was intended and by doing so we can add years to our existence on earth and pleasure to our lives.

AIDS/HIV as a STD

But these entry points have been used and have been misused and society is paying the costly price. One of the most destructive STDs is AIDS, which has and is leaving unprecedented destruction in its path. This has caused a tremendous amount of financial and emotional ruin to families across the globe. Imagine, the breadwinner of a family is dead from AIDS, and leaves the wife and children with no emotional and financial support. The entire future of the children may be derailed and to make matters worse, the wife may also die from AIDS, leaving the children as orphans to fend for themselves. This is the destructive power of sexual deviation.

Here is the World Health Organization's (WHO) situation and trend report on HIV/AIDS: *HIV continues to be a major global public health issue, having claimed 40.1 million [33.6-48.6 million] lives so far. In 2021, 650 000 [510 000-860 000] people died from HIV-related causes globally. There were approximately 38.4 million [33.9-43.8] million] people living with HIV (PLHIV) at the end of 2021 with 1.5 million [1.1-2.0 million] people becoming newly infected with HIV in 2021 globally. The WHO Africa Region is the most affected region, with 25.6 million [23.4-28.6 million] people living with HIV in 2021. Also, the WHO Africa*

Region accounts for almost 60% of the global new HIV infections.[71]

This report is based on the fact that people interact with some governmental agency or hospitals for the data to be collected. The fact is that most people in developing countries hardly interact with hospitals unless they are very sick and desperate. Going to the hospital just for a physical exam when you are not sick is considered a waste of resources. This data may show about a third of the situation and the simple truth is that no one knows for sure but what we do know is that, it is far worse than the data seem to reveal. There are lots of orphans around the globe because both parents have died of AIDS.

But where did AIDS originate from and how did it get into the human population? Here is what is reported on the CDC's website on the origin of HIV: *HIV infection in humans came from a type of chimpanzee in Central Africa. Studies show the HIV may have jumped from chimpanzees to humans as far back as the 1800s.*[72] The CDC's study says that " HIV may have jumped from chimpanzees to humans," and I find this to be quite fascinating that the key and operative word here is "jumped," and this requires further investigation. This is the theory of how the virus got to humans, according to the CDC: *It was probably passed to humans when humans hunted these chimpanzees for meat*

[71]https://www.who.int/data/gho/data/themes/topics/topic-details/GHO/data-on-the-size-of-the-hiv-aids-epidemic#:~:text=In%20 2021%2C%20650%20000%20%5B510,with%20HIV%20in%2020 21%20globally.

[72]https://www.cdc.gov/hiv/basics/whatishiv.html#:~:text=Where %20did%20HIV%20come%20from,is%20called%20simian%20im munodeficiency%20virus.

and came in contact with infected blood.[73] I noticed a couple of observations here on how the HIV virus got to humans: This report uses the phrases, "passed to humans," and "came in contact with infected blood." And so by eating infected meat, humans came into contact with HIV. According to the government's own website wholly dedicated to HIV: *You can only get HIV by coming into direct contact with certain body fluids from a person with HIV who has a detectable viral load.*

These fluids are: Blood, Semen (cum) and pre-seminal fluid (pre-cum), Rectal fluids, Vaginal fluids, Breast milk. For transmission to occur, the HIV in these fluids must get into the bloodstream of an HIV-negative person through a mucous membrane (found in the rectum, vagina, mouth, or tip of the penis), through open cuts or sores, or by direct injection (from a needle or syringe).[74]

So if HIV were to be acquired through a chimpanzee coming into contact with humans then two things must happen for humans to become infected: (1) The chimpanzee must be carrying the HIV virus and (2) The blood of the chimpanzee must come into direct contact with human blood. According to the CDC's own report, there was no evidence that the humans who came into contact with the supposed chimpanzees, had open cuts or sores for there to be a blood to blood contact with the humans.

The hypothesis that physical contact between chimpanzees and humans is the origin of HIV is suspect at

[73]https://www.cdc.gov/hiv/basics/whatishiv.html#:~:text=Where%20did%20HIV%20come%20from,is%20called%20simian%20immunodeficiency%20virus.
[74]https://www.hiv.gov/hiv-basics/overview/about-hiv-and-aids/how-is-hiv-transmitted#:~:text=You%20can%20only%20get%20HIV,seminal%20fluid%20(pre%2Dcum)

best because there is hardly any consensus in the science community of how the infection occurred. Here is an article published on science daily: *No one knows exactly how it happened. It may have entered through a cut or a bite wound, the blood of a chimpanzee seeping into an exposed fingertip or forearm or foot.*

But in the early 1900s, probably near the West African rainforest, it's thought that a hunter or vendor of bush meat, wild game that can include primates, acquired the first strain of a simian immunodeficiency virus that virologists consider the ancestor of HIV. A new study by the University of Nebraska-Lincoln has supported this hypothesis by reporting the first in vivo evidence that strains of chimpanzee-carried SIVs can infect human cells. They include the SIV ancestor of HIV-1 M, the strain responsible for the global HIV pandemic and another ancestral strain of HIV found only among residents of Cameroon.[75]

So far, no clinical evidence has been presented that a real human being and a real chimpanzee came into contact and the blood of the chimpanzee infected the human. There is also no clear evidence that chimpanzees naturally carry the HIV virus and if they do, then it could have been transmitted into humans through some other means. There is even some levels of skepticism amongst researchers if the chimps even have the virus.

Read this: *While chimpanzees are not badly affected by simian immunodeficiency virus (SIV), the researchers say the findings suggest that some subspecies may have evolved a degree of tolerance to the virus. "Unlike humans, who when infected by HIV suffer devastating health*

---

[75]https://www.sciencedaily.com/releases/2016/07/160722092947.htm

consequences, chimpanzees can remain healthy when infected with the SIV virus," said the study's senior author, Dr Aida Andres (UCL Genetics Institute and Max Planck Institute for Evolutionary Anthropology).[76]

This study raises more questions than answers: Even if the chimps do have the virus, Is HIV innately part of the chimp's DNA or is it infected from a foreign source? The study is suggesting that the chimps may have evolved a degree of tolerance, implying that the chimp may have been infected from a foreign source. It is now no surprise that sex with animals or zoophilia has been proven to be the source of STD's into the human population and here is a quote: *"We know, for example, that gonorrhea came from cattle to humans. Syphilis also came to humans from cattle or sheep many centuries ago, possibly sexually."The most recent and deadliest STIs to have crossed the barrier separating humans and animals has been HIV, which humans got from the simian version of the virus in chimpanzees.*

The most common STI among animals today is Brucellosis or undulant fever present in domestic livestock, dogs, cats, deer and rats. It is transferable to humans by drinking contaminated milk or direct contact with the infected animals and can be very dangerous to humans, which is one reason why milk is pasteurized.[77]This is the destructive power of sexually deviant conduct. So, let's assume that the chimp or some other subspecies of the chimp innately carries HIV/AIDS, then how did it cross over to humans? Sexual intercourse with any animal is an extremely

---

[76]https://www.ucl.ac.uk/news/2019/dec/chimpanzees-may-have-evolved-resistance-hiv-precursor
[77]https://www.animalresearch.info/en/medical-advances/diseases-research/stis-sexually-transmitted-infections/

dangerous, shameful, and abominable act that puts the perpetrator and the entire global health population at risk.

Almost all other STDs have crossed from the animal population into the human population through human sexual intercourse with animals and so why should HIV/AIDS be any different? Gonorrhea, syphilis and others have been documented to have entered the human population through sexual intercourse between humans and animals. And for AIDS/HIV to be transmitted there must be a direct blood contact between the infected and the non-infected person. Remember Genesis 2:24, sexual intercourse joins a man and a woman. The semen that is emitted by the man into the vagina of the woman, goes into the bloodstream of the woman and that is how infection takes place because there is direct blood contact. The injection of semen creates a direct link into the bloodstream between the man and the woman and that is how infections occur, including HIV.

There is so far little or no evidence that AIDS can be transmitted through oral sex. Unless there is a cut or a wound in the mouth, then AIDS is rarely transmitted through saliva or the mouth. The reason is simply because there is no blood contact but not so with vaginal sex. The sperm or semen is injected into the vagina and there is direct blood contact between the man and the woman and either party can be infected. So, sex with an animal puts the blood of the animal in direct contact with the blood of the human and they are now joined in the blood and in spirit with the animal. The human and animal are now one flesh just as man and woman are one flesh. Animals have deadly fluids that are not found in the human population and any sexual act with animals imports all those deadly fluids into human populations. This is not the Creator's design for sexual intercourse. Here below are some risk factors associated with bestiality:

Image of a chimpanzee portrayed as the source of HIV/AIDS

Risks Factors from Sex with Animals

1. Rabies is a viral disease from dogs that is fatal in humans. It is transmitted from the saliva of dogs, horses and cats. Immediately after the symptoms set in, the human has little chance of survival if not treated.

2. Echinococcosis is a parasitic tapeworm found in the feces of dogs, cats and sheep. This disease is asymptomatic and does not manifest until after a few years. These worms cause cysts to develop in the kidneys, heart and brain of the person so affected. If not treated, it can lead to death.

3. Injury The reproductive organs of these animals are not made to fit into that of a woman or man and have caused a lot of injuries; some men have had ruptured rectum from sex with pigs and others have experienced head injuries from sex with horses. The reproductive organ of an aroused dog is like a light bulb that would injure the vagina. Let's not even imagine the size of a horse's reproductive organ. It can cause serious tears and injuries.

4. Allergic reaction Receiving the semen of a dog or horse can trigger allergic reactions because it's a foreign substance that the body tries to expel. Imagine a person with a peanut allergy eating peanuts, and not getting treated immediately. A woman in Ireland who had sex with a dog died from anaphylaxis. According to the Mayo Clinic, "Anaphylaxis causes the immune system to release a flood of chemicals that can cause you to go into shock and the blood pressure drops suddenly and the airways narrow, blocking breathing. Signs and symptoms include a rapid weak pulse; a skin rash, nausea and vomiting."

5. Leptospirosis This disease is gotten from the urine of animals like dogs and cats. When it is in the immune system, it can lead to meningitis and 10% of the time, meningitis is deadly.[78]

Sexually deviant behaviors come at a very severe cost to humanity. Misuse of sex is deadly to humanity and grieves the heart of the Creator. One simple act of sex with an animal in some obscured town or village anywhere in the world, has the potential to destroy a very large portion of the global population as that sexual act contracts some STD, and it spreads throughout the global population. Your one sexual act has the potential to affect the global population if and when a STD is contracted and spreads through multiple

---

[78]https://www.pulse.ng/lifestyle/womens-health/5-health-risks-of-sxual-intercourse-with-animals/2sdxc3r

sexual partners and potentially, millions of sexual contacts. Gonorrhea is another very common STD that has been infecting the human population for quite some time and has damaged millions of lives.

Gonorrhea as a STD

What really is gonorrhea and how is it transmitted? According to the CDC, gonorrhea is a sexually transmitted disease (STD) caused by infection with the Neisseria gonorrhoeae bacterium. N. gonorrhoeae infects the mucous membranes of the reproductive tract, including the cervix, uterus,fallopian tubes in women, and the urethra in women and men. N. gonorrhoeae can also infect the mucous membranes of the mouth, throat, eyes, and rectum.[79]According to the CDC, gonorrhea is considered the second leading STD, only behind Human Papillomavirus (HPV) infection. And so, how widespread is this virus?

The CDC estimates that gonorrhea is a very common infectious disease and estimates that approximately 1.6 million new gonococcal infections occurred in the United States in 2018, and more than half occurred among young people aged 15-24. Gonorrhea is the second most commonly reported bacterial sexually transmitted infection in the United States. However, many infections are asymptomatic, so reported cases only capture a fraction of the true burden.[80] This report does not capture the true picture of the situation as most infected people may not engage the healthcare system and as such, are never

---

[79]https://www.cdc.gov/std/gonorrhea/stdfact-gonorrhea-detailed.htm
[80]https://www.cdc.gov/std/gonorrhea/stdfact-gonorrhea-detailed.htm

counted. According to a (WHO) report, about 78 million people are infected with gonorrhea each year. [81]

I recently consulted with a doctor for my routine yearly physical exam and he was very surprised that I had no STDs, and he confided to me that my case is rare. He confided in me that about 98% of his patients have all kinds of STDs, from HIV down the list to all other sorts of STDs, and these are all married men and women. The problem is much bigger than any report is able to capture and because sexual promiscuity has become the order of the day, so have STDs. Gonorrhea is ravaging the global population but how is it acquired?

According to the CDC: Gonorrhea is transmitted through sexual contact with the penis, vagina, or anus of an infected partner. Ejaculation does not have to occur for gonorrhea to be transmitted or acquired. Gonorrhea can also be spread perinatally from mother to baby during childbirth [82] Unlike AIDS/HIV that requires blood contact with the infected person for transmission to occur, gonorrhea simply only requires sexual contact with an infected person and the un-infected becomes infected.

How did Gonorrhea enter the Human Population?

We are told that the bacterium, Neisseria gonorrhoeae or gonococcus, is transmitted through sexual

---

[81] https://www.ncbi.nlm.nih.gov/pmc/articles/PMC6329377/

[82] https://www.cdc.gov/std/gonorrhea/stdfact-gonorrhea-detailed.htm

contact through the penis, vagina, anus, or mouth, but the first cause is rarely mentioned. How did the first ever human infection with gonococcus occur? Either humans are innately born with gonococcus or the bacteria must be a foreign invasion. Both scenarios cannot be true! Here is an article about this very issue: *STDs in animals and humans have a historical relationship. "Two or three of the major STDs have come from animals," says Alonso Aguirre, a veterinarian and vice president for conservative medicine at Wildlife Trust.*

"We know, for example, that gonorrhea comes from cattle to humans. Syphilis also came to humans from cattle or sheep many centuries ago, possibly, sexually.[83] Since gonococcus is a bacteria that is naturally foreign to the human ecosystem and is present in the animal ecosystem,if humans have physical and sexual interactions with those same animals then gonococcus was transmitted from animals to humans.

It has been established that gonorrhea, syphilis and AIDS/HIV are acquired through interaction with animals, sexually or otherwise. But that is not it! *The most common sexually transmitted disease among animals today is brucellosis, or undulant fever, which is common among domestic livestock and occurs in mammals including dogs, goats, deer, and rats.*[84]This report says brucellosis is sexually transmitted among animals but the world renowned Mayo Clinic says that it infects humans as well and here is what is said: *Brucellosis is a bacterial infection that spreads from animals to people. Most commonly,*

---

[83]https://www.discovermagazine.com/planet-earth/how-often-do-animals-get-stds
[84]https://www.discovermagazine.com/planet-earth/how-often-do-animals-get-stds

people are infected by eating raw or unpasteurized dairy products. Sometimes, the bacteria that cause brucellosis can spread through the air or through direct contact with infected animals.[85]The point here is that the facts have been clearly established that this is the most common sexually transmitted disease among animals. The fact that humans are having sexual intercourse with animals is also not in dispute. The fact that brucellosis is being transferred from animals to humans should not be in dispute. And when an infected human engages in intercourse with another human then there goes the spread of brucellosis into the global human population.

Gonorrhea linked to Prostate Cancer

Gonorrhea and other STDs are not only harmful to your health but it may also lead someone to paying the ultimate price with their life. I just ran into some very interesting findings about gonorrhea and prostate cancer. There is always a price to pay for going against the plan of God. And here is the link between gonorrhea and prostate cancer: *Prostate cancer is the most common neoplasm of American men and the second most common cause of cancer-related deaths. Research suggests that infection and subsequent inflammation may be an important risk factor in the pathogenesis of prostate cancer. In this meta-analysis, we examine the current epidemiological evidence for the association between specific sexually transmitted disease (STDs) and prostate cancer. This meta-analysis provides evidence of a higher rate of prostate cancer in men with a history of an exposure to gonorrhea, HPV, or any STD.*

---

[85]https://www.mayoclinic.org/diseases-conditions/brucellosis/symptoms-causes/syc-20351738

117

Further research, especially with cohort studies, is required to confirm this potentially modifiable risk factor.[86]

The risk in any sexually deviant behavior is evidently not worth the reward of any momentary, temporary pleasure that may be achieved. This all began with bestiality and then gonorrhea, from gonorrhea or other STDs to cancer and then death. This is the power of sex, the irresistible force. This list of STDs is long and this very short study cannot exhaust all the available STDs out there but we can only whet your appetite as to the dangers and risks associated with any form of sexually deviant behavior and before we close this chapter, we will look at few more STDs that are common and affect more people.

Human Papillomavirus Infection (HPV) as a STD

This is the most common STD and affects and infects more people than any other and yet it is quiet and rarely makes headline news. It is rarely talked about and yet it is responsible for the deaths of more people. Here is how it is described: *HPV infection is a viral infection that commonly causes skin or mucous membrane growths (warts). There are more than 100 varieties of human papillomavirus (HPV). Some types of HPV infection cause warts, and some can cause different types of cancer. Most HPV infections don't lead to cancer. But some types of genital HPV can cause cancer of the lower part of the uterus that connects to the vagina (cervix). Other types of cancers, including cancers of the anus, penis, vagina, vulva, and back of the throat (oropharyngeal), have been linked to HPV infection. These*

---

[86]https://pubmed.ncbi.nlm.nih.gov/15988645/#:~:text=Conclusions%3A%20This%20meta%2Danalysis%20provides,this%20potentiall y%20modifiable%20risk%20factor.

infections are often transmitted sexually or through other skin-to-skin contact. [87]

The effects of HPV are staggering and its after effects are devastating as it is reported to be the source of several kinds of cancers that are taking the lives of millions of people. Here are some stats on HPV: *It is responsible for over 80% of cervical cancers in women and 70% of throat cancers in men. About 79 million Americans, mostly in their late teens, are infected by the virus. The virus inserts its own generic code into an infected cell and either destroys it to release viral particles or transforms it into cancer cells, giving it viral properties such as unlimited growth. Cervical cancer kills more women worldwide than any other type of cancer apart from breast cancer. It accounted for 270,000 deaths in 2012, 85% of which were in developing countries and 530,000 new cases were declared in 2008 by the International Agency of Research on Cancer.* [88]

It is reported by this study that about half of all sexually active women are infected by HPV but only small percentages go on to develop some sort of cancer. This is a staggering number of deaths caused by a sexually transmitted disease and yet it hardly makes the headline news and it is hardly part of the kitchen table daily discussion. A disease that infects 79 million youths and yet it is not even on the front page news is astonishing. The situation is more likely to get worse than is currently reported since only those who engage the healthcare system are counted.But what is the origin of HPV and how did it invade the human population? Studies have shown that this

[87]https://www.mayoclinic.org/diseases-conditions/hpv-infection/symptoms-causes/syc-20351596
[88]https://www.animalresearch.info/en/medical-advances/diseases-research/human-papillomavirus-hpv/

same virus is found in animals as well. It is normally called papillomavirus (PV) and when found in humans, it is called human papillomavirus. By its very name, it suggests that this virus is available in both the human and animal population. Here is an article posted on a respected website: *Papillomaviruses (PV) are associated with epithelial malignancies in animals, including cancer in humans. Limited knowledge exists regarding the evolutionary history of non-human PV. We assessed the phylogeography of PV with emphasis in wildlife hosts.*[89]

This article uses the phrase, "epithelial malignancy in animals," and the word, "malignancy," has to do with a tumor or growth, sometimes cancerous. This article is saying that research has shown the availability of cancer in humans and the epithelial malignancy in animals. So, it's no longer a question of animals having PV but how did it cross over into the human population? Some research has shown that PV got into the human population through sex with Neanderthals. A Neanderthal is described to be a now-extinct animal that lived in Europe and parts of Asia.

Now, here is what is said: One version of the human papillomavirus, which leads to most cases of cervical cancer, evolved in humans as a result of sex with Neanderthal, a new study shows. The American Cancer Society estimates that more than 13,000 women in the United States will be diagnosed with invasive cervical cancer this year and 30 percent will die from the disease. HPV is responsible for nearly every case of cervical cancer worldwide. Although over 200 types of the virus exist, the National Cancer Institute indicates just two-HPV16 and PHV18- account for about 70 percent of all cervical cancers.

---

[89]https://www.frontiersin.org/articles/10.3389/fevo.2019.00406/full

HPV16 infection can also lead to anal cancer and cancer that develops in the throat, at the base of the tongue and the tonsils. "There is no more carcinogenic agent that causes cancer in humans than HPV, especially HPV16," said Robert Burk, who led the research.[90]

This research says the PV got into the human population through sex with a Neanderthal, probably centuries ago and assuming that it is accurate, how did it get into the animals that are infected today? It is quite possible that human obsession with bestiality has imported an unknown and unprecedented number of STDs into the human population, including HPV. It seems like every so often, there is a new STD to invade the human population and recently, the newest arrival is a STD called monkeypox.

Monkey-pox as a STD

Monkeypox virus has been in the news recently but it is not really a new virus, as it was first noticed in the human population over 50 years ago. According to the CDC: *Monkey-pox was discovered in 1958 when two outbreaks of a pox-like disease occurred in colonies of monkeys kept for research. Despite being named "monkey-pox," the source of the disease remained unknown. However, African rodents and non-human primates (like monkeys) might harbor the virus and infect people.* [91] So, the CDC has established the fact that some non-human primates, like monkeys, innately carry the virus that has been identified as monkey-pox.

But what is really monkey-pox? According to the World Health Organization (WHO), monkey-pox is a viral

---

[90]https://www.discovermagazine.com/health/scientists-trace-evolution-of-hpv-to-sex-with-neanderthals
[91]https://www.cdc.gov/poxvirus/monkeypox/about/index.html

zoonosis (a virus transmitted to humans from animals) with symptoms similar to those seen in the past in smallpox patients, although it is clinically less severe. With the eradication of smallpox in 1980 and subsequent cessation of smallpox vaccination, monkey-pox has emerged as the most important orthopoxvirus for public health.[92]

So, the fact has been established that some monkey-like animal carries the monkey-pox virus and it has also been established that the virus is transmitted from animal to human, but how is it transmitted? What is the means of its transmission? The CDC has identified physical contact as a means of transmission but sexual intercourse seems to have been identified as its primary means of transmission.

Here is a Washington post article on monkey-pox: More than 6,600 cases of monkey- pox have been detected in the United States, prompting the Biden administration to declare a public health emergency Thursday to galvanize awareness. The virus primarily spreads through exposure to an infected person's rashes or lesions, and this is the first outbreak in which contact during sex appears to be the significant driver. While infections are heavily concentrated among men who have sex with men,others can contract the virus through nonsexual contact and sharing contaminated items.[93]

This article reports the facts that monkey-pox is largely transmitted through homosexual intercourse (mainly gay men).But the true picture of the situation is not really captured in this article! *New data published in Morbidity and Mortality Weekly Report and gathered by the Centers*

[92]https://www.who.int/news-room/fact-sheets/detail/monkeypox
[93]https://www.washingtonpost.com/health/2022/08/04/monkey pox-gay-safe-sex/

for *Disease Control and Prevention (CDC) shows that 99% of monkey -pox cases in the United States are in males, and 94% of cases report recent male-to-male sexual or intimate contact.* [94] This report clearly shows that monkey-pox is mainly transmitted through sexual intercourse and almost always through male-to-male sexual intercourse.

The evidence is overwhelming that monkey pox is transmitted through male-to-male sexual acts and not just physical contacts between males.There must be something different about a male sticking his penis into the anus of another male that results in monkey- pox! Is it the contact between the sperm and stool or feces in the anus or what? This is quite puzzling because there is no evidence of a reported case of monkey-pox contracted through heterosexual vaginal sex. No evidentiary explanation to my knowledge has been provided by the CDC or WHO for why 99% of monkey-pox cases are acquired through homosexual male-to-male sexual relationships!

Without any scientific research and evidence, it is quite possible, based on inference, that some species of animal innately has the monkey- poxvirus in their stool or faces and there was some anal sex between an animal and a human male in times past. This virus was most likely contracted through a sexual act between the animal and human male. The human male now engages in sex with another human male and the virus invades the human population. Faces or stool have bacteria that can be transmitted through physical contact and that is why there is a small amount of transmission through physical contact but the vast majority is transmitted through anal male-to-male

[94]https://www.cidrap.umn.edu/news-perspective/2022/08/monkeypox-cases-reach-7500-us-99-cases-males

sexual activity. This is the destructive power of sexually deviant behavior.

Hepatitis as a STD

Hepatitis is another STD that infects hundreds of thousands of people yearly. And here is how the CDC defines it: Hepatitis means inflammation of the liver. The liver is a vital organ that processes nutrients, filters blood, and fights infections. When the liver is inflamed or damaged, its function can be affected. [95]Heavy alcohol use, toxins, some medications, and certain medical conditions can cause hepatitis. However, hepatitis is often caused by a virus. In the United States, the most types of viral hepatitis are hepatitis A, hepatitis B, and hepatitis C.[96]For the purpose of this study, we are only concerned about viral hepatitis that is mostly transmitted through sexual intercourse. But where does viral hepatitis come from and how did it enter the human population?

Dogs are one of the few animals that have been identified to be carrying viral hepatitis and here is how they become infected: *Dogs most often become infected with canine hepatitis by consuming feces, saliva, nasal discharge or urine from infected dogs. In some cases, dogs can develop severe chronic hepatitis as a result of damage caused by the accumulation of copper in the liver's cells.*[97]It is no surprise that the eating of human or other dog feces and other discharges from the animal or human body will lead to such a deadly viral infection. Can you imagine a

[95]

[96]   https://www.cdc.gov/hepatitis/abc/index.htm

[97]

https://www.guilfordjamestownvet.com/site/blog-greensboro-vet/2021/03/31/types-hepatitis-in-dogs-symptoms-treatments human male sticking his penis into the anus of another male and coming into direct contact with feces? No wonder we are faced with monkey-pox and a host of other STDs. Guess what might just happen when a human kisses a dog in the mouth and comes into direct contact with dog saliva? Or a human male engages in anal sex with a dog? Another viral hepatitis is imported into the human sexual ecosystem.

Syphilis as a STD

Syphilis is another STD that is infecting a lot of people but what is it all about? According to the CDC, syphilis is a sexually transmitted infection (STI) that can cause serious health problems without treatment. Infection develops in stages (primary, secondary, latent, and tertiary). Each stage can have different signs and symptoms.[98] So, syphilis has the potential to cause health problems if not quickly diagnosed and treated, but how does it spread? The CDC says, you can get syphilis by direct contact with a syphilis sore during vaginal, anal, or oral sex. Syphilis can spread from a mother with syphilis to her unborn baby. You cannot get syphilis through casual contact with objects, such as: toilet seats; doorknobs, swimming pools, hot tubs, bathtubs, sharing clothing, or eating utensils. [99]

The CDC concludes by saying that STDs cannot be completely avoided unless there is a complete abstention from vaginal, anal or oral sex. This is quite a surprising and remarkable statement from the CDC. The CDC would normally promote safe sex as opposed to abstinence but this is a rare instance. So, syphilis has been established to be a viral sexually transmitted infectious disease but what is its

---

98   https://www.cdc.gov/std/syphilis/stdfact-syphilis.htm
99   https://www.cdc.gov/std/syphilis/stdfact-syphilis.htm

origin and how did it enter the human population? There is no evidence that syphilis innately inhabit the human population and so, how did it enter the human population?

Another research has revealed that syphilis also has animal origins and connections: Two or three of the major STIs [in humans] have come from animals. We know, for example, that gonorrhea came from cattle to humans. Syphilis also came to humans from cattle or sheep many centuries ago, possibly sexually.[100] It has been proven that animals like cattle, sheep and likely others, innately or through infections, have the viral syphilis. It has also been proven that humans engage in sexual intercourse with cattle, and other animals. It is also true that the type of syphilis that is found in the animal population is also found in the human population. It is also true that humans do not innately have syphilis and from here, I will draw the logical conclusion that it entered the human population through sexual intercourse.

Chlamydia as a STD

Chlamydia is another STD that is ravaging the human population but what is it all about? Here is how it is defined by the CDC: *Chlamydia is a common STD that can cause infection among both men and women. It can cause permanent damage to a woman's reproductive system. This can make it difficult or impossible to get pregnant later. Chlamydia can also cause a potentially fatal ectopic*

100

https://www.understandinganimalresearch.org.uk/news/sti-day#:
-:text=STIs%20in%20animals&text=%E2%80%9CTwo%20or%20t
hree%20of%20the,centuries%20ago%2C%20possibly%20sexuall
y%E2%80%9D.

pregnancy (pregnancy that occurs outside the womb). [101] It is quite evident that this viral infection can have dire consequences if allowed to linger around without seeking immediate medical attention.

Like all other STDs, Chlamydia is transmitted through sexual intercourse and here is the CDC's take on that: You can get Chlamydia by having vaginal, anal, or oral sex with someone who has Chlamydia. Also, you can get Chlamydia even if your sex partner does not ejaculate (cum). A pregnant person with Chlamydia can give the infection to their baby during childbirth.[102] So, like all other STDs, how did this infiltrate the human population? Does it also have an animal connection? Chlamydia has been a threat to koala populations for some time now and here is a report on that: Chlamydia is a major threat to koala population-More than half of the koalas admitted to the Australia Zoo Wildlife Hospital are sick with Chlamydia.

And over the next year, the hospital will check admitted koalas for microchips so that they can gather data on whether the growing vaccination efforts are effectively preventing or treating Chlamydia.[103] It is also clear that this virus is also present in the animal as well as human population. And it is transmitted through sexual intercourse in human population and must have entered the human population through bestiality.

101

https://www.cdc.gov/std/chlamydia/stdfact-chlamydia.htm
102

https://www.cdc.gov/std/chlamydia/stdfact-chlamydia.htm
103

https://www.smithsonianmag.com/smart-news/australia-begins-vaccinating-hundreds-of-koalas-against-chlamydia-in-trial-180978900/

Other Viruses that are STDs

There is potentially an endless list of viral STDs and we cannot discuss all of them in this limited study. The evidence has shown that just about every viral STD has been brought into human population through bestiality. Herpes is another STD that is readily common in animals and humans. Here is evidence of its presence in animals: *Herpes virus infection is an important cause of disease in dogs, cats, humans and many other animal species. Infection occurs via mucosal surfaces of the respiratory and genital tracts or via epithelial surfaces such as the cornea of the eye. Herpes simplex virus (HSV) -induced keratitis is the leading infectious cause of visual impairment and blindness in humans.*[104]

The domestication of animals is posing a problem for animal rights advocates and animal lovers. Having sexual contact with animals is one thing, but living in close proximity to animals is quite another. Just the human daily contact with urine and feces from dogs, cats and other domesticated animals poses a real health care challenge. Someone has to clean after these animals and even kissing a dog or cat in the mouth and coming in contact with its saliva and then transferring that kiss to another human being poses a real healthcare challenge. Some even go to bed with their animals. An unlimited number of diseases can easily be imported into the human population just by animal-human camaraderie. There are other STDs that you can study for

---

[104]

https://www.vet.cornell.edu/departments-centers-and-institutes/baker-institute/our-research/animal-health-articles-and-helpful-links/ocular-herpesvirus-infection#:~:text=Herpesvirus%20infection%20is%20an%20important,the%20cornea%20of%20the%20eye
.

yourself, like: Pelvic Inflammatory Disease (PID)*is the most frequent uterine disease following any parturition in cows and mares*[105]; bacterial *vaginosis is found and carried by dogs*[106]; trichomoniasis is a STD carried by bulls and cows.

This chapter seeks to show that any sexual intercourse that is outside of the creator's intended plan is very destructive and millions of lives have been cut short because of human deviation from God's marvelous plan for sex. Mankind has decided to use sex primarily for pleasure and the end result is a world on fire. Many other diseases, including most cancers, are linked to STDs and this is the destructive power of STDs. Sexually deviant behavior did not just happen in a vacuum but has been given birth from the nature of human sin and this sin influences what we see and perceive, and what we think and believe.

[105]

https://vetsci.org/DOIx.php?id=10.4142/jvs.2016.17.3.413
[106]

https://vcahospitals.com/know-your-pet/vaginitis-in-dogs#:-:text
=What%20are%20the%20clinical%20signs,often%20appear%20or
ed%20and%20swollen.

Chapter 5

The Power of Sight and Thought in Sex

Sight and thought are extremely powerful forces that greatly impact sexual decisions. We use sight to admire gorgeousness and beauty in a person and that will attract or detract us from that person. The eyes are the most important organ of the body after the heart and the brain, without which, our quality of life drops tremendously. Every action that we take most often begins with sight. Seeing, perceiving, understanding, and hearing are all involved in sight. Sight has a very powerful effect on our lives because it brings us very close to the object that we are perceiving.

The very first method that we use in appraising any object is sight. Now, sight can be physical, metaphorical or spiritual. So, in the context of sex, it's all about sight. Seeing a very beautiful girl, woman or a very handsome young man, arouses all kinds of thoughts and emotions of what might happen if the woman or man says yes to you. Looking at their body structure, body size, height, weight, hairstyle, dressing, walking style and movement, breast and buttock (callipygian, a term for a finely developed buttocks) size for women, or the man's handsome looking smile that attracts a woman.

It is difficult to go to the beaches during summer as the beaches are filled with young men and women half naked. The eyes are bombarded with such images and just about every sexually deviant thought and behavior begins with sight and is nurtured in the thoughts and conceived in the heart. Most Paraphilia begins with visual images of sexual acts that manifests itself in deviant sexual acts after those thoughts take root in the heart.

Here is a report from WebMD: Paraphilias are abnormal sexual behaviors or impulses characterized by intense sexual fantasies and urges that keep coming back. The urges and behaviors may involve unusual objects, activities, or situations that are not usually considered sexually arousing.[107]Seeing and harboring sexual fantasies in the heart, leads to other sexually deviant behaviors like: exhibitionism, fetishism, frotteurism, pedophilia and voyeurism.The paraphilialist is unable and unwilling to detach him or herself from sexual images that have been seen and stored in their heart. Sight is good but it may also lead to our ultimate destruction. All that we see and perceive, is filtered through our thoughts and sooner, becomes our beliefs and once they are believed then it will sooner or later flow out through our actions. We have been talking about sight in general terms but I will critically look at physical and spiritual sight.

The Power of Physical Sight

Physical sight is using the body organ called "eyes" to see another physical object, like the beauty of God's creation. Here is an eye definition from the Cleveland Clinic: *Your eyes are organs that allow you to see. Many parts of your eye work together to bring objects into focus and bring visual information to your brain.*[108]So, from this clinical definition of the "eye," we see a connection between what we see and what we think. There are transmission lines between the eye and the brain. We often think of the brain as the place of origin of thought but read a quote from the Lord Jesus Himself: *For out of the heart come evil thoughts, murders, acts of adultery, other immoral sexual acts, thefts, false testimonies, and slanderous statements,* Matthew

107

https://www.webmd.com/sexual-conditions/guide/paraphilias-o verview
108

https://my.clevelandclinic.org/health/body/21823-eyes#:~:text=Yo ur%20eyes%20are%20organs%20that,can%20cause%20changes %20in%20eyesight.

15:19. This quote establishes a connection between our thoughts and our hearts.

The point is that our thoughts originate from our hearts, since all thoughts, good or evil, proceed from the heart. Thankfully, neurologists have identified a human organ called the "gut brain," and here is what is said: *Scientists call this little brain "enteric nervous system (ENS). And it's not so little. The ENS are two thin layers of more than 100 million nerve cells lining your gastrointestinal tract from esophagus to rectum.*[109] Neurologists have also established the fact that there is constant communication between the "gut brain or belly brain," and the brain (head brain),and so these neurologists only confirm through physical evidence what Jesus was saying in the above verse.

The heart, (biblically speaking)is not just a blood-pumping body organ but is actually the origin of thoughts and the regulator of emotions. So, why is this important? This is extremely critical information, because the eyes transmit visual information to the brain (head brain), which is in constant communication with heart (gut brain or belly brain) and these images come in contact with the thoughts of the heart (gut brain) and will sooner show up in our actions. This matter is so serious that Job had this to say: *I have made a covenant with my eyes; Why then should I look upon a young woman?* Job 31:1. So, Job understood this principle so vividly that he took drastic steps to deal with it.

He even treated his eyes as some entity outside of his body, that he will take an oath, sign a contract, and make

---

[109]

https://www.hopkinsmedicine.org/health/wellness-and-preventio
n/the-brain-gut-connection#:-:text=Scientists%20call%20this%2
0little%20brain,tract%20from%20esophagus%20to%20rectum.

an agreement between the rest of his body and his eyes. The purpose of the contract, covenant, and agreement was never to look upon a young woman with lustful intent. Why would Job take such a drastic decision? Job feared God and he had come to understand that an improper use of his eyes can lead him into a bunch of physical and spiritual trouble. If we are not very careful, sight is the very thing that sets the ball rolling in causing us to conduct our lives against the will and desire of God and here is an example: *that the sons of God saw that daughters of mankind were beautiful; and they took wives for themselves, whomever they chose.* Genesis 6:2.

There is an intense theological debate about the identity of the "sons of God and the daughters of men" in this passage but that is not a concern for us today. Our concern is that they "saw," and noticed that they were beautiful and the wrongful use of their sight led them to illicit marriages that God did not approve of. The context of Genesis 6 is about the wickedness and sinfulness of mankind and so there is nothing good about the intentions of the men seeing the daughters of men and noticing their beauty. Looking is okay but the intention for looking is sometimes the problem.

Wrong use of sight led to the fall and ultimate separation between God and mankind and all sexual deviations, other sinful conducts are a direct consequences of wrong use of sight and here is how it all went down: *When the woman saw that the tree was good for food, and that it was a delight to the eyes, and the tree was desirable to make one wise, she took some of its fruit and ate; and she also gave some to her husband with her, and he ate,* Genesis 3:6. All these events began by "sight," the woman"saw" the tree was good and she disobeyed what God had warned Adam not to do in Genesis 2:17. The entire human race is still suffering the effects of that disobedience that was put into motion by sight. This is how sin entered the world and all sin, including all sexually deviant sin, began right here in Genesis 3:6 and the result has been death and destruction ever since.

Just about every sexual sin begins with sight and here is another case in point: *But I say to you that everyone who looks at a woman with lust for her has already committed adultery with her in his heart*, Matthew 5:28.This verse raises the bar from simply looking to looking with intent! Simply looking is not a sin but looking with lustful intent is sinful. The idea of lust means that the act of adultery has already been nurtured and committed in the heart. When a young and beautiful girl passes in front of a bunch of young men, their eyes will be fixed on the woman's breast size, face and buttocks or the rear end. And they will make commentaries amongst themselves about the girl.

Why do you think that breast and buttocks implants are a very large industry? Women know that men spend a lot of time looking at their chest when they are approaching or at their rear end when they have just passed. There is a very huge demand to look from men and then the women are feeding the supply with dresses that will expose their chest as much as practicable and also expose their buttocks or rear end with extremely tight dresses that expose the size and shape of their buttocks. Sex is on the mind of the sexes and everything is centered on sex. Women on the other hand are more detailed and emotional.

They may discuss among themselves and other girls or women about the emotional part of sex. They may discuss the size and depth of the man's penis and may even ridicule their mate or sometimes, even their husband whose penis is considered small and with no depth. Some women would openly let other women know that a certain man's penis is very tiny and gives no pleasure and that they needed a man with a large penis, something large, strong, and that has depth and penetration. Where else would anyone go without looking at a beautiful or handsome member of the opposite sex?

So long as no sex act is being contemplated then looking is okay but not staring at someone for a prolonged amount of time, because when you do, then those sexual thoughts begin to take root. Then you move from looking to lust, then at that point sin has already taken place even though no physical adultery has occurred but it has already happened in the heart. The eye is often called "the window to the soul," and that is why you can sometimes look straight into another person's eyes and it may reveal something about their emotional state of mind. The eye does not reveal the emotional state of a person but most importantly, reveals the spiritual condition of the person.

You will see the world around you based on the condition of your heart. Your eyes are directly linked to your heart and if your eye is good then your whole body will be good and this is what the Lord Jesus said: *The eye is the lamp of the body; so then, if your eye is clear, your whole body will be full of light. But if your eye is bad, your whole body will be full of darkness. So if the light that is in you is darkness, how great is the darkness?* Matthew 6:22-23. It also says that: *Your word have I hid in my heart that I might not sin against thee,* Psalms 119:11.

I have earlier established the fact that the images that are seen by the eyes are directly transmitted to the heart and we are told to hide God's word in our hearts for the purpose of keeping us from sinning against God. So, whatever is in our hearts, will be reflected through our eyes. Our eyes will see the world based on the condition of our heart. With God's word hidden in our hearts, we have the ability, given by God, to see bad things and it will have minimal effect on our body because our hearts are good, we see clearly and our bodies are full of light.

This physical sight is extremely important in the context of sex because sight is the first in a series of actions that may lead to pleasurable or destructive sexual behavior. The person whom you are either having sex with now or are married to, began by sight as you were seeing and admiring them. You saw him or her, you desired him or her, and the rest was history. But physical sight was the first in a series of actions but there is more to life than having 20/20 vision.

The Psalmist made this profound request to God: *Open my eyes, that I may see wondrous things from your law*, Psalms 119:18. There is no evidence that King David, the author of Psalms 119, had any vision problems and if that was not the case, and of which I don't believe that it was, then what was he talking about? David was not blind, he had physical vision but he needed to see clearer and deeper into the things of God. It is quite possible to have 20/20 vision and yet be blind. Yes, you heard me right! So, physical sight is good but you will need more than that to navigate the pitfalls of life. You will need more than physical sight to see into things of God.

The Power of Spiritual Sight

Sight is physical, which is the natural use of sight to see physical things but it can as well be spiritual. Spiritual sight is a God-given ability and/or discernment to see that which is not physically apparent. This ability is exclusively God's but He graciously grants such ability to whomever He wills. By nature, humans are physical beings and we like to feel and touch things so that it makes sense in the natural realm of things, but the unseen world is foreign to the natural human understanding. It is quite a daunting task to talk about spiritual sight outside the context of spiritual darkness and blindness.

It is quite possible to have a 20/20 vision in the physical realm and be blind. Anyone who does not truly know Christ and is a follower of Him is a blind person, spiritually speaking. The bible frequently talks about people who are not physically blind, who need their eyes opened and here is one such case: *Then Elisha prayed and said, "O Lord, please open his eyes so that he may see." So the Lord opened the eyes of the young man, and he saw, and behold, the mountain was full of horses and chariots of fire all around Elisha*, 2 Kings 6:17.

The context here was that Elisha, his assistant and the Israelites were surrounded by the Syrian army and their chariots. Elisha's assistant looked outside and reported to Elisha that the Syrian Army And their chariots were everywhere and they were in trouble. Elisha's assistant physically saw that the opposing army was advancing towards them and they were out-numbered. He was terrified at the physical sight of the opposing army, knowing that they did not have the manpower and equipment to fight. And here is how Elisha responded: *And he* (Elisha), answered, *Fear not: for they that be with us are more than they that be with them*, 2 Kings 6:16. These are two people looking at the same situation, but one is seeing physically and the other is seeing spiritually.

His assistant probably said to himself something like, "What are you talking about? We are about to die!" and the clear distinction was that Elisha was seeing spiritually and his assistant was seeing physically. The assistant was not blind physically, but he was not able to see what Elisha was seeing. Elisha was seeing outside the physical realm but his assistant was seeing in the physical realm. Elisha prayed and interceded for God to grant his assistant eyes to see what he was seeing.

And when God granted Elisha's request, his assistant's vision was transported from the physical realm into the spiritual. God opened the eyes of the young man, and he saw what Elisha was seeing: and behold, the mountain was full of horses and chariots of fire all around Elisha and his assistant. The young man moved from spiritual blindness (even though he saw physically) to spiritual sight. But not so for the Syrian Army, the enemies of God and those who were encamping to kill Elisha and the Israelites. They moved from physical sight to physical blindness: *And when they came down to him, Elisha prayed unto the Lord, and said, Smite this people, I pray thee, with blindness. And He smote them with blindness according to the word of Elisha*, 2 Kings 6:18.

So sex can only be seen the way God sees it and if we are given new eyes and vision to see it the way that God sees it then we will have a fulfilling sex life. Elisha's prayer to God resulted in physical blindness so that they could no longer see and fight against Elisha. If someone has physical sight but is spiritually blind then they cannot see sex the way that God sees it. They will have a deviant view of sex simply because they are spiritually blind. Blindness (spiritual blindness) is a picture of being dead in sin and separated from God. It is a state of depravity and being under the power and control of Satan and here is a vivid description of that: *To open their eyes, so that they may turn from darkness to light and from the power of Satan to God, that they may receive forgiveness of sins and a place among those who are sanctified by faith in me*, Acts 26:18.

The people in this context had physical sight but the text says they needed their eyes opened because they were in darkness and under the power and control of Satan. Just as darkness represents being under Satan's control, light represents being under God and Christ's control. Light represents someone that has received forgiveness of sin and is now a Christian and darkness represents someone that is not, hence the two kingdoms: light and darkness; anyone who sees sex in a perverted manner, then, in all likelihood, is still in darkness and needs to get their spiritual eyes opened so that they may see and be translated from the kingdom of darkness into the kingdom of light. It is impossible to have a correct view of sexual intercourse unless you also have 20/20 spiritual eyes to see clearly but also bad eyes lead to bad thoughts.

The Power of Thoughts in Sex

Thoughts are a very powerful force that can enhance or wreck our lives in general and our sex life in particular. What we see and perceive will be embedded in our thoughts. If someone spends a lot of time watching pornography, then they will think pornographically since the images that have been watched are stored in their head brain and the belly brain (gut). We are the sum product of what we think. We have already established the fact that thoughts come from the heart, but those thoughts are heavily influenced by images that are seen, recorded and stored in the heart (gut brain). What you think may, in large part, affect your outlook on life and that is why millions of people are on some type of anxiety or depression prescription or non-prescription medication for the purpose of numbing their feelings and controlling their thinking. All sexual battles are fought in the brain and so right thinking leads to right living.

Unrealistic expectations can damage anyone's thought life. You may believe that sex with a certain person may result in a certain amount of happiness and you may quickly realize that it was not the case and you are left abandoned and rejected. And as a result, shame is brought into the equation. There is a feeling of worthlessness that creeps in and before you know it, the person is depressed and even suicidal. People engage in sex with all kinds of unrealistic expectations that hardly ever materialize. Rational thinking has been replaced by emotionalism. Facts do not matter because emotions have taken over.

People make emotional decisions about sex because pleasure is driving their thinking and instant gratification is the goal. People spend their entire life in regrets over bad thinking sexual decisions and the consequences cannot be reversed. What they were expecting to gain from that bad thinking sexual encounter was not worth the price paid decades later. Millions have died from AIDS/HIV and other STDs from bad thinking sexual decisions. Millions are currently paying the price of severe health issues because of bad thinking sexual decisions.

Millions of unwanted babies have been aborted because of bad thinking sexual decision. People are making sexual decisions without pondering all the possible ramifications. The guilt and shame that comes with aborting a baby, and that baby is not just a bunch of tissue! That baby is a person at the moment of conception and terminating the life of the baby is murder, plain and simple. The baby does not achieve personhood at some later date, but personhood is innately in the child's DNA at conception and even before.

141

All the attributes of a person are in that fetus and all that is needed is development and growth.

So, abortion is the killing of a person and the taking of life, made in the image of God.The baby is a complete human being with unlimited value and potential who is brutally murdered in the womb. Wrong thinking about sex has led to the murder of millions if not billions of babies. Millions are living with an unbelievable amount of emotional trauma because of bad thinking sexual decisions. It is very critical to think right about life in general and about sex, in particular then you will live right. And here is a quote about right thinking: *Finally, brothers, whatever is true, whatever is honorable, whatever is right, whatever is pure, whatever is lovely, whatever is commendable, if there is any excellence and if anything worthy of praise, think about these things,* Philippians 4:8.

The apostle Paul was admonishing his audience to think true thoughts and what does it really mean to think true thoughts? So to think true thoughts means that our thinking about any given matter or subject should be in-line with God's thinking. We will be in error if we are not thinking God's thoughts. We have to see sin the way that God sees it and we have to see sex the way God sees sex. The above text also talks about thinking honorable thoughts.

The Greek word translated here as honorable, has the idea of reverend and venerable thoughts – thoughts that are reflected in character and reverence. Then the text talks about thinking the right thoughts. The word,"right," has been translated from the Greek word, "dikaia"and has the idea of thinking upright, virtuous, righteous thoughts. If anyone has righteous thoughts about sex, then they cannot have a deviant view of sexual intercourse. They will act and do right.

The text above also talks about thinking pure thoughts. The word that is translated here in most of our English translations as "pure," comes from the Greek word,"hagnos", which means "holy," "sacred," "undefiled," and this is a uniquely Divine attribute. We are called to think as God thinks. The apostle Paul finally admonishes his audience to have this pattern of thinking in their lives. It is impossible to have sexually impure thoughts and think pure thoughts simultaneously. How does anyone get to think pure thoughts? Humans naturally think impure thoughts until it pleases God to grant them a new heart and a heart transplant. We have already established the fact that generally, the human thought life is corrupt and evil because the source of our thoughts is evil and corrupt. Our thoughts originate from our hearts (Matthew 15:19),which are evil and corrupt.

A corrupt heart is incapable of thinking pure and righteous thoughts and this is what God told the prophet Ezekiel in regards to a new heart: *Moreover, I will give you a new heart and put a new spirit within you; and I will remove the heart of stone from your flesh and give you a heart of flesh. And I will put My Spirit within you and bring it about that you walk in My statutes, and are careful and follow My ordinances,* Ezekiel 36:26-27.God is the first-ever heart transplant surgeon who never lost a patient during and after surgery.

In order to think pure and righteous thoughts, two things must happen first: (1) a heart transplant by God must have taken place and (2) the Spirit of God placed alongside the new heart and in addition to a heart transplant and the Spirit of God, new abilities are also included. The ability to walk in the statutes of God and follow His ordinance. New abilities to see sex the way that God sees it. New abilities to abstain from all forms of sexually deviant and immoral conduct. New abilities to do the will of God. New abilities to see clearly and think clearly about sex. Now thoughts may sometimes not be as dangerous until they are believed.

Thoughts lead to Beliefs

We can sometimes hardly control what thoughts go through our minds so long as those thoughts do not become beliefs. Actions that we take about sex or any other matter are based on sets of beliefs that have been influenced by what we see and think about the subject matter. Thoughts do not become actions until those thoughts are believed and trusted. We are literally products of our belief system. So you can see bad images, and think about them all day long, but until you believe what you watched then you will not act on them.

So, if someone is having sexual intercourse with an animal, then it is because they have seen or heard someone else having sex with an animal and that has influenced their thinking over time, and that thinking has turned into a belief system and taking action on that belief is pretty easy because they are convinced that it is the right thing to do. Homosexuality is based on what people have seen, read and thought about and over time those thoughts became beliefs. Likewise are adultery and fornication, which are based on what people have watched, what friends and families do, read about, and think about. Now, over time those thoughts turn into a belief system and those beliefs are easily acted upon.

No one can take any action unless they believe in that action and that is why it is critically import to protect and guard what goes into your belief system because your actions will depend on it and here is what the author of

Proverbs said: *Above all else, guard your heart, for everything you do flows from it,* Proverbs 4:23. Wow! This is the assessment by Solomon, the author of the book of proverbs. He began by using the phrase, "above all else," to mean that this should be the number one issue in your life, and nothing else comes before it.

Solomon must have known something that we don't and it is no surprise that he is called the wisest man that ever lived. Your number one goal in life is to guard your heart, and protect it from all enemies, foreign and domestic. It is like depositing money in the vault of the United States Federal Reserve Bank. Thieves cannot break-in nor can the money be destroyed by fire. Likewise, and in like manner, guard your heart. Solomon is not talking about guarding your heart from some heart attack or some cardiac disease, but he is talking about putting a guard around the images and information that goes into your heart.

I guess you must have heard the computer information system jargon: "garbage in, garbage out," meaning that the computer output is a function of its input. What you put in is what you get out, no more, no less. So, you are to guard your heart and you may ask the logical question, why? Am I not free to do as I please? Solomon had an answer ready for you: *for everything you do flows from it.* Solomon is saying that do not kid yourself; whatever images and information that you allow into your heart will sooner or later show up in your actions. Solomon was only echoing what the Lord Jesus Himself said in Matthew 15:19 that evil thoughts come from the heart.

So, what information and images that you feed into your heart and you believe it then it will soon show up in your actions. So, having the right kind of sight will lead to the right thoughts about sexual intercourse and those right and pure thoughts will eventually lead to the right belief and right belief will lead to right actions about sexual intercourse. This is the summation by Solomon of the duty of mankind on the earth: This is the end of the matter; all hath been heard: *Fear God, and keep His commandments; for this is the whole duty of man*, Ecclesiastes 12:13. This was also succinctly put by the Westminster Shorter Catechism: *Man's chief end is to glorify God and enjoy Him forever.*[110]

So, seeking temporary pleasures through deviant sexual behaviors is not God's plan for mankind and for you. God wants you to glorify Him in your sexual intercourse, obey His commandments, fear Him and in so doing, you will enjoy Him forever. Perform sex to the glory of God. God is watching you! Let all that you do, in word or deed, be for His glory. Seek no glory for yourself for He will not share His glory with another. There is no better way to do this than in a God-ordained heterosexual, monogamous marital union. The marital union is the most powerful institution on the planet, but what is a marital union?

---

[110]

https://en.wikipedia.org/wiki/Westminster_Shorter_Catechism#:~:text=Q.,and%20to%20enjoy%20him%20forever.

Chapter 6

The Power of Marriage

Marriage is the unit which helps to establish a family, a village, a town, a city, a state, a country, and then the world. A nation, state, city, or the world may come to ruin without strong and stable family units, called marriages. The stronger the marriages, the stronger that nation and its people will be.When this unit is shattered and nonexistent, then a lot of societal ills are brought to the surface.

The breakup or the nonexistence of the family unit called marriage has led to a host of problems like these: Approximately 1 million divorces are recorded every year in Europe and another 850 000 in the USA. It is estimated that slightly more than half of all divorces involve children under the ages of 18. In addition, an increasing number of parents are not officially married, and if they break up, their children face similar life changes as children of married parents getting a divorce. Parental break-up is in most cases due to long-term conflicts in the family, and detrimental effects of divorce and the underlying conflicts on the mental well-being of children as well. [111]

There is a saying by Pope John Paul II that says, "As the family goes, so goes the nation and so goes the whole world in which we live."[112] This quote pretty much sums it all up,that the morals of a single family has the potential to influence the morals of the entire world over time.

---

[111]

https://academic.oup.com/eurpub/article/27/5/829/3760077

[112]

https://www.brainyquote.com/quotes/pope_john_paul_ii_138667

Remember that the world began with just one family, the family of Adam and Eve.

The family then is the nucleus that holds it all together without which, all hell breaks loose. The morals of a nation, and by extension the world, are derived from the morals of the family. You may often hear the saying, "an apple does not fall far from the tree." A child will most likely grow up to mimic the morals of his or her family of origin. Children do not suddenly manufacture morals other than the fact that they are born with a corrupt nature. Adolf Hitler did not suddenly come up with his morals but must have been heavily influenced by the morals of his family. The morals of a nation are positively or negatively influenced by the morals of the family. Marriage is the power that holds it all together. The marriage union is the power that holds it firmly knit together. The marriage union is what holds the family firmly knit and held together. But what really is a marriage?

Image of a happy marriage

What is a Marriage?

The meaning of marriage remains highly debated and controversial. This word can have a legal, cultural, religious and theological understanding but the underlying meaning of the word is the same, in my humble opinion. The basic thrust of this word is to join, mix. Its application and context may be different but its underlying meaning remains the same. The word, "marriage," actually appears in the bible but is missing in some foundational passages on marriage like Genesis 2:24, Matthew 19:5, Mark 10:7, Ephesians 5:31.

The word that is primarily translated as marriage in the New Testament and in most of our English translations is the Greek word "gamos," and in just about every context in which it is found, it means feast, banquet, a wedding banquet, as in John 2:1, Matthew 22:8,10, and in Revelation 19:7, it is used to refer to the intimate and everlasting union of Christ with His church. This word also appears in LXX in

Genesis 29:22, to mean feast, and in Ester 1:5, 2:18, 9:22 to mean banquet.

This meaning of marriage has to do with the ceremonial aspects, like presenting the bride and the groom to the invitees, the drinking and the dances, and whatever ceremonies are involved to celebrate or in celebration. And sometimes, it could just mean a banquet celebration. So, in today's terms, what really is a marriage? Is it the signing of papers at the county clerk's office? Is it the exchanging of wedding rings? Is it the pronunciation made by some religious official in some religious building? What is it?

This word is translated in the Old Testament from the Hebrew word, "mishteh,"and this *Hebrew word appears between 43 to 45 times in the entire Old Testament and about 19 of those were in the book of Esther*[113] and that should make Esther the book of festivals. The word has several other Old Testament appearances. The following definitions for marriage have been obtained from the merriam-webster's dictionary:*1.(a) the state of being united as spouses in a consensual and contractual relationship recognized by law. (b) the mutual relation of married: WEDLOCK. (c) the institution whereby individuals are joined in a marriage. 2. an act of marrying or the rite by which the married status is effected, especially: the wedding ceremony and the attendant festivities or formalities. 3. an intimate or close union: the marriage of painting and poetry- J.T. Shawcross.*[114]

---

[113]

https://www.biblestudytools.com/lexicons/hebrew/kjv/mishteh.html

[114]   https://www.merriam-webster.com/dictionary/marriage

This definition uses various synonyms like "united," in (1a), "mutual," in (1b), "joined," in (1c), "marrying," in (2) and "intimate, union," in (3). So, whatever marriage is or means, must have to do with uniting, mutual, joining and marrying. This is quite an interesting use of synonyms to define the meaning of marriage. The word "join," is used in key biblical passages to define marriage. The Greek word, "proskollao," has been translated from the Hebrew word, "dabaq"in Genesis 2:24 in the LXX or the Septuagint.

This same word appears outside the marriage context in Joshua 23:8, to mean to "glue to God, cleave to God, cling to God, unite to God, cling tightly or hold fast" and is also transported into the New Testament in the marriage context in Matthew 19:5, Mark 10:7, and Ephesians 5:31. This Greek word carries with it the idea to mean: *to glue upon, glue to, to join one's self to closely, cleave to, stick to.*[115]So, the biblical definition of marriage has the concept of joining permanently and that concept is undergirded in its basic meaning.

The idea of joining permanently without any possibility of separation. It is like welding two pieces of metal together. Heat and fusion has occurred and the metals have melted and its elements intertwined and the possibility of a clean separation does not exist again, ever. This is the idea behind this word and joining may take on several significance and importance.

Philosophical Arguments for Marriage

The idea of joining to mean marriage is quite fascinating to say the least! The premise of using the word,"join," to apply to anything or in any context would

---

[115]   https://www.studylight.org/lexicons/eng/greek/4347.html

necessarily imply that the things or components being joined are distinct and different. They must possess distinct essences and qualities otherwise joining would be unnecessary. Someone may ask why you can't join two identical pieces of wood together. That is also an interesting observation! I guess, you could fasten or attach the pieces together but not necessarily join them with the same meaning of this biblical word in mind. They must be distinct and different in essence for real joining to take place. There is no need to really join anything unless they are different in essence.

A better example would be joining or mixing two identical types of tomatoes and the result will have no effect because they are identical pieces in quality and essence. The purpose and goal of joining is that the resultant effect will be altered and different. What would really be the goal and purpose of a male human being and another male human being of identical essence of being joined? What are they trying to accomplish? Why would a female human being be joined to another female human being? What is the goal to be accomplished? They really can't be joined because they are the same in essence and quality. Remember that the purpose and goal of joining anything together is to accomplish a different resultant effect.

If they are the same in essence of being then the resultant effect is zero and nothing is accomplished. The same is true if a female is to be joined to another female then the resultant effect is also zero. Even the very word, "marriage," implies the merging of two distinct things to form a new entity. So, for a marriage to exist, the parties to it or the things being married must possess innately different and distinct qualities. Like the marriage between sports and poetry and not sports and sports or poetry and poetry.

The Merriam-Webster dictionary definition above mentioned, "marriage of painting and poetry," and that is why this can be rightly called a marriage. The marriage of sports and the media would be another example. If all this is true, of which I believe that it is, then why the term, "same sex marriage?" The word, "same," and "marriage," cannot be in the same phrase. If the sexes are the same then it cannot be called a marriage or a union. Because, for it to be truly a marriage or a union, the sexes have to be opposing. The idea of same sex marriage is truly an oxymoron. Another term that is often used is "same sex union," and again, the word, "same sex, and "union," are mutually exclusive with no possibility of cohabitation. But what about the fact that the sexes are different and does it really matter?

Biological Arguments for Marriage

Is biology a factor to be considered when it comes to marriage? We have made a philosophical argument that there must be a difference in essence and quality for any marriage, joining or union to occur but what kind of difference are we talking about? No true union can occur without a difference in biology. Two people with identical body parts cannot marry because all their body parts are the same. The very word "marriage," means to join, or unite two parts, things that are completely different.

There is no need to call it "marriage," if they are identical in body parts. The female body parts are innately female and can never be replicated in a male, even through surgery. A female has two breasts and a male has zero and the female breasts provide at least two critical functions: provide sexual pleasure for the male husband and provide nourishment for an infant child. These critical biological differences can never be acquired by a male. These are uniquely female biological differences.

The reproductive body parts of a female are unique and different. Take for example, the vagina, which provides at least three vital functions: the release of urine waste and other body fluids, a location for the male penis to be inserted into the female for reproduction, and an exit for a child to be born into the world. These are innately and uniquely female body parts and cannot be replicated in a natural born male. These distinctions are vital and crucial for any semblance of marriage to even be contemplated.

The womb and the uterus, where the conception of a child takes place, are also natural female body parts, which no natural born male can ever possess. These are also uniquely and natural female biological differences. The male penis protrudes from the lower parts of the stomach and between the legs and its function is to provide intercourse between a male and a female. This is an innately male body part and it cannot be replicated in a female. The sperm which comes out of the male during sexual intercourse is unique to the male and the eggs of the female in the ovaries that are produced only in the female are unique,essential, and required differences for any idea of marriage to even be contemplated or conceived. These biological arguments make the case that in order for a marriage to occur, there must be a biological differentiation in the sexes or partners involved and that difference is also seen theologically.

Theological Arguments for Marriage

Marriage is not only supported by a philosophical and a biological argument but also a theological one, in the areas of headship, trinitarianism, the marriage between God and Israel,and the Lord Jesus Christ and the church. The marriage relationship has profound theological significance. God, the Father, God, the Son and God, the Holy Spirit are the same in essence but different in function and role. And by "essence," I am talking about the intrinsic nature, quality, character and being of the Father, Son and the Holy Spirit being co-equal and the same.

There is no difference in their quality of being. Philip, one of the disciples of Jesus, did not initially get this theological understanding and here is what he had to say: *Philip said to Him, "Lord, show us the Father, and it is enough for us." Jesus said to him, "Have I been with you for so long a time, and yet you have not come to know Me, Philip? The one who has seen Me has seen the Father; how can you say, Show us the Father?* John 14:8-9. Philip had been with Jesus for a long time (not sure how long) but a long time (possibly three years)and yet, he did not truly know who He was. (Quite scary to say the least, to be with Jesus and not know Him).

It is possible to be around Jesus or in a church for a long period of time and not really know Jesus, and that was the case with Philip. He did not know His true identity. He had no idea that he was in the presence of God for all that time and did not know it. The point here is that Jesus was claiming co-equality with the creator of the universe in essence, intrinsic nature, quality and character. So, John 14:8-9 establishes the fact that they are equal but in other places, it talks about their difference in role or function and here is a quote: *But I want you to understand that Christ is the head of every man, and the man is the head of a woman, and God is the head of Christ*, 1 Corinthians 11:3. This text says that God is the head of Christ and man is the head of woman. The headship issues here are only in terms of roles and function but not in terms of essence. So, the

155

same is true between the husband and wife. They are co-equal before God in matters of salvation and their standing before God but are different in roles and function. Here is what the text says: *There is neither Jew nor Greek, there is neither slave nor free, there is neither male nor female; for all are one in Christ Jesus,* Galatians 3:28.

The key takeaway from this verse is that, "for they are one in Christ Jesus." A male and a female stand before God as co-equals in matters of salvation but with different roles and functions, while on earth and in a marital relationship. So, the male and female marital relationship is a picture of God and Christ. God is co-equal with Christ and man is co-equal with woman. God is co-equal with Christ in essence and man is co-equal with woman in essence. This relationship mirrors that of our earthly marriages. There is no mention of same sex couples being co-equal with God or Christ. A male (man) and another male (man) are not co-equal with God and Christ and likewise a female (woman) and another female (woman). There is no theological need for such a comparison. There is also a theological trinitarian link in marriage.

Trinitarian Arguments for marriage

Some of you may say that there could not possibly be any trinitarian connection in marriage and that is fair and valid skepticism. The writer of Ecclesiastes seems to suggest that there could be a third person in a God ordained heterosexual monogamous marriage relationship and here is how the text reads: *Two are better than one because they have a good return for their labor; for if either of them falls, the one will lift up his companion. But woe to the one who falls when there is not another to lift him up! Furthermore, if two lie down together they keep warm, but how can one be warm alone? And if one can overpower him who is alone, two can resist him. A cord of three strands is not quickly torn apart.* Ecclesiastes 4:9-12.

The book of Ecclesiastes is written in the genre of poetry and in the area of wisdom sayings by the author Solomon. So, verse 9 through 12 has to be taken in the context of a heterosexual monogamous marriage union. And of importance to us is verse 12 which makes the progression by raising a hypothetical possibility, and the progression is "if," one is able to overpower him who is alone, two can resist him. And this fits perfectly well with the genesis of the argument in verse 9, which says, "two are better than one because they have a good return for their labor." The argument that the writer is making is that marriage is a force to be reckoned with but a God ordained marriage is a very powerful and unbreakable force.

Notice the progression in the argument in verse 12: *one can overpower, two can resist and three is not quickly torn apart.* But what is the identity of the third person represented at the end of verse 12? Here is what one commentator described as the identity of the third person in this passage: *Here-in is seen an adumbration of the doctrine of the Holy Trinity, the Eternal Three in One; of the three Christian virtues, faith, hope and charity, which go to make the Christian life; of the Christian's body, soul, and spirit, which are* consecrated *as a temple of the Most High.*[116] I do agree with this commentator that the Trinity is in view but disagree that the Trinity in the passage means hope, faith and charity.

---

[116]

https://biblehub.com/commentaries/ecclesiastes/4-12.htm

These are attributes of the Godhead and I do not see that idea being thought anywhere else in Scripture. I believe that the third person in the "cord of three strands," is a person of the Godhead not an attribute of the Godhead. Most likely the Spirit of Christ or the Holy Spirit. In a God ordained marriage, husband and wife have the Holy Spirit living inside of them (Romans 8:9) and are sealed (Ephesians 4:30) with it and never to leave. In Romans 8:9 alone, the Holy Spirit is identified as the Spirit of God and the Spirit of Christ. So, the Spirit of God and the Spirit of Christ is synonymous with the Holy Spirit.

Now, if the Holy Spirit is in the marriage then there is no possibility of it being quickly torn apart. If God is for the marriage then who can be against the marriage? You often hear the phrase, "two are better than one," but a better phrase would be, "three are better than two". Without the aid and help of the Holy Spirit, it is very difficult and impossible to sustain a marriage. I do not see how any other form of marriage would fit the description in Ecclesiastes 4:9-12. Verse 11 talks about," if two lie down together they keep warm, but how can one be warm alone"?

I am sure that two men or two women can lie down together and make each other warm. I would want to believe that the opposite is true but there is no evidence from the text that a homosexual relationship is in view or even contemplated. So, the theological doctrine of the Trinity is also reflected in the marriage relationship. And by marriage I mean a God ordained marriage by followers and disciples of Jesus Christ. So, two people of the same sex should repel each other as opposed to attract each other, naturally.

Electromagnetic Argument for Marriage

Someone may simply raise the question, what does electromagnetism have to do with marriage? That is a very fair and logical question! The question that we are trying to answer in this chapter is, what constitutes a marriage? Does it really matter, the sexual orientation of the people involved? Does it mean that any two people of any sex or gender can get together in a marital union? How do people of the same sex get attracted and drawn to each other for the purpose of sexual intercourse and even a marital union?

What is the force and chemistry that attracts and draws humans of the same or opposite genders to each other? Have you ever held two pieces of magnets in your hand to test their polarity? Poles are the movement of electromagnetic waves. There is a famous phrase in physics and electromagnetism, which says: "like poles repel and unlike poles attract," and that simply means the magnetic force will attract to each order if the poles or polarities are different and will repel from each other if the poles are the same. Even in simple power generation theory, there is a positive and negative terminal.

No power will be generated if it is all positive or all negative poles or polarity. Both are required for power to be generated. So, naturally, when a male is attracted to a female, sparks are flying everywhere and the amount of power being generated could light up a city. The amount of power is so strong that nothing can stop it. Have you ever tried to stop your eighteen year old daughter from seeing her boyfriend? How did it go? Who won and who lost? This is the force that is generated when unlike poles attract. There is no evidence that a force of that magnitude exists in a homosexual relationship.

The entire nervous system is thrown into a panic mode at receiving the news that your beloved boy or girlfriend is about to dump you for your close friend! Your power generation is thrown into overdrive. You cannot even think right! You cannot function. You suddenly start thinking that your life is over. You are even suicidal.

The science of electrical engineering says" that like poles repel".. There is a natural rejection and push away from the poles. Two human beings of the same sex are considered like poles and have no natural power. They cancel each other out. They are supposed to repel each order because of identical polarity. It is like having a positive and another positive terminal or a negative and another negative terminal. No power can be generated. No union can occur because there is no female and male terminal and no power can be generated. There is power in a heterosexual union and marriage is defined in such a union. So, societies and the world communities over time have accepted heterosexual marriages of one man and one wife as normative, yet, communities around the world view polygamy as an alternative view of marriage.

Monogamous vs. Polygamous Marriages

The debate about the number of women that any man should marry has been going on since the early biblical times, and is ongoing with no chance of abating any time soon. How many women should any man marry? And is it normative to

Image of a Polygamous marriage

marry multiple women? It seems to me that the human desire for more sex may be a driving force behind the need for more sexual partners. I listened to a lady who is in a monogamous marital union and she said, "I don't see myself having sex with just one man for the rest of my life; that is so boring."

So, sexual dissatisfaction may be another driver behind the need for more than one lifetime marriage sexual partner. There is a craving for more, and more, and more. I have talked to several men who are in monogamous marital unions and yet they are still looking at a woman lustfully, right in front of me, and telling me what they can do with the woman. I will say something like this to them, "I thought that you are married," and I will get a response like this, "Yeah, but one is not enough, I need to quench my thirst." Really!

So, the wife who is at home or the husband at home is not able to provide you with sexual satisfaction but someone else out there will? This is a much larger problem than I am able to fully understand. Proponents of polygamy would sometimes argue that polygamy prevents people from other sexual sins, like adultery. The argument here is that instead of committing adultery, they would rather legally marry multiple women, so that there would be no need for adultery. Really? Who are you kidding? I personally know an endless list of men who are polygamous outside the United States and in other countries, and yet they have fathered an endless number of children outside those polygamous marriages. David Koresh, who was the leader of the Branch Davidians, who was killed during an FBI raid on his compound in 1993, was also a well-known polygamist in the United States.

He is reported to have had 16 children.[117] He is also reported to have had sex with just about any woman or girl who entered and lived in his compound in Waco, Texas. If you read his life story, he had an obsession with sex, and that may be true for most if not all men who are engaged in polygamous marriages.

So, polygamy is not the answer to adultery. If anyone has a desire for more sex, then being legally married to multiple women will not stop that desire. If you are not satisfied with one, then you will not be satisfied with a hundred. Solomon is recorded to have had 700 wives and 300 concubines (1 Kings 11:3) and no evidence is recorded that he had anything close to happiness and contentment in those marriages and the reverse is likely true. Some proponents of polygamy have argued that the practice is actually sanctioned by the bible – after-all, several biblical persons, including Solomon, were in polygamous marital

---

[117]   https://en.wikipedia.org/wiki/David_Koresh

unions. This is a very fair and valid observation and objection.

The biblical Patriarchs, such as Abraham, Isaac, and Jacob, were all in polygamous marriages. The king of Israel, King David, had a host of sexually deviant conducts, including polygamy. The Old Testament is filled with polygamous marriages and that causes us to wonder, was God really okay with that? After all, it is all over the Old Testament! Some proponents of polygamous marriages have used Paul's teachings on marriage in 1 Corinthians 7:2 as proof in the text that polygamy is expressly sanctioned in the bible and here is the text: *But because of sexual immoralities, each man is to have his own wife, and each woman is to have her own husband.*

The word, "each," is an adjective in the singular, substantive, functioning as a noun and the subject of this part of the phrase (man was added by the translators as it is not in the original Greek text) and the object of "each" is "wife," also a feminine singular noun. Secondly, the word, "each," next to "woman," is also a feminine singular adjective, in the substantive, functioning as a noun and its object is "her own husband," in the singular. Some proponents of polygamous marriages have attempted to say that this passage is teaching that, "each man," singular, is to have his "own wife," plural. They conclude that the man can have many wives but the woman can have only one husband. The grammar and linguistics of this verse and the entire context of 1 Corinthians 7 refutes any such interpretation. The context of 1 Corinthians 7 does not support that interpretation and that idea is not even taught anywhere else in the bible.

Yet, others have turned to several Old Testament examples of polygamous marriages and concubine relationships as irrefutable evidence that polygamous marriages are sanctioned by God. That is quite a logical way to arrive at the conclusion, right? I mean, let's be real; it is all over the Old Testament! It is like telling your best buddy that the bible is against drinking alcohol and proponents of alcohol consumption will respond by saying something like: why did Jesus turn water into wine and the people at the wedding feast in John 2 drank it all until it ran out?

There is a difference between allowing something and permitting or approving of it to happen. Let's say that you have a stubborn female child and you have warned her about the dangers of having sex outside of marriage and she does it anyway! So, you did not permit or approve of the conduct of your child, but you passively allowed it because of the stubbornness of their heart. Divorce is allowed by God but not permitted or approved because of the hardness of the human heart.

The guidelines for marriage is clearly stated in Genesis: *Therefore shall a* man leave his father and his mother, and shall cleave unto his wife: and they shall *be one flesh.* Genesis 2:24. The man is abandoning his natural family and joining unto [his] wife. The personal pronoun, "his," is intentionally placed at that location to emphasize the fact that the man is not cleaving or joining unto "women," as unto many wives, but unto "his," "wife," singular.

This is not even just an Old Testament concept, but it has application for all people, and all dispensations for all times. The way that you may know what I have said is true is that this same verse is quoted by Jesus in Matthew 19:5, Mark 10:7 and by Paul in Ephesians 5:31.This is the foundational teaching on marriage, on which all other teachings are derived. There is no room for all other marital

164

deviant views and even polygamous marriages have impacted society in ways unimaginable.

Sociological Impact of Polygamy

Believe it or not, polygamy is a deviation and leaves a profound, lasting and damaging impact on the fabric of society. I see no real difference between polygamy and adultery since they all produce the same results: unfaithfulness and others. Children born in polygamous homes are living in a hell of fire. There are step-mother and step-father issues; there are step-brother and step-sister issues; there are real problems bonding strangers or half-brothers and half-sisters together to form a family unit; there are really deep emotional and bonding issues that are sometimes irresolvable until death in most cases.

There are deep feelings in the soul of being different and not being fully part of the family. The father never sits down to consider all the societal ramifications of polygamy before engaging into it. These are extremely selfish actions in all its forms. Families and society function smoothly and harmoniously in monogamous marriage relationships. So when the children are of the same father but of different mothers, then sooner or later, they will begin to identify themselves through their mother's lineage and all hell breaks loose if and when the father dies.You may hear about the children of Hagar and the children of Sarah, but they are all Abraham's children. There is difficulty with unity even among children from a monogamous marriage, so what do you expect would be the case in a polygamous marriage?

There is hardly any semblance of unity and would hardly be. Abraham was married to Sarah but also bore a child named Ishmael with Hagar, Genesis 16:1-16, 21:8-21. At the suggestion of Sarah, Abraham's wife, Abraham agreed to have a child by Hagar, Sarah's maid. This is what happens when we get outside of the plan of God. God had promised Abraham that he would have a son through Sarah, but they had doubts about the plan of God and considered it unrealistic because they were outside the age of child bearing, and so they took matters into their own hands.

The results of their decision are still being felt more than two thousand years later. The wars between the Jewish and the Arab people are somehow linked to polygamy. The children of Sarah (Jewish People) are fighting the children of Hagar (Arab People). They both claim that Abraham was their father and they are correct in the physical sense. Think about the twelve tribes of Israel that originated with four wives or two wives and two concubines of Jacob, namely Leah, Rachel, Bilhah and Zilpah, Genesis 29:32-35, 30:17-21. Almost all land wars in Israel are a result of polygamy. These are mostly wars between brothers and sisters of the same father but different mothers. The lineage of the father has some importance when the father is alive but when the father dies, almost all lineages revert back to their mothers. The children band in groups based on the lineage of their mothers.

Even today, there are all kinds of battles being fought over land and property as a result of polygamy. King David, king of Israel, was a famous polygamist and his house was on fire. This is true that there are battles in just about every home because of the human sin problem but polygamy takes the problems to another level. Children from polygamous homes may have to fight a perpetual war among themselves long after their parents are gone. Isaac and Ishmael, Abraham's children from a polygamous home, are still fighting today, approximately 2000 years later.

We all remember the adultery in David's life with Bathsheba but that was not all; there was also rape in the family. Amnon, one of David's sons, raped Tamar, one of David's daughters, 2 Samuel 13-1-22. David was their father but they were of different mothers. Absalom, another son of David, who was of the same mother as Tamar, killed Amnon for raping his sister, 2 Samuel 13:23-38. The human race already has enough problems in monogamous marriages and throwing polygamy into the mix exacerbates the societal problems to unbelievable levels. All kinds of societal ills are linked to polygamy and other sorts of sexual deviations.

You are free to do as you please and God is kind, patient, and long-suffering, but His kindness will not last forever. He is giving you a very long rope to examine your ways. Monogamous, God ordained, heterosexual, marital union, is God's prescription for marriage. Men are not the only ones seeking a polygamous marital union, but even women, in some cultures around the globe,are also seeking polyandry.

Polyandry Marriages

We have been making the case for monogamous heterosexual marriages as opposed to polygamous, but this is another strange dimension in the name of marriage. In polygamous marriages, the man is legally married to multiple women but in polyandry marriages, a woman is legally married to multiple men. I have grown up hearing about polygamous marriage but never knew that anything ever existed as polyandry until recently. When I first heard about it, my initial gut reaction was, 'no way! This must be false and cannot really be true!' So, I went online and checked and all my fears and doubts were confirmed. This is real, and humans are depraved to the core of their being.

The level of degradation in the meaning of marriage is mind-blowing. I never really knew how bad things had gotten if a woman would be living in the same house with multiple men as her legal spouses. Are the men normal, or is this really a severe psychological and mental disorder? It is very difficult for me to come to terms with the remotest possibility that a normal, natural man or woman would knowingly and willingly share their spouse with another man or woman. One of the husbands or co-husbands would sit in the living room and watch another husband take the wife and get into the bedroom and close the door and start having sex and the other husbands are watching TV in the living room, really? This is beyond my comprehension!

Image of Polyandry marriages

Are their minds really on the TV? I mean, the same is true for a polygamous marriage! How can a woman, who says that she really loves her husband, watch and see another woman taken into a room where they undress, strip naked, and have sex? The woman, women, co-wives or co-wife, watch and accept it as normative behavior. In a normal monogamous marriage, if a spouse finds out that the other spouse has betrayed the trust and love between them then the marriage is just about over, but not so in a polygamous or in polyandrous marriages. Why not?

What is really going on in the psyche of people who engage in polygamous and polyandrous marriages? Where is the jealousy and rage that happens in normal monogamous marriages? Why this unusual and unnatural level of acceptability? A normal monogamous marriage is already filled with drama, sometimes, but the potential of increased levels of drama in such marriages is out of this world. Polyandry is really not new for it has been around for a while and here is a quote:

There are examples of historical and contemporary polygamy within many cultures and religions. For example, "both polygamy and polyandry were practiced in ancient times among certain sections of the Hindu society," which includes Brahmin Hindus. Even today, there is no Hindu law against these customs. The main factors discouraging polygamy are the cost and the time required to raise the family well."[118]

So, these marriages have been existing from ancient times and they are also present in various parts of the world and here are the facts: *Polyandry is, in fact a rare phenomenon, if not rare as once thought, and understanding of the variables that define the term is evolving. The two best-known areas in which polyandry*

118

https://www.christianity.com/wiki/christian-terms/what-is-polyg amy-and-what-are-examples-today.html *was studied and continued to be practiced into the 21st century are the Plateau of Tibet (a region shared by India, Nepal, and the Tibet Autonomous Region of China) and the Marquesas Islands in the South Pacific. In a report published in 2012, however, anthropologists Kathrine Starweather and Raymond Hames identified 53 additional non-classical societies throughout the world (including North America and South America) that also practice polyandry, whether formal (i.e. recognized by marriage and co-residence) or informal (when two or more are considered the co-fathers of offspring and are invested in the care of both mother and child or children).[119]*So, folks, this is real and it is happening next-door to you. This is not a fairy tale and it may be happening right next to you.

Anthropologists may try to carve out some sociological reasoning and support for polygamy and polyandry but such support is not warranted. You may hear things like polygamy will help reduce the unmarried population for women, since unmarried women out-number unmarried men. Or a woman may need to marry multiple men to guarantee her economic support. These reasons are a camouflage at best because the real reasons are an entrenched, embedded, and erroneous belief system.

What you truly believe can rarely be altered by your economic situation. While some have said that polygamy and polyandry are not explicitly prohibited in the bible, and so, it must be okay, but is that really the case? The whole chapter of Leviticus 18 is about a list of sexual prohibitions and astonishingly, polygamy and polyandry are not on that list. Paul's expository exposition on marriage in 1 Corinthians 7, clearly supports and defends the monogamous position

---

[119] https://www.britannica.com/topic/polyandry-marriage

but no mention of polygamy or polyandry. Jesus spoke extensively about marriage in Matthew 19, Mark 10 and other New Testament passages but no mention of polygamy or polyandry. So, why does the bible seem to be silent about approving or disapproving of such marriages?

Here is what I believe is going on! Prohibition against adultery and fornication are well established all over the Old and New Testament. The term fornication includes all forms of sexually immoral conduct. So, a male, having multiple wives and a female having multiple husbands would normally fit into the category of adultery as marriage was never intended to be a shared experience but an exclusive one.

There was no need to mention polygamy or polyandry as a separate category, since these would naturally fall under the general category of fornication and adultery. The monogamous marriage is a reflection of the relationship that God has with mankind. Marriage is the mirror between God and man. God instituted marriage to mirror His dealings with mankind and first, God was married to Israel.

God's Marriage to Israel

Some may find it strange to hear that God was married to Israel but what does that all really entail? God Himself is identified as the Husband of Israel. We have already established the meaning of marriage to mean, "joined," "united," "glued," and so, God is joined to the Nation of Israel. This is not just a physical union but it is a much deeper spiritual union. So also is the union between a man and a woman, which is also a spiritual union. The man and the woman are joined and as a result, they are now one flesh.

Their individual identities are maintained but they are somehow united or joined in the spirit. So, likewise, is God married or joined to Israel. Here is a text that identifies God as the husband of Israel: *For your husband is your Maker, whose name is the Lord of hosts; And your Redeemer is the Holy One of Israel, who is called the God of all the earth,* Isaiah 54:5. This verse is using marriage to point to a much bigger spiritual truth. As important as earthly marriages may be, God is speaking to Israel and by extension, to the rest of mankind, that your real husband is God Himself. In other words, you are married to God.

The earthly husband and wife marriages are only a shadow of the real and ultimate marriage to God Himself. So, anyone who is physically married on earth but is not married to God and He is not their husband, then that would mean that they are spiritually single and unmarried. The text identifies the name of the husband since it simply said in the first line, "your husband is your maker," and in the second line, your maker is identified as the "Lord of hosts." Just in case someone was wondering and asking the question, "who is your maker," then this second line answers that question.

There is the idea of redemption that is built into the concept of marriage as mentioned in the third poetic line in this verse, which expands the identity of husband to that of the redeemer, who is also the Holy One of Israel. God is their redeemer in the Old Testament dispensation but this verse is also looking forward to the Messiah, the Lord Jesus Christ, who is also married to the church in that dispensation. The human earthly marriage is pointing to a redemptive story. The goal and purpose of mankind is to be married to Christ, so, make Him your husband today.

God's marriage to Israel was instituted by a covenant but what is really a covenant? In today's marriages, we often hear of the term "marriage contracts," but how is it different from a covenant?

Marriage Covenant vs. Contracts

The word covenant is likely amongst one of the most important words in the bible with a vast array of meanings. In the Old Testament, the Hebrew word, "Berith,"is often translated in our English bible translations as "covenant." This meaning of the word would actually depend on the context in which it was used. The word means treaty, or an *alliance between nations or people as in Genesis 14:13, Genesis 31:44.,agreement, pledge as in 2 Kings 11:4, alliance of friendship, like David and Jonathan as in 1 Samuel 18:3,20:8, or alliance of marriage as in Proverbs 2:17, Malachi 2:14.*[120]

This Hebrew word is also translated in the LXX (the Greek translation of the Old Testament*) as "disthekes," and appears about 30 times in the New Testament and 14 of those in the book of Hebrews alone. This Greek word means (1) a disposition, arrangement, of any sort, which one wishes to be valid, the last disposition which one makes of his earthly possessions after his death, a testament or will. (2) Compact, covenant, a testament. God's covenant with Noah, etc.*[121]

This Hebrew word, in a marriage context, carries the idea of an alliance, union, joining together. A covenant is basically an agreement between two parties to perform

---

[120]   https://biblehub.com/bdb/1285.htm
[121]

https://www.biblestudytools.com/lexicons/greek/nas/diatheke.html

some action. A covenant could be conditional or unconditional and when it is unconditional, then both parties are not required to fulfill the terms of the agreement for it remains in effect. A conditional covenant or a contract will require both parties to fulfill the terms of the agreement for it to remain in effect. Contracts signed in our courts today, including marriage contracts, are examples of conditional covenants.

The Abrahamic covenant in Genesis 12:1-3 is an example of an unconditional, unilateral covenant. If you read the text, there was no requirement that Abraham needed to take or not take, for the covenant to be nullified. Abraham was passive in the fulfillment of the covenant. The agreement only stated what God would do and no action was required of Abraham. Here is the covenant which God made with Abraham: *Go from your country, And from your relatives, And from your father's house, To the land which I will show you; And I will make you into a great nation, And I will bless you, And make your name great; And you shall be a blessing; And I will bless those who bless you, And the one who curses you I will curse*

. And in you all the families of the earth will be blessed, Genesis 12:1-3. This is a unilateral covenant or agreement between God and Abraham, but the entire covenant only stipulates what God will do and no action was needed to be taken by Abraham for the covenant to be fulfilled. God promised Abraham that he would possess the land, and here is what Abraham said: *But he said, "O Lord God, how am I to know that I shall possess it?"* Genesis 15:8. Abraham may have had doubts about what God had promised, so God moved to assure Abraham that what He promised would come to pass.

174

So, God moved to ratify the covenant and here is how it happened as God was speaking with Abraham: He said to him, "Bring me a heifer three years old, a female goat three years old, a ram three years old, a turtledove, and a young pigeon." And he brought all these, cut them in half, and laid each half over against the other. But he did not cut the birds in half, Genesis 15:9-10.After the animals have been slaughtered and put in place, here is what happened next: Now it came about, when the sun had set, that it was very dark, and behold, a smoking oven and flaming torch appeared which passed between these pieces. On that day the Lord made a covenant with Abram, saying, To your descendants I have given this land, From the river of Egypt as far the great river, the river Euphrates:, Genesis 15:17-18.

So, cutting a calf in half and passing between the two pieces was a means of taking an oath and saying that if the words of the covenant are not kept then may you be as the body of the calf cut in two parts. Here is the text: *And I will give the men that have transgressed my covenant, which have not performed the words of the* covenant which they had made before me, when I cut the calf in two, and passed *between the parts thereof, The princes of Judah, and princes of Jerusalem, the eunuchs, and the priests, and all the people of land, which passed between the parts of the calf; I will even give them into the hand of their enemies, and into the hand of them that seek their life: and their dead bodies shall be for meat unto the fowls of the heaven, and to the beasts of the earth,* Jeremiah 34:18-20.

The ratification process of a covenant requires both parties to pass between the two pieces of cut calf but in God's covenant with Abraham, it is recorded that, "a smoking oven and a flaming torch appeared which passed between these pieces," (Genesis 15:17). The smoking oven and flaming torch is the presence of God passing between the two pieces of cut calf. One commentary says that: *The symbol of a burning lamp is linked with the* salvation *of God's people (Isaiah 62:1) and* describes *the eyes of God (Daniel 10:6). In addition, when God descended on Mount Sinai in the fire, its "smoke ascended like the smoke of a furnace" (Exodus 19:18).* [122] So, God Himself passed between the two cut pieces of calf, taking an oath against Himself to fulfill the tenants of the covenant. This is like taking a vow in a traditional human marriage.

If Abraham had also passed between the two cut pieces of calf then there would have been no hope for Abraham and the rest of mankind because he would have failed, and hence the rest of mankind would have no hope. The multiple aspects to this covenant, the marriage between God and His elect. First, it is a union, marriage between God and Abraham, then Israel as a nation, then to the church or God's elect. It is also a redemption covenant between God and His elect. Abraham is recorded as having believed in God and it was credited to him as righteousness, Genesis 15:6, and the Apostle Paul made application of this text in Romans 4:-5.

So, this is a marriage covenant but the ultimate purpose is the redemption of His elect throughout all dispensations. God also used the rainbow in the clouds as a memorial to His covenant with Noah and here is what God said: *When the bow is in the clouds, I will see it and remember the everlasting covenant between God and every living creature of all flesh that is on the earth,* Genesis 9:6. In the Old Testament, these covenants, with different people or

---

122

https://www.bibletools.org/index.cfm/fuseaction/Topical.show/R
TD/cgg/ID/6870/Smoking-Oven-as-Symbol.htm

with the nation of Israel, always carry a union, a marriage between God and Israel, with the goal of redeeming His people.

In this marriage context, God is the husband and Israel is the wife. God calls Israel His wife by covenant and here is that exchange: *But you say, "Why does he not?" Because the Lord was witness between you and the wife of your youth, to whom you have been faithless, though she is your companion and your wife by covenant. Did he not make them one, with a portion of the Spirit in their Union? And what was the one God was seeking? Godly offspring. So guard yourselves in your spirit, and let none of you be faithless to the wife of your youth,* Malachi 2:14-15.

This text and many like it, declares that God was a husband to Israel and God was married to a faithless wife. The goal of God in this marriage with Israel was to seek a Godly offspring but the wife was adulterous and a covenant breaker, and here is what Jeremiah said about God making a new covenant: *"Behold, days are coming,"declares the LORD, "when I will make a new covenant with the house of Israel and the house of Judah, not like the covenant which I made with their fathers in the day that I took them by the hand to bring them out of the land of Egypt, My covenant which they broke, although I was a husband to them, declares the Lord,* Jeremiah 31:31-32.

Because of the adulterous character of God's wife, Israel, God decided to institute a new covenant with Israel. We will not really get into the contents of this new covenant in this book as our primary focus here is to establish the fact that God was married to the nation of Israel. This marriage between God and Israel is a mirror or a reflection of the marriage between Adam and Eve, in Genesis 2:24 and all other marriages after that. This is a monogamous marriage, one man and one woman. Can you imagine God being in a polygamous marriage?

The marriage between God and Israel is also monogamous. God is the husband and Israel is the wife. So, just as there are deviant marital relationships in the human realm there were also deviant covenantal or marital relationships between God and Israel. Here is what the Lord said about Israel: *Then the Lord said to me in the days of Josiah the King, "Have you seen what faithless Israel did? She went up on every high hill and under every green tree, and she was a harlot there. I thought, After she has done all these things she will return to Me; but she did not return, and her treacherous sister Judah saw it. And I saw that for all the adulteries of faithless Israel, I sent her away and gave her a writ of divorce, yet her treacherous sister Judah did not fear; but she went and was a harlot also,* Jeremiah 3:6-10.

Proponents of polygamy may read this text and conclude that God was somehow married to two wives: Israel and Judah, but that would be furthest from the truth. There were times when Judah and Israel were divided kingdoms and this was one of those, and Josiah was king of Judah. This was of less significance because God's covenant with Abraham applies to the Jewish people and by extension, to all humanity. So, God's covenant with Abraham did not only apply to Israel but more importantly to the elect for all times, in both the Old and New Testament. This covenant of blessing applies to all who were elected by God to salvation. Paul argues in Romans 9 and Galatians that the children of God are not those with national lineage to Israel as a nation, but all who will believe in the atoning work of Jesus Christ on the cross of Calvary.

Here is what Paul said: Not as though the word of God has not taken effect. For they are not all Israel, which are of Israel: Neither, because they are the seed of Abraham, are they all children: but in Isaac shall your seed be called, Romans 9:6-7.Paul is making the argument that your national or natural lineage to Israel or Abraham will not get you into a marriage union with Jesus Christ. Just as God was married to Israel, so the Lord Jesus was married to the church.

Jesus Christ Married to the Church

It is almost impossible to understand the marriage between Jesus Christ and the church without fully understanding the marriage customs in which He lived. He was a Jew and lived under Jewish marriage customs and traditions, and God has used those customs to greatly impact the marriage between Christ and the church. There are basically three parts to a Jewish marriage: The engagement, the betrothal, and the wedding feast.

Two feasts are observed during a Jewish marriage and they are the betrothal and wedding feasts and here are some comments on them: *Until late in the Middle Ages, marriage consisted of two ceremonies that were marked by celebrations at two separate times, with an interval between. First came the betrothal [erusin]; and later, the wedding [nissuin]. At the betrothal, the woman was legally married, although she still remained in her father's house. She could not belong to another man unless she was divorced from her betrothed. The wedding meant only that the betrothed woman, accompanied by a colorful procession, was brought from her father's house to the house of her groom, and the legal tie with him was consummated. Marriage, as with any type of purchase, consisted of two acts. First the bride price was paid and an*

179

agreement reached on the conditions of the sale. Sometime later, the purchaser took possession of the object. In the Jewish marriage, the "mohar," (Hebrew word for the purchase price) was paid and a detailed agreement reached between the families of the bride and groom. This betrothal was followed by the wedding, when the bride was brought into the home of the groom, who took actual possession of her. [123]

The concept of a betrothed woman being legally married to the groom is not some invented Jewish tradition but it is actually rooted in the Old Testament law: *The root of the word ("to betroth"), from which the Talmudic abstract ("betrothal") is derived, must be taken in this sense; i.e., to contract an actual though incomplete marriage. In two of the passages in which it occurs the betrothed woman is directly designated as "wife" (2 Sam. 3:14, "my wife whom I have betrothed" ("erasti"), and Deut, xxii. 24, where the betrothed is designated as "the wife of his neighbor"). In strict accordance with this sense the rabbinical law declares that betrothal is equivalent to an actual marriage and only to be dissolved by a formal divorce.* [124]

So, a betrothal is a full legal marriage even though no sexual intercourse has taken place. In this sense, only a promise to get married, marriage contract, and dowry, brings the bride and groom into a covenantal marriage union. It is no surprise that this law was applied to Joseph and Mary in Luke 1:27. It was between the betrothal period that Mary was found to be with child. They had been

---

[123]

https://www.myjewishlearning.com/article/ancient-jewish-marriage/

[124]

https://www.jewishencyclopedia.com/articles/3229-betrothal

together for one year and during this betrothal period, she turned up pregnant before the wedding ceremony and consummation of the marriage. But during this stage all other formalities have been completed, like paying off the dowry.

The father of the groom pays the bride price to purchase the bride. At the end of the betrothal period, this is what happens: It was a common custom for the bride to join the groom's father's household, rather than the groom and the bride establishing their own household. So, if the bride and groom were of a marriageable age, the groom would return to his father's house after the betrothal to prepare a bridal chamber.

This process traditionally took a year or more (the length of time is dictated and determined by the groom's father). When the time was complete and fulfilled, the groom would return to fetch his bride. The bride would not know the day or hour of her groom's or husband-to-be's return, so the groom's arrival was usually announced with a trumpet call and a shout so that the bride had some fore-warning.[125] So, at the beginning of Matthew 25, Jesus made this very fascinating analogy in this parable that mirrors the Jewish marriage tradition. Just as in the Jewish marriage tradition, the groom returns to take his bride at a time unknown to the bride.

So, Christ will return to take His bride, the church, at a time unknown to the bride, the church. In the Jewish traditional marriage, the time when the groom will return to take his bride is only known to the father of the groom. It is not even known by the groom. Hear what Jesus Himself said about this: *But about that day and hour no one knows, not even the angels in heaven, nor the son, but the Father alone,*

---

[125]   https://www.gotquestions.org/marriage-customs.html

Matthew 24:36. Wow! Amazing stuff! One of the points in the parable of the ten virgins in Matthew 25:1-13, is that the bride must be prepared to be taken by the groom at any moment.

The bride must be waiting expectantly for the groom to arrive at any moment. It could be tomorrow or it could be two thousand years, but the bride has to be ready at all times because His return is imminent. He will come for his bride as a thief breaks into a house to steal. The house owner would have been well prepared if he knew the date and time of the thief's coming to break-in. So, the house owner must live his life in his house as though the thief may break-in at any moment. You must be prepared to be taken by the groom, even today! This is a very amazing and fascinating analogy between the Jewish marriage tradition and the marriage between Christ and the church. Now, it is required that the groom pays the dowry or the bride price as part of the betrothal process in the Jewish marriage tradition.

This bride price is called the "mohar," (Hebrew word) and is paid by the father of the groom to the father of the bride. The bride price and any associated gifts are paid during the betrothal/engagement portion of the marriage. The marriage consists of two principal ceremonies: The Erusin, (Hebrew word for betrothal) which is the betrothal/engagement part and the Nissuin, Hebrew word for the wedding ceremony) which is the wedding ceremony or marriage supper. The "mohar,"is settled during the "Erusin," and followed by a feast to commemorate the event and issuance of the ketubah or the marriage contract as shown below.

The Ketubah or Marriage Contract.[126]

Is it any surprise that Jesus was crucified on the Passover day? The Passover is the most celebrated of all Jewish feasts in the Old Testament and Jesus lived on earth under the Old Testament dispensation. Once every year, every Jew went to Jerusalem to celebrate the Passover. It was during this feast that the new covenant was inaugurated.

There was a marriage and betrothal ceremony taking place. Just as the father of the groom is paying the dowry and the bride price to the father of the bride, so the Father in heaven is sending the groom of the church (Jesus Christ) to offer His blood on the cross of Calvary, as a bride price or dowry, to purchase His bride, the church. In this analogy, the Father of the groom and the Groom Himself are separate but the same. The Father and the Son (Groom) are one and this too is a mystery. Here is what Jesus said: *And He had taken some*

126

https://www.myjewishlearning.com/article/ancient-jewish-marriage/

bread and given thanks, He broke it and gave it to them, saying, "This is My body, which is being given for you; do this in remembrance of Me." And in the same way He took the cup after they had eaten, saying, "This cup, which is poured out for you, is the new covenant in My blood, Luke 22:19-20. This bride price, dowry,(mohar), His blood, which was paid to purchase the redemption of the elect, His bride, the church. This is the betrothal/engagement ceremony between the bride and groom. There is also the betrothal ring, given by the father of the groom to the father of bride shown below:

Jewish wedding ring above. [127]

[127]

https://www.myjewishlearning.com/article/ancient-jewish-marriage/

This is the first of two marriage ceremonies, "Erusin," also involves a marriage contract, which is the covenant, being inaugurated with His blood. Like in the Jewish traditional marriage, the bride price is paid by the father of the groom to the father of the bride but who receives the bride price for the betrothal of Christ to the church? This question poses a real dilemma, because in order for the bride to be transferred from the control of someone who owns the bride, the father of the bride, a bride price or a dowry must be paid but who received the bride price for the church to become the bride of Christ?

Some have said that God receives the bride price. If that is true as many believe that it is, then God will have to be the Father of the groom (Jesus Christ) and the bride (the church, the elect, fallen humanity). This is quite a fascinating thought that God will have to be the Father of the groom and the bride. If it is true then is there really a need for a bride price to be paid if God already owns the bride and groom? The purpose of the bride price is to provide a ransom and release the bride from the control of her father to the control of the groom. No such ransom will be needed if the bride is already in the control of the groom.

A ransom has to be paid before God can be the Father of the bride and groom. So, if God is already the Father of the bride, then what is the purpose of the ransom? It is widely believed that the ransom was paid to God and not to Satan and here is one such view: *God's holy character requires that sin be punished. Sin makes us the objects of God's wrath until the penalty of sin is paid. By laying down His own life,* Jesus paid the price on our behalf, satisfying God's demand. This payment was *made, not to Satan, but*

God.[128] I would like to believe this to be the case but the logic and the evidence is inconclusive.

If this is the case then that would mean the unregenerate or unsaved are already in God's camp, but is that really the case? It is quoted as saying: *He has delivered us from the power of darkness and transferred us to the kingdom of His Son,* Colossians 1:13. This text is saying that the unregenerate or unsaved are under the power and control of darkness. There are two kingdoms: kingdom of darkness and kingdom of His son. This would imply that the unsaved are in another kingdom and once the bride price is paid, then they are transferred into the kingdom of His Son or kingdom of light. But what kingdom could the unsaved be in?

The unsaved seems to be firmly under the control of Satan; listen to what the text says: *To open their eyes so that they may turn from darkness to light, and from the power of Satan to God, that they may receive forgiveness of sins and an inheritance among those who have been sanctified by Faith in Me,* Acts 26:18. The idea that humans are under the power of Satan is not very comfortable, so most theologians are running to rescue God by asserting that the bride price could not have been paid to Satan. I am very much in sympathy with that position because I kind of know why there is some tension to protect the character of God. Some may say that paying the bride price to Satan will kind of equate Satan to God. That is the furthest from the truth. God is in absolute control of all things and has no competition.

128

https://www.moodybible.org/beliefs/positional-statements/substitutionary-atonement/#:~:text=Sin%20makes%20us%20the%20objects,not%20to%20Satan%2C%20but%20God.

So, let's say that the king of a country were to get married to a common citizen of that country. In keeping with tradition, the king will be required to come down from his royal palace and visit the commoner, the father of the bride-to-be, and pay the bride price. The king is still the king and the commoner is still the commoner, but the bride will not be released until the bride price is paid. God does not need Satan's permission to do anything and He does as He pleases. The unsaved are not only under the dominion of Satan, but he is actually the father of the unsaved just as God is the Father of the saved. People act as their father. You may act as the devil because the devil is your daddy. You cannot act as God unless He is your daddy and some of His nature and attributes have been imputed into you.

I know that a lot of people are also very uncomfortable with this position but let's let the bible speak: You belong to your father, the devil, and you want to carry out your father's desires. He was a murderer from the beginning, not holding the truth, for there is no truth in him. When he lies, he speaks his native language, for he is a liar and the father of lies, John 8:44. In this context, Jesus was responding to the Pharisees who were having doubts about who He really was, and by extension, this applies to the rest of humanity. In the preceding verses in John 8, the Pharisees were debating Jesus, saying Abraham was their father, but He told them bluntly, that Abraham was not their father because if he were, then they would have done what he did.

The devil or Satan is the father of all the unsaved or unregenerate and before anyone becomes saved, they have no desire for God and the things of God but only endeavor to carry out the desire of the devil, their father; but not only that! It is impossible to do the will and desire of God unless one belongs to God. Satan is also called "the ruler of this world," John 12:31. The world system or the cosmos is under his rule and dominion. Isaiah 61:1, speaking of the Messiah, prophetically, goes to proclaim liberty to captives and freedom to prisoners. If these people are captives and prisoners then someone is guarding the prison and ransom will have to be paid to secure their release. His blood was that ransom and once that is paid, the wedding ceremony is next on the agenda, and this is called the marriage supper of the Lamb.

The Marriage Supper of the Lamb

The marriage supper is considered to be the long anticipated feast that the groom and the bride are waiting for. Imagine that you paid the bride price and there was the feast to commemorate the intentions of both parties to come together (betrothal ceremony), but the wedding feast is still some time in the future. In the Jewish marriage tradition, the time between the betrothal feast and ceremony is determined by the father of the groom; it is usually one year, but not always one because it is up to the father of the groom. So, during this waiting period, the bride is living in her father's house and likewise the groom is living in his father's house.

There is no sexual intercourse between them during this period. The marriage is not yet consummated, even though they are a legally binding couple. If any of the parties to the wedding decides, for whatever reason, that they want to withdraw from the marriage, then the party who wants to get out would have to file for a formal divorce and this is a period that is filled with tension and anxiety. In that tradition, a marriage is more than the bride and the groom joining together. A marriage is a family affair and it is the joining of two families together.

It is a big deal for both families. One family is sending their precious daughter away into the arms of a complete stranger. Daddy or mommy's little girl is about to be released into the arms of another man. You may often hear the saying, "Dads are attached to their daughters and moms are attached to their sons." So, it is quite emotional to release a child and let go. Another family is sending their son away into the arms of another woman.

The mom, dad, and other siblings are very emotional in releasing and separating from one of their family members. Both families are feeling the emotions of joy and anxiety. Now, to make matters worse, the bride has no idea when the groom will return to take her for the marriage ceremony. The bride has to be waiting, ready, knowing that the groom can return at any moment. This, too, raises the level of anxiety and anticipation to another level. This Jewish marriage tradition is a reflection of the highly anticipated wedding ceremony between Christ and his bride, the church. The normal union between a man and a woman, outside of Jewish tradition, also reflects the union between Christ and the church. The love relationship between husband and his wife is a direct reflection of the love relationship that Christ has for his church.

The human marriage is a mirror of the marriage between Christ and His church. Here is what the apostle Paul had to say: Husbands, love your wives, even as Christ loved the church, and gave himself for it; That He might sanctify and cleanse it with the washing of water by the word, That He might present it to himself a glorious church, not having spot, or wrinkle, or any such thing; but that it should be holy and without blemish. So ought men to love their wives as their own bodies. He that loves his wife, loves himself. For no man ever yet hated his own body; but

189

nourishes and cherishes it, even as the Lord loves the church. For we are members of his body, of His flesh, and His bones. For this cause shall a man leave his father and mother, and shall be joined unto his wife, and they two shall be one flesh. This is a great mystery: but I speak concerning Christ and the church, Ephesians 5:25-32.

Paul used this analogy of the husband loving his wife as a picture of Christ's love for His church. This human and earthly marriage union serves as a reflection of the heavenly union between Christ and His church. In verse 27 of Ephesians 5, Paul talks about the goal of Christ, which is to present His bride, the church, spotless and without wrinkles. A spotless bride can only happen after the wedding feast or ceremony has taken place and when the bride has been taken to live permanently in the father of the groom's home.

Remember the words of the groom: In My Father's house are many dwelling places; if it were not so, I would have told you; for I go to prepare a place for you. And if I go and prepare a place for you, I am coming again and will take you to Myself, so that where I am, there you also will be, John 14:2-3. Just as in Jewish traditional marriage, the Lord Jesus Christ has completed what He was sent by the Father to do. He is the groom, sent by the Father as the bride price or dowry to purchase,redeem or buyback the bride.

He had finished the betrothal and now, He is telling His bride, "Look, do not be sad or anxious, because I will see you soon, and I will return soon and take you to my father's home for the wedding ceremony."Remember what He said: "it is finished," John 19:30 but what is finished? He said that "it is finished," but He was still alive and His work was completed. He had just finished paying the redemption price, dowry or the bride price. He had only finished part of the marriage ceremony and is now getting ready for part two, which is the marriage supper of the Lamb.

This marriage supper of the lamb also mirrors the Jewish traditional marriage ceremony. In the ancient Jewish marriage tradition during the biblical times, the marriage ceremony is called "nasium or huppah," or it is also called the "home-taking,"and huppah is understood to mean a "room," usually a special room in the father of the groom's home. Here is what tradition tells us: *The groom arrives at the huppah before the bride. Since the huppah is considered [according to traditional understanding] the symbolic home of the groom, he must be there first to welcome his bride into his home. The tradition is said by some to go back to the very first wedding, when, the Torah says, God took Eve "and brought her to Adam." Eve, since she was created after Adam, is considered in Jewish thought to represent a higher form of life than Adam, since she was able to carry a fetus in her body. As the first one created, Adam is said to have been waiting under the huppah in the Garden of Eden when Eve was brought to him.* [129]

This is an amazing human analogy that God Himself would take the bride and bring her to the groom. The groom was waiting for the bride just as the groom (Jesus Christ) is waiting for His bride (the church), in a special chamber(huppah) in His father's house, in Heaven. This is a special wedding ceremony and there has never been nor will there ever be anything like it. Imagine being invited to a wedding, and to a city, where the streets are built of gold? And everything that you may see and touch is made of gold. The invitation ticket costs about a billion dollars per ticket,

---

[129]

https://www.myjewishlearning.com/article/arriving-at-the-huppah-or-wedding-canopy/

and someone special secured a ticket for you. The angelic hosts are in charge of the praise and worship team. You are considered blessed among humanity; if you are invited,then it is because someone secured your ticket because the cost of the ticket was and is beyond the reach of anyone alive or living.

Those Invited to the Wedding Feast

The wedding feast is set in motion when the bridegroom returns to take his bride from the home of her father to the home of the father of the bridegroom. In the traditional Jewish wedding, the arrival of the bridegroom is preceded by a trumpet blast. This blast is so loud that all in that town will hear it, including the bride. This trumpet blast will not only alert the bride that the bridegroom is on his way but also summons the people to gather for the wedding feast.

This is fascinating and amazing stuff! This blowing of the trumpet in a traditional Jewish wedding ceremony is a clear picture of the arrival of Jesus Christ (bridegroom) to take home His bride (the church). This trumpet blast is actually called the feast of the trumpet. There are several Jewish feasts in the Old Testament and these feasts point to Jesus for its final fulfillment. These feasts are a fascinating picture of God's plan for redemption. There are four feasts in the spring and three in the fall. The spring feasts have already been fulfilled in Christ Jesus.

These are the feasts of Unleavened Bread, Passover, First Fruits and Weeks. The final three feasts happen in the fall and they are: Trumpets, the Day of Atonement, and Tabernacles, and these three fall feasts happen within a brief fifteen-day period. The feast of Unleavened Bread (Leviticus 23:6) points to Jesus as one who is without sin. Paul said that,

"A little leaven leavens the whole lump," Galatians 5:9. Leaven is a picture of sin and the feast of Unleavened Bread points to His sinless life. The feast of the Passover (Leviticus 23:5) points to Jesus as the sinless lamb of God and that is why John said: "behold the Lamb of God who takes away the sin of the world," John 1:29.

The feast of the First Fruits (Leviticus 23:10) points to Jesus as the first fruit from the dead, 1 Corinthians 15:20, guaranteeing the resurrection for all who sleep in the dust. The feast of Weeks (Leviticus 23:16) also known as the feast of Pentecost, occurred 50 days after the feast of First Fruit Acts 1:9-11 as Jesus was taken up into heaven. These are all Old Testament feasts that have already been fulfilled in Jesus. These are the spring feasts and the fall feasts are yet to be fulfilled. Jesus has departed from His bride and will return soon to take His bride home to His Father's house. The next feast in line to be fulfilled is the feast of Trumpets (Rosh Hashanah). This feast is mentioned in (Leviticus 23:24) and is a picture of the announcement and coming of the bridegroom to take His bride. This begins with a trumpet blast as seen below.

The Shofar or Trumpet[130]

This trumpet blast is to announce the arrival of the bridegroom to take home his bride and to consummate the marriage. So, it is famously called the Feast of Trumpets and it is actually a feast that comes with fanfare and jubilation. It is like announcing the arrival of the President of the United States of America, but this is a zillion times bigger and better and nothing can be compared to it. Some have said that the feast of Trumpets points to the rapture in the New Testament (1 Thessalonians 4:13-18 and 1 Corinthians 15:52)

. If you were to view the rapture and the second coming of Jesus Christ as two separate events, then you may see another fall feast, the Day of Atonement (Yom Kippur)(Leviticus 23:27), as pointing to the second coming of the Messiah. Proponents of this view will have to conclude that the trumpet sounded and the groom came and took His bride to heaven and at a later date, returned again for the second coming. Is that really the case? The fundamental question is whether the rapture and the second coming of Christ are separate events. The widely held view is that they are distinct and separate events.

There remain a lot of unanswered questions! All the spring Jewish feasts, the Passover, Unleavened bread, First Fruits, and feast of Weeks or Pentecost, were fulfilled in Christ in under two months. They were designed to be fulfilled together and this too was part of the betrothal ceremony. The Groom came for His bride and has fulfilled all the rituals that qualifies Him as the rightful Groom. He fulfilled the feast of Unleavened Bread to show He was the sinless Lamb of God and the bride required a sinless Groom and He was and is the only one that met those qualifications.

---

130   https://www.myjewishlearning.com/article/shofar/

He fulfilled the feast of the Passover in that He Himself was the sacrificial lamb to be sacrificed for His bride. He was the bridegroom and also the dowry or bride price to be paid to purchase His bride. He fulfilled the feast of the First Fruit in that He was the first to be resurrected bodily to signify that His bride will also be resurrected. If His bride is not resurrected then the wedding will not be consummated and there will be no wedding between the Groom and the bride. He fulfilled the Feast of Weeks or Pentecost to show that the Groom must return to the father of Groom's house to prepare to receive His bride.

So, all these spring feasts were fulfilled sequentially, and within a period of under 60 days. So, why would the fall feasts be any different? Why would Christ return at the rapture to take His bride home and then return at a later date for His second coming? No one can really tell us the time between the rapture and His second coming! The fall feasts were completed in the Hebrew month of Tishri or Tishrei of the Jewish civil calendar, and there was no lengthy amount of time between the Feast of Trumpets (Leviticus 23:24)(the rapture) (1 Thessalonians 4:13-18, 1 Corinthians 15:52 and the Day of Atonement (the second coming), not even the Feasts of Booths or Tabernacles (Leviticus 23:34), which is widely believed to be when Christ will permanently dwell among His people. All these fall feasts were completed in about twenty-three days and there seems to be no reason why its fulfillment in Jesus would require an extensive amount of time between them for their fulfillment. Now, all these events are set in motion by the sound of the trumpet, but what does that really signify?

Feast of Trumpets

The feast of Trumpets is also called *Rosh Hashanah*, which means "the Head of the year." It is called "Head of the Year " because it marks the beginning of the Jewish civil Calendar year. The feast of Trumpets is one of the most fascinating of feasts, in that it lasts for ten days and leads right into the next feast, Yom Kippur or Day of Atonement. The blowing of the Trumpet, also called Shofar or the Ram's horn, is a very important and significant part of Jewish life.

The Shofar or Trumpet was used to warn the people of impending danger from an enemy nation but most importantly, to warn the people of God's Day of Judgment. This was the interaction between the God of Israel and the prophet Ezekiel about the use of the Trumpet: *then whoever hears the sound of the trumpet and does not take warning, if the sword comes and takes him away, his blood shall be on his own head. He heard the sound of the trumpet, but did not take warning; his blood shall be upon himself. But he who takes warning will save his life. But if the watchman sees the sword coming and does not blow the trumpet, and the people are not warned, and sword comes and takes any person from among them, he is taken away in his iniquity; but his blood I will require at the watchman's hand*, Ezekiel 33:4-6.

The trumpet or the shofar was often used to warn the people of Israel of an invading nation coming to war against Israel. God used this as a picture of His coming judgment on the world. Just as Ezekiel was to warn the people, we, the redeemed, are also to warn every human of God's coming judgment lest their blood will be on our hands if we fail to warn them. So, this sounding of the trumpet is announcing the "Day of Awe," "Day of Vengeance," "Day of the Lord," and "Day of Atonement."

It is often portrayed as a joyous occasion because the Lord is coming for His bride but it is not so joyous for those who are headed for eternal condemnation. In the New Testament, some have identified the feast of trumpets as being fulfilled in the rapture, thus making the rapture and the second coming two separate events but is that really the case?Let's look at a few uses and applications of the trumpet: The trumpet was used to summon the congregation to come together, Numbers 10:1-7. It was also to summon those who are perishing to come and worship and here is a quote: *It will come about in that day that a great trumpet will be blown, and those who were perishing in the land of Assyria and who were scattered in the land of Egypt will come and worship the Lord in the holy mountain at Jerusalem*, Isaiah 27:13.

The phrase, "in that day," is most likely referencing the day of the Lord, which is also considered to be the second coming of Jesus, which also happens to be the Day of Atonement. So, on that day, not just any trumpet will be blown but the "great trumpet" will be blown. So, who then is the blower of that great trumpet? A trumpet blown by any of the prophets, including Moses, is not called the "great trumpet;" so, it must be very special but who is the blower?

Here is another text that shows the trumpet being blown on the Day of Atonement, which is the second coming of Jesus: And you shall count seven Sabbaths of years for yourself, seven times seven years; and the time of the seven Sabbaths of years shall be to you forty-nine years. Then you shall cause the trumpet of the Jubilee to sound on the tenth day of the seventh month, on the Day of Atonement you shall make the trumpet to sound throughout

197

your land, Leviticus 25-8-9.This also makes the point that the trumpet will also be blown on the Day of Atonement, which is the second coming. Also the forty-nine years represent the feast of weeks which is also Pentecost. And Pentecost which represents Christ's ascension and return to heaven, His Father's house, and then the next event on the calendar will be Christ's return with trumpet blasts for His bride to consummate the marriage with a wedding feast.

So, the trumpet is blown on the first day of the month of Tishri, the beginning of the feast of Trumpets, commemorating the beginning of the year or head of the year, Rosh Hashanah. Then ten days later, there is a trumpet blast on the Day of Atonement. These ten days are an entire period of celebrations and warnings and it is quite possible that the trumpet was very loud because Leviticus 25:9 says, "Make the trumpet sound throughout all your land." No human could blow such a trumpet that would sound throughout all the land. The context was the land of Israel but by extension, we are talking about a global trumpet blast and sound. It is also quite possible that this was not and it is not going to be an intermittent trumpet blast but it may be a very long blast that may last days.

This was and is possibly a very long lasting blast of the trumpet that lasted, possibly ten days or longer. The whole earth is guaranteed to hear this coming sound of the trumpet and here is the one who will blow the trumpet: *For the Lord Himself shall descend from heaven with a shout, with the voice of the archangel, and with the* sound of the *trumpet of God: and the dead in Christ shall rise first: Then we which are alive and remain shall be caught up together with them in the clouds, to meet the Lord in the air: and so shall we ever be with the Lord. Wherefore comfort one another with these words*, 1 Thessalonians 4:16-18.

This is the key text that probably gave rise to the debate of the rapture and second coming of Jesus Christ being the same or separate events. A lot has centered on the meaning of the word "rapture," or "caught up," and this simply means to be violently or suddenly taken and transported into Heaven. This text has been used as support for the rapture being separate from the second coming but is that really the case? It is becoming very difficult to see them as separate events when at the end of verse 17, it says, "to meet the Lord in the air: and so shall we ever be with the Lord."

The phrase, "ever be with the Lord," implies the finality of His coming and not to come again. It did not say that we will be with the lord when He comes again for us. This signals our final dwelling place and no chance of another return again. We shall ever be with the Lord, the finality of His coming and no chance of another coming. The rapture and the second coming seem to be clearly identical events. Here is another text that is also often used in support of the rapture as an event that is distinct and separate from the second coming: *In a moment, in the twinkling of an eye, at the last trumpet: for the trumpet shall sound, and the dead shall be raised incorruptible, and we shall be changed. For this corruptible must put on incorruption, and this mortal must put on immortality,* 1 Corinthians 15:52–53.

This text is often used as proof in defense of the rapture, but does it really make the case for the rapture? If the rapture is an event that occurs before the second coming of Christ, then the trumpet blast that happens at the rapture would not be the last trumpet because there is another event on the horizon. The text above says that, "at the last trumpet," to mean that there were multiple trumpet sounds and as a matter of fact, it would seem like the blowing of a trumpet was part of Jewish life and culture. Trumpets are so important in Jewish life that an entire feast was dedicated to trumpets alone, called feasts of Trumpets. Trumpets were blown at weddings, and by prophets to warn the people, but this is identified as the last trumpet; meaning that there will never again be a trumpet sound after this.

The implications could be that no one will be alive after this point because no one will be alive to hear or blow the trumpet blasts. No more weddings and no more prophets will be alive or anyone else for that matter. This is the last trumpet to ever sound again on the earth. Why would it be the last trumpet if there will be a second coming? And if the second coming is still in the future after the rapture then that means that people are still living on the earth and that will not really fit the reality of the last trumpet. This text and many like it make a compelling case for the rapture and the second coming being the same event and I clearly understand that there are many who would disagree. So, after the feast of Trumpets, the Day of Atonement is next on the calendar.

Day of Atonement

The Day of Atonement is considered to be the holiest among Jewish feasts. This is also called Yom Kippur in Hebrew. It is also and rightly called the Day of Atonement, since the feast lasts about 25 hours or an hour longer than our typical 24 hour calendar day. This feast or festival points to Jesus's second coming when atonement is fully realized. At the betrothal, at the Passover feast, the dowry or the bride price was paid but the bride was not yet taken to the home of the Father of the bridegroom.

This may again be rightly called "Day of Atonement," because it is on this day that the atonement is considered

200

complete. It is on this day that believers in Christ are resurrected and instantly changed. This is how the apostle Paul puts it: *So when this corruptible shall have put on incorruption, and this mortal shall have put on immortality, then shall be brought to pass the saying that is written, Death is swallowed up in victory. O Death, where is your victory? O grave, where is your sting?* 1 Corinthians 15:54-55.

The atonement is complete at the cross of Calvary but will be consummated at the resurrection when the bride is resurrected and ushered into Heaven, the home of the bridegroom's Father. The Day of Atonement is looking at the completion of salvation and not the start of salvation and here is how Paul puts it: *And that, knowing the time, that now is high time to awake out of sleep: For now is our salvation nearer than when we first believed,* Romans 13:11. Salvation is often mentioned in the bible in three ways: present or partial, progressive, and ultimate. At the moment that you believe the gospel's message, you are saved and passed from death to life; present or partial salvation. As you live out your faith on a daily basis in obedience to God, then you are being saved or sanctified, meaning that you are progressively being saved, Philippians 2:12-13.

Then our salvation is complete and consummated when we receive our glorified spiritual bodies, Romans 13:11. This verse in Romans says that our salvation is nearer than when we first believed, meaning that there is a future aspect to our salvation that has not yet been realized and consummated. This is an extremely important concept to understand if you are to clearly understand the Day of Atonement and its significance.

Here is how the writer of Hebrews puts it: So Christ was sacrificed once to take away the sins of many. To those who eagerly wait for Him, He will appear a second time, without sin for salvation, Hebrew 9:28. This is probably one of the clearest passages on the Day of Atonement. This verse makes the case for the appearance of Christ: First, to deal with the issue of sin from the spiritual death's side and will appear again, on that day to completely eradicate sin by giving us a resurrected spiritual and sinless body. Notice that the text did not say that He will appear at the rapture but a second time.

Below are several acts of Christ that were initiated but not yet consummated:

Adopted now (Rom. 8:15) – Consummating Adoption to come (Rom. 8:23)

Redeemed now (1 Cor. 1:30) – Consummating Redemption to come (Php. 3:14, Rom. 8:23).

Regeneration now (Titus 3:5) – Consummating Regeneration to come (Rom. 8:18-21, Php. 3:12-14)

Kingdom within you now (Lk. 17:21, Col. 1:13, Eph. 2:6) – Consummating Kingdom to come (2 Tim. 4:1, Rev. 3:21)

On Mount Zion now (Heb. 12:22) – Consummating ascent upon Mount Zion to come (Rev. 14:1-5)

Resurrection now (Rom. 6:4) – Consummating Resurrection to come (1 Cor. 15:50)

Eternal Life now (1 John 3:15, 5:12-13) – Consummating Eternal Life to come (2 Cor. 5:1-4, 1 Tim. 6:12)

Overcoming power now (Eph. 2:5, 1 John 5:4) – Consummating Overcoming power to come (1 Cor. 15:54-57)

Defeat of Death now (Rom. 8:2, 6, Eph. 2:5) –
Consummating Defeat of Death to come (1 Cor.
15:54-57)

In the Light now (Eph. 5:8) – Consummating Eternal
Day of Light to come (Prov. 4:18, 2 Peter 1:19, Rev.
21:23-25)

Seeing God now (2 Cor. 3:17-18, 1 Cor. 13:12, Heb. 11:27) –
Consummating revelatory sight to come (1 John 3:2)

Perfect Now (Heb. 10:14) – Consummating Perfection to
come (Php. 3:12, 1 Cor. 13:10, Prov. 4:18)

"As He is" now (1 John 4:17) – Consummating
conformity, "as He is" in glory, to come (1 John 3:2, Rev.
2:27)

Knowing Him now (1 John 2:4, John 17:3) –
Consummating knowing, "even as also I am known" to
come (1 Cor. 13:12)

Elect now (2 In. 1:1, 13, 1 Pet. 1:2) – Consummating
Election to come (2 Peter 1:10)

Called now (1 Cor. 1:26) – Consummating Calling to
come (Php. 3:14)

Chosen now (1 Peter 2:9) – Consummating Choice to
come (Matt. 22:14, Rev. 17:14)[131]

These are acts of God that are awaiting a future
consummation and so is the Day of Atonement. The
atonement was mentioned in the Old Testament: *But the
goat on which the lot fell to be the scapegoat shall be*

131

http://www.thecondescensionofgod.com/present-progressive-sal
vation-explained.html

presented alive before the Lord, to make atonement upon it, and let it go as the scapegoat into the wilderness, Leviticus 16:10. The scapegoat was to be the sin bearer to carry the sin of the people into the wilderness. This scapegoat will be condemned and those whose sin, the scapegoat carried will be atoned and their sin forgiven and they are set free.

But this was only a picture of what was to come because the blood of bulls and goats can only cover sin but cannot take it away, Hebrews 10:4. Christ, Himself, became the scapegoat and the sin of those He came to redeem were put on Him and here is how the writer of Hebrews puts it: *Not with the blood of goats and calves, but with His own blood He entered the most Holy place once for all, having obtained eternal redemption,* Hebrew 9:12. He is the perfect sin bearer because He was sinless. He who knew no sin became sin for us, 2 Corinthians 5:21.

Image of a scapegoat taken from Wikipedia [132]

So, the Day of Atonement is the day of the Lord's second and final return to consummate all that He had started and bring it to completion. This day is not distinct from the rapture as many say that it is but they are identical events. Most pretribulationalists see the rapture and second coming as distinct and separate events, and that Christ will return and rapture the church before the tribulation and will return later for the second coming. Proponents of such views, like Dr. Richard Mayhue, Professor of Theology at The Master's Seminary, in California made these arguments in his article titled, "Why a Pretribulational Rapture ?" in which he argued that the rapture and the second coming are separate events.[133]Some will say that Matthew 24 is a rapture passage but is that really the case? John Walvoord seems to argue that a pretribulational rapture is taught in Matthew 24, as elaborated in his article, "Is a Posttribulational Rapture Revealed in Matthew 24?"[134] I do not believe that we are smarter than the disciples of Jesus, they certainly believed in posttribulational rapture of the church and that the church will be raptured at the second coming of Jesus. Here was a question asked by the disciples: *Now as He sat on the Mount of Olives, the disciples came to Him privately, saying, "Tell us when will these things be? And what will be the sign of Your coming, and the end of the age?"* Matthew 24:3.

132

https://en.wikipedia.org/wiki/Scapegoat#/media/File:William_Hol
man_Hunt_-_The_Scapegoat.jpg
133

https://tms.edu/educational-resources/journal/archive/why-a-pr
etribulational-rapture/
134   https://biblicalstudies.org.uk/pdf/gtj/06-2_257.pdf

The disciples asked a very interesting question right from the beginning: They wanted to know two things: (1)"the sign of His coming," and (2)"the end of the age." The sign of His coming may be called "the rapture" by some,while "the end of the age," is also seen as the second coming by others. But the fundamental question that is posed here is: are these two separate events or the same event? The question here also is the use of the Greek word,"kai," that stands between, "sign of your coming and the consummation or end of the age." How is "kai" functioning in this context? The Greek word,"kai," can be translated into *English* as *and, also, even, indeed, but it is considered a primary article, having copulative and sometimes a cumulative force.*[135]

This Greek word has broad and expanded uses but the basic idea behind the use of the Greek word,"kai," is that it either connects or compliments. It either connects two independent ideas or acts as a compliment to the main idea. So, is "kai," used here to connect "the sign of His coming" and "the coming or consummation of the age," or to complement and expand on the idea of "the sign of His coming," which is "the coming or consummation of the age?"I happen to believe that the Greek word "kai" in this passage and context should have been translated into English as "also," making, "the coming of the age," a complimentary or cumulative force to "the sign of His coming," thus, making the rapture and the consummation of the age or the second coming the same event.

This understanding sets the tone for the rest of Matthew 24 as Jesus's response to the question posed by the disciples. The Lord Jesus will spend the rest of His time, answering this question for the entire chapter of Matthew

---

135

https://www.biblestudytools.com/lexicons/greek/nas/kai.html

24.Here is excerpt of how Jesus responded: *Immediately after the tribulation of those days the sun will be darkened, and the moon will not give its light; the stars will fall from heaven, and the powers of the heaven will be shaken. Then the sign of the Son of Man will appear in heaven, and then all the tribes of the earth will mourn and they will see the Son of Man coming on the clouds of heaven with power and great glory. And He will send His angels with a great sound of a trumpet, and they will gather together His elect from the four winds, from one end of heaven to the other,* Matthew 24:29-31.

Verse 29 of Matthew 24 begins by saying, "immediately after the tribulation of those days," the return of Christ is to begin. This verse makes the point that the return of Christ is posttribulational, as the verse clearly states. But note that, there is no gathering of His elect at the rapture but at the second coming. Some have even advanced the idea that this chapter applies only to the nation of Israel and not to the church. Why would this apply to Israel alone when it clearly says, "then the sign of the Son of Man will appear in heaven, and then all tribes of the earth will mourn and they will see the Son of Man coming on the clouds?"

This is clearly a passage about the second coming and not the rapture unless they are the same events. This is about the Day of Atonement and not the feast of Trumpets. This is about the consummation of the marriage between the bride (the church) and groom (Christ). He is coming to take his bride but also for judgment. This is what is said at the end the chapter concerning judgment: The Lord of that servant shall come in a day when he is not looking for Him and in an hour that he is not aware of it, And shall cut him asunder, and appoint him his portion with the hypocrites, there shall be weeping gnashing of teeth, Matthew 24:50-51.He is coming for His bride and to gather His elect, both Jew and gentile who believe. He is coming to gather them as a hen gathers her chicks under her wings, where we shall forever be with Him.

Feasts of Booths or Tabernacles

The feast of tabernacles or booths is the last of seven feasts which the Israelites were commanded by God to observe. Sometimes called the feast of ingathering or shelter, it is the third and final feast in the fall that they were to observe. This feast is also known as "sukkot," and it is celebrated on the 15th day of the Hebrew month, Tishri. This is the seventh month on the Hebrew calendar and it normally occurs at the later part of September and mid-October. The feast of the Day of Atonement is on the 10th of the same month and the feast of Tabernacles is five days later, which is on the 15th day of that month. The concept and being of a deity is somewhat abstract to the human mindset.A being that cannot be seen, touched or smelled; a being who seems so very far away that any human being who suddenly gets a glimpse of Him will drop dead instantly; a being, so amazing that He knows all things, knowable and unknowable. His power and potency knows no bounds.

There is no place where He is not and He needs not to travel there but His glory fills the universe. It is in this context that the God of all the earth instituted the feast of Tabernacle. This feast foreshadows a time when the God of the universe will no longer be distant but will actually dwell or tabernacle among His people. He will be our God and we shall be His people. This feast reminded the Israelites of their deliverance from Egypt to the Promised Land, and also provides a vivid picture of our deliverance from sin to salvation.

This is also agreed by most scholars to be symbolic of Christ's second coming, when He will separate the wheat from the tares or chaff and dwell or tabernacle forever with His bride. Here is what God said to the Israelites concerning this very important feast: *You shall dwell in booths seven days; all that are Israelites born shall be in booths. That your generations may know that I made the children of Israel dwell in booths, when I brought them out of Egypt; I am the Lord your God,* Leviticus 23:42-43.

The Israelites were taken from bondage to booths and the feast serves as a reminder that God brought them out of Egypt. The basic idea behind the feast of ingathering or tabernacle is that God is gathering His elect from the four corners of the earth and tabernacling among them. Once the Day of Atonement is complete and sin is completely eradicated, then God is ready to draw near to His people.

That is why the Day of Atonement is a precursor to the gathering of His elect. The elect have received their resurrected glorified spiritual bodies, and are ready to enter the New Jerusalem, where no sin dwells. But before we get to this New Jerusalem, God was very gracious to give us a picture of His presence on earth. In the old testament, the Ark of the Covenant was tasked with showing a physical and tangible presence of God upon the earth, the shekhina glory as it is referred to. God spoke with Moses from between two Cherubs (Numbers 7:89) because He could not speak with him face to face.

The Ark was built and carried with the Israelites as they traveled from Egypt through the desert. The Ark was later placed in the tabernacle of meeting (Exodus 40:21) and later into the temple (Exodus 25:22).

Here is one description of the role of the Ark in Jewish life: It was accessible only once a year, and then, only by one person. On Yom Kippur, the High Priest (Kohen Gadol) could enter the Holy of Holies to ask forgiveness for himself and for all the nation of Israel (Leviticus 16:2).

The relationship between the Ark and the shekhina is reinforced by the recurring motif of clouds. God's presence is frequently seen in the guise of a cloud in the Bible (Ex. 26:16), and the Ark is constantly accompanied by clouds: When God spoke from between the Cherubs, there was a glowing cloud visible there Ex. 40:35); and when the High Priest entered the presence of the Ark on Yom Kippur, he did so only under the cover of a cloud of incense, perhaps intended to mask the sight of the shekhina in all its glory Lev. 16:13). The holiness of the Ark also made it dangerous to those who came in contact with it.

When Nadav and Avihu, the sons of Aaron, brought a foreign flame to offer a sacrifice in the Tabernacle, they were devoured by a fire that emanated from the Lord (Lev, 10:2). During the saga of the capture of the Ark by the philistines, numerous people, including some who merely looked at the Ark, were killed by its power. Similarly, the priests who served in the Tabernacle and the Temple were told that viewing the Ark at an improper time would result in immediate death (Num. 4:20).[136]

It is vividly clear that the Art represented the presence of God upon the earth. It is also clear that mankind,

---

136

https://www.jewishvirtuallibrary.org/the-ark-of-the-convenant

in its sinful state, is unable to come close to a Holy God. Mankind is not even able to look upon a Holy God without suffering severe consequences, including death. Removal of sin is necessary for sinful mankind to dwell or tabernacle with a Holy God. Image of the Ark of the Covenant is shown below:

The Ark of the Covenant

The Ark of the Covenant contains two tablets of stone (on which the Ten Commandments were given to Moses on Mount Sinai) 2 Chronicles 5:10. But the writer of Hebrews, in the New Testament, says that the Ark also included the golden pot that had manna, Aaron's rod that budded, and the tablets of the Covenant, Hebrews 9:4.

The presence of God among His people was also manifested in the new testaments. The plan of God is to always be among His people. The feast of ingathering or tabernacle foreshadows a time when God will gather His elect, His bride, the church, and tabernacle with her forever. The first advent of Jesus is also a foreshadowing of His second advent. Jesus, in His incarnation, left His home in glory and temporarily came to dwell among His people. Jesus was born at a very interesting time and circumstances that foreshadows His future ingathering with His people.

Here are the circumstances surrounding His birth: While they were there, the time came for her to give birth. And she gave birth to her firstborn son; and she wrapped Him in cloths, and laid Him in a manger, because there was no room for them in the inn. In the same region there were some shepherds staying out in the fields and keeping watch over their flock at night, Luke 2:6-8.This text gives rise to two very interesting observations: (1)He was born and laid in a manger; and(2) the shepherds were keeping watch over their flock at night. He was in a manger because there was no room in the inn and the reason given for lack of room was because the people were ordered to each travel to their place of birth so that a census could be taken. So, being born in a manger may not also be accidental or coincidental after all.

A manger is normally a location in an animal stable outside the main building where animals are kept. In the Old Testament, the Israelites were told to leave their homes and set up tents and dwell in them to commemorate the feast of tents or tabernacle. Is it any surprise that Jesus was born in a tent-like structure? In all likelihood, this was a partial fulfillment of the feast of Tabernacle. God is gathered among His people and that is why He was born in a tent. The lack of room in the inn was no accident, but was actually in accordance with the plan and purposes of God. The timing was right.This decree by Caesar Augustus may have coincided with some other Jewish feast. This is purely a speculation at this point but the facts are that the shepherds were watching over their flock at night. That tells us that this period in which the shepherds were watching over their flock has to be during the warm weather, likely from May through October.

Here is a report from the Israeli Science and Technology Directory on the weather in Israel: The rainy season extends from October to early May, and rainfall peaks in December through February. Heavy snow falls only in the Northernmost part of Golan Heights, where Mount Hermon Summit (2,224 m above sea level) generally remains snow covered from December to March. In other parts of the country, snow is observed rarely. [137] It is very unlikely that shepherds would be watching over their flock in December, in the midst of heavy rain, cold, winter, or a combination of the three.

That puts December 25th as Jesus' date of birth in question. Every significant event in the life of Jesus is fulfilled from some Jewish feast. An event like the birth of Jesus is very important that was foretold in the Old Testament, and cannot just happen on December 25th, with no real theological and cultural significance. The birth of Jesus and His coming into the world signifies God coming to dwell among His people. The Old Testament had the Ark of the Covenant in their midst to signify God's presence in their midst.

There is no conclusive evidence as to the origin of December 25th as the day of the birthday of Jesus. The origin of that holiday and its December date lie in the ancient Greco-Roman world, as commemorations probably began sometime in the 2nd century. There are at least three

---

[137]

https://www.science.co.il/weather/Israel-climate.php#:~:text=The%20rainy%20season%20extends%20from,the%20North%20to%20the%20South.

possible origins for the December date:*The Roman Christian historian Sextus Africanus dated Jesus's conception to March 25th (the same date upon which he held that the world was created), which, after nine months in his mother's womb, would result in a December 25 birth.*

In the 3rd century, the Roman Empire, which at the time had not adopted Christianity, celebrated the rebirth of the Unconquered Sun (Sol Invictus) on December 25th. This holiday not only marked the return of longer days after the winter solstice but also followed the popular Roman festival called the Saturnalia (during which people feasted and exchanged gifts). It was also the birthday of the Indo-European deity Mithra, a god of light and loyalty whose cult at the time was growing popular among Roman soldiers.[138]

The birth and first advent of Jesus also signifies the physical presence of God in the midst of His people. Here is how John puts it: *And the Word became flesh, and dwelt among us, (and we beheld His glory, the glory of the only begotten of the Father) full of grace and truth,* John 1:14. The interpretation here is simply that God took on human form and became flesh and blood. He can be seen and touched. The dichotomy is that He never relinquished His divine attributes and at the same time, was fully human. He was fully human and fully God simultaneously, and yet sinless or without sin. He was incapable of sinning yet He was dwelling among sinful creatures like us. The Greek word "skenoo," that is translated into English in this text as "dwelt," also means Tabernacle, Tent, Spread, and Abode. The

---

138

https://www.britannica.com/story/why-is-christmas-in-december#:~:text=The%20Roman%20Christian%20historian%20Sextus,in%20a%20December%2025%20birth.

Hebrew word "Ohel," is translated into the LXX as "skenoo," So Exodus 40:34-35 is fulfilled in John 1:14 and will completely be fulfilled in Rev. 21:3, when God is gathered to His elect.

In all likelihood, the birth of Jesus happened at the beginning or during the feast of Tabernacle, which is the 15th day of the Hebrew month of Tishri, which is the 7th month in Jewish calendar, which corresponds to September/ October in our current calendar. The exact date is not given to us but this is the likely period of His birth but at the end of the Day of Atonement and the very beginning of the feast of tabernacle or ingathering, lines up with the biblical evidence and Jewish feasts timelines that have already been fulfilled.

This God is tabernacling with His people in His first advent but He will finally tabernacle with His people at His second advent and here is what the text says: *And I heard a loud voice from heaven saying' "Behold, the tabernacle of God is with men, and He will dwell with them, and they shall be His people, God Himself will be with them and be their God*, Revelation 21:3. This is the final fulfillment of the feast of Tabernacle. The chapter is titled, "The Power of Marriage," for very good reason, because it is the unit and fabric of society. Without the human marriage that started with Adam and Eve, there will be no multiplication of humans and hence, no marriage or union between Christ and His *bride, the church, so marriage is the most powerful force in the universe.Sexual* intercourse has to be properly used; else, it may lead to destructive and addictive sexual behaviors.

The Destructive Power of Sexual Addiction

Sexual intercourse is probably, by far, the most pleasurable experience in human existence. It is the most sacred and intimate experience in human existence. Sexual intercourse is very powerful; and if it is powerful then it has the potential to be pleasurable, explosive and destructive. The potential to be useful and destructive. A kitchen knife that is normally used to help prepare food to sustain life, can also be used to harm and kill a human being, who is created in the image of God. A knife can be powerful and destructive; likewise, so is sex if not used in its proper context, with restraint.

Sexual addiction has the potential and power to destroy lives in ways that are unimaginable. This is a very huge societal problem and yet it hardly makes headline news. Most people would hardly believe that sexual addiction is even a problem. Society is well aware of things like alcohol addiction, drug addiction, food addiction, power addiction, gambling addiction and various forms of addictions that are out there. The simple truth is that any form of addiction is destructive to the person involved and to the society at large and so, the idea that sex can be addictive, is news to many.

Sexual addiction is a little different from other forms of addictions in that it is considered as part of a normal human activity and so people are very reluctant to even admit that they have a sexual addiction problem. There is also the societal stigma of labeling someone as a sex addict. Even the psychological and psychiatric communities are struggling to identify sexual addiction as a mental health issue.

So what really is sexual addiction? Here is a definition from the National Library of Medicine: Compulsive sexual behavior (CSB) is a common disorder featuring repetitive, intrusive and distressing sexual thoughts, urges and behaviors that negatively affect many aspects of an individual's life.[139]This is quite an interesting and fascinating definition and description of sexual addiction. It is interesting because it links two very important parts of human life, namely thoughts and behavior, but the definition does not tell us if the behavior is a result of the thoughts or if the thoughts are a result of the behavior.

The fact remains that this is a big issue and millions of lives are affected. Here are some stats on sexual addiction: The number of people in the United States living with sex addiction is currently estimated at 12-30 million. Both men and women can be affected, though little research exists on female sex addiction. Men with sex addiction have an average of 32 sexual partners, while females have an average of 22 sexual partners. A strong correlation exists between sex addiction and childhood trauma. Surveys of people with sex addictions show that during childhood:

72% were physically abused

81% were sexually abused

97% were emotionally abused

Sex and Porn Addiction

Sex and porn addiction often go hand-in-hand. Many people with sex addiction also turn to porn to satisfy their desires.

---

[139]   The new PMC design is here! Learn more about navigating our updated article layout. The PMC legacy view will also be available for a limited time.

Many people with sex addiction say that they are dependent on porn and become distressed when they go for long periods of time without viewing it.[140] As you can tell from these statistics, sexual addiction is a big deal and the real picture is probably a lot worse than what is portrayed here. Most sex addicts may never want to take a survey and openly admit that they are a sex addict. Sexual addiction is also closely linked to pornography, in that porn may be used as a visual sexual stimulant to feed the fantasy of the sex addict. The power and force that drives a sex addict literally takes over the thoughts and decision-making faculties of the individual. A sex addict can be compared to an alcoholic or a drug addict. An addict, in general, is incapable of any restraint on their conduct and behavior.

This is very foreign to the mind of an average person to understand. Let me say it one more time: An addict, in the true sense of the word, is incapable of altering their behavior on their own. Why will the president of the United States of America, who is married, have sex with a young intern in the oval office, knowing that his marriage and presidency was at stake? Where was the moral compass? Why could he not reason within himself that the few minutes of pleasure would not be worth the risk? Do not be quick to pass judgment on him because there are millions more who would have done worse, given the same opportunity. I am actually speaking of President Bill Clinton and his sex issues that are well documented in the public domain.

Even the then speaker of the House of Representatives who was leading the Clinton's impeachment

---

140

https://www.therecoveryvillage.com/process-addiction/sex-addiction/sexual-addiction-statistics/#:-:text=The%20number%20of%20people%20in,average%20of%2022%20sexual%20partners.

did not also have clean hands himself, and here is ABCNEWS: In 2007, House Speaker, Newt Gingrich, admitted to cheating on his first and second wives, including having an affair while leading the Clinton impeachment proceedings. Gingrich's first marriage was to his former high school teacher, Jackie Battley, in 1962. Gingrich married his second wife, Marianne Ginther, months after he divorced Battley in 1981. Gingrich divorced Ginther in 2000 and soon married Callista Bisek, who he began an affair with when she was a former congressional aide.[141]The then Mayor of Washington DC, Marion Barry, was caught and busted by the FBI smoking crack cocaine on live television. It is assumed that he knew that the FBI was on his trail and tracking him, but he simply could not stop and why is that?

He lacked the capacity to stop, plain and simple. Addicts do not stop their actions because of some law that has been passed or even knowledge that they are being tracked by the FBI.That is why no law can stop a real, not a marginal addict, from performing his or her sexual acts. They are overpowered and cannot be stopped from within, and help has to come from without. Sexual addiction is not limited to males, as females are also unable to put a lid over their sexual desires. One such example is a Minnesota congresswoman, who was caught in a web of sexual activities. She seems too out of control to even contemplate the damage that her actions may have had on her family and career.

---

[141]

https://abcnews.go.com/Politics/photos/political-sex-scandals-43 202982/image-newt-gingrich-43223585

Chapter 7

The Power of Sexual Addiction

The power of sex is so strong that humans are unable and unwilling to resist and any sense of logical reasoning is out of the window. Here is what happened to the Minnesota congresswoman: *A Washington, DC, mom says her political-consultant husband left her for Rep. Ilhan Omar, according to a bombshell divorce filing obtained by The Post. Dr. Beth Mynett says her cheating spouse, Tim Mynett, told her in April that he was having an affair with the Somali-born US representative and that he even made a "shocking declaration of love"for the Minnesota* congresswoman before he ditched his wife, alleges the filing, submitted in DC *Superior Court on Tuesday.*

The physician, 55, and her 38- year-old husband – who has worked for left-wing Democrats such as Omar and her Minnesota predecessor, *Keith Ellison –have a 13-year-old son together. "The parties physically separated on or about April 7, 2019, when the Defendant told the Plaintiff that he was romantically involved with and in love with another woman, Ilhan Omar," the court papers say. Defendant met Rep. Omar while working for her," the documents state. "Although devastated by the betrayal and deceit that preceded his abrupt declaration, Plaintiff told Defendant that she loved him, and was willing to fight for the marriage.*[142]This is the destructive power of sexual addiction that is taking down families around the globe.

It does not matter one's status in life, this is a real destructive power. It leaves the offended parties abandoned, confused and rejected. Children are caught in the middle and they too probably feel confused, abandoned and rejected. So, sexual addiction does not just happen in a vacuum, but it is a reflection of something deeper. The deep uncontrollable compulsion and seemingly unstoppable desire for more sex reflects a deep rooted problem that is driving the desire. Such a person dreams, eats and thinks about sex 24/7. So, what is at the root of this desire?

The Root Cause and Remedy of Sexual Addiction

So, the cause of sexual addiction or any other form of addiction for that matter is a very fascinating subject. Addiction takes over the thinking faculties of anyone that it gets hold of, such that such a person is rendered impotent in the face of this foe. Some have argued that the addict has the will power within them to stop his or her destructive behavior, while others disagree. If you were to consult a psychiatrist, then you may be told that it is a medical issue that needs medications to fix it; psychologists would certainly disagree, calling it a psychological issue that needs to look at the person's family of origin history and suggest some talk therapy or cognitive behavior therapy (CBT) sessions with the person.

142

https://nypost.com/2019/08/27/my-husband-dumped-me-for-re
p-ilhan-omar-dc-mom-says-in-divorce-filing/

Then if you were to talk to a theologian, pastor or some faith person, you may hear a faith perspective thrown into the mix. Here is a definition of compulsive sexual behavior (CSB), as defined by the world's renowned Mayo Clinic: *Compulsive sexual behavior is sometimes called hypersexuality, hypersexuality disorder or sexual addiction. It's an excessive preoccupation with sexual fantasies, urges or behavior that is difficult to control, causes you distress, or negatively affects your health, job, relationships or other parts of your life. Compulsive sexual behaviors may involve a variety of commonly enjoyable sexual experiences. Examples include masturbation, cybersex, multiple sexual partners, and use of pornography or paying for sex.*

When these sexual behaviors become a major focus in your life, are difficult to control, and are disruptive or harmful to you or others, then they may be considered compulsive sexual behavior. No matter what it's called or the exact nature of the behavior, untreated compulsive sexual behavior can damage your self-esteem, relationships, career, health and other people. But with treatment and self-help, you can learn to manage compulsive sexual behavior. [143]

This is a medical response to sexual addiction. This medical response says that "When these sexual behaviors become a major focus in your life, they are difficult to control." This medical response calls it "sexual behaviors," and they are rightly behaviors but where did they come from? Behaviors do not suddenly appear out of thin air! Behaviors originate from a thought pattern and the behavior is dependent on the thought and it is a derivative of that

---

[143]

https://www.mayoclinic.org/diseases-conditions/compulsive-sexual-behavior/symptoms-causes/syc-20360434 thought. So, for any behavior to be altered, the thought about that behavior must first be altered. It normally progresses like this: from a thought to a belief; and from a belief to an action. Thought + Belief = Actions. You can think about something but if you do not believe it, then it will not show up in your actions. You cannot act on what you do not first believe and that is why your life and death hangs in the balance in your belief system. Wrong belief is detrimental to your health. The behavior of sexual addicts and all other addicts, for that matter, are rooted in a deep-seated and entrenched belief system.

The medical response ended by asserting that "but with treatment and self-help you can learn to manage compulsive sexual behavior." And by the word, "treatment," the doctors are most likely talking about medicating the sex addict or persons with other forms of addictions in order to curtail or stop their out of control sexual desires or other addictive behaviors. If these behaviors are linked to thoughts, then can thoughts be medicated to change behavior? How can some one's thoughts be treated with medication to change behavior? This is the medical approach in dealing with sexual addiction and all other forms of addictions for that matter. The mind cannot be medicated to wellness. Medications only provide a numbing effect that alters the feelings with no real tangible effect. This is a mind altering solution that brings no real relief.

Now, let's look at sexual addiction through the lenses of a psychologist. Here is a description of sexual addiction posted on a prominent site: *The concept of sexual addiction has been thought of in a variety of ways. A sexual addiction does share many of the hallmarks of clinical addiction. One of these hallmark is that the person will be unable to control their behavior even if the negative consequences are clear (or even likely).As opposed to someone with a healthy sex drive, a person with a sex addiction will spend a disproportionate amount of time seeking or engaging in sex while keeping the activity secret from others. People with a sex addiction will be unable to stop the behavior unless there is some sort of intervening event. As a result, personal and professional relationships may suffer. There may even be an increased risk of sexually transmitted infection, including HIV, if a person is unable to rein in their sexual impulses.*[144]

The key take away from this assessment is the acknowledgement that sexual addiction is not unique but is in many ways similar to other addictions. The common denominator for all addictions is that "the person will be unable to control their behavior." There is a sense of helplessness in addictions as the person is completely rendered impotent to get out of that predicament through any self-effort. It is like watching a person drowning in a river because they don't know how to swim and you are standing by the side of the river and shouting, "swim to the shore!" and they simply cannot obey your command because they simply can't swim. Likewise, if someone is suffering from sexual addictions or other forms of addictions for that matter, they cannot stop on their own. That is why moral laws may be good, but are useless for such a person. That is why most legal systems, including the bible, recognize insanity as a defense against actions that are committed unwillingly.

I am not advocating a license to enable certain behaviors but only recognizing the reality of the dilemma. If

---

[144]

https://www.verywellmind.com/sex-addiction-symptoms-23290 82 the truth be told, we know someone, or have a relative, or we ourselves are suffering from some form of addiction, including sexual addiction, and are unable to stop, but why is that? But what is the cause of sexual addiction according to psychologists? Here is their take on this: *There are a number of theories as to why a sexual addiction occurs. Some of these involve conceptualizing a sex addiction as a form of impulse control, obsessive-compulsive or relational disorder. They also include the idea that in some individuals sexual addictions emerge as a consequence and a way of coping with early traumas, including sexual trauma.*[145]There seems to be a lack of concrete response from the psychological and psychiatry communities as to the origin of sexual addictions, and other forms of addictions.

This article identifies a number of theories as to why a sexual addiction occurs but no single cause is identified. It identifies impulse control, obsessive-compulsive or relationship disorder and early childhood sexual trauma as possible causeS of sexual addictions. There is clear confusion about the cause of sexual addiction from the psychological community as to the cause and origin of sexual addiction.

Here is the view from the psychiatry community as to the cause of sexual addiction: *The causes of long-term uncontrollable sexual urges and behaviors are not well understood. People of all ages may experience the condition and for different reasons. It's probably that a combination of factors leads to compulsive sexual behaviors, including: chemical imbalances in the brain; underlying or co-occurring mental health conditions,*

145

https://www.verywellmind.com/sex-addiction-symptoms-23290
82

childhood experiences; childhood relationships with parents or guardians; other lifestyle influences. Preliminary research Trusted Sources suggests an imbalance of dopamine, a neurotransmitter in the brain, may also impact sexual behaviors. [146]There seems to be some sort of agreement between psychologists and psychiatrists that sexual addiction is linked to uncontrollable sexual urges and they also agree that the behavior and its root causes are not well understood. The psychologists see them as emotional issues and the psychiatrists see them as medical issues. You may have heard the term: "chemical imbalance in the brain," to mean that some type of medication is needed to correct the imbalance, hence the role of a psychiatrist is needed to correct the imbalance.

Getting Help through a Psychologist or Psychiatrist

People seek help based on their belief systems. So, if someone believes that sexual addiction is caused by their feelings and emotions about sexuality, then they are likely to seek out a psychologist for help; but if they believe that some chemical imbalance in the brain is causing them to have uncontrollable sexual desires then they are more likely to talk to a psychiatrist. Here are the medical or psychiatrist and psychologists' suggestions: *Sexual addiction requires treatment from a medical professional experienced in the field, such as a psychologist, psychiatrist, or sex therapist. Treatment can vary based on the underlying cause, but will typically be conducted on an outpatient basis with counseling and behavior therapies.*

---

[146]

https://psychcentral.com/lib/what-is-sexual-addiction#causes

If the sex addiction is associated with an anxiety disorder or mood disorder, medications may be prescribed as part of the treatment plan. There are currently no established recommendations on the appropriate use of medications to treat a sex addiction outside of the realm of these clinically classified disorders.

There are also a growing number of sex addiction support groups, some of which deal with co-addictions (such as sex and substance abuse) and other types of treatments which are built on a 12-step recovery model. [147] It is quite interesting that in the second paragraph of this article, it is stated that, "there are currently no established recommendations on the appropriate use of medication to treat a sex addiction," and yet it is treated as such. If it is linked to some other disorder like anxiety or depression, then they seem to suggest that medication may be appropriate. Psychologists and psychiatrists agree that the cause is unknown, yet many are being medicated. Yet others seek help from a psychiatrist through other programs, including the 12-step recovery model and here is that program:

Honesty: After many years of denial, recovery can begin with one simple admission of being powerless over alcohol or any other drug a person is addicted to. Their friends and family may also use this step to admit their loved one has an addiction.

Faith: Before a higher power can begin to operate, you must first believe that it can. Someone with an addiction accepts that there is a higher power to help them heal.

---

[147]
https://www.verywellmind.com/sex-addiction-symptoms-2329082

Surrender: You can change your self-destructive decisions by recognizing that you alone cannot recover; with help from your higher power, you can.

Soul searching: The person in recovery must identify their problems and get a clear picture of how their behavior affected themselves and others around them.

Integrity: Step 5 provides a great opportunity for growth. The person in recovery must admit their wrongs in front of their higher power and another person.

Acceptance: The key to Step 6 is acceptance—accepting character defects exactly as they are and becoming entirely willing to let them go.

Humility: The spiritual focus of Step 7 is humility, or asking a higher power to do something that cannot be done by self-will or mere determination.

Willingness: This step involves making a list of those you harmed before coming into recovery.

Forgiveness: Making amends may seem challenging, but for those serious about recovery, it can be a great way to start healing your relationships.

Maintenance: Nobody likes to admit to being wrong. But it is a necessary step in order to maintain spiritual progress in recovery.

Making contact: The purpose of Step 11 is to discover the plan your higher power has for your life.

Service: The person in recovery must carry the message to others and put the principles of the program into practice in every area of their life. [148]

This program has been used to combat several kinds of addictions, from alcohol to drugs, and now sex addiction has been added into the mix. The 12-step recovery model is the closest that it gets in acknowledging that addictions of any kind are spiritual problems. This model seems to subscribe to some form of generic spirituality without any absolute attachment to any particular deity. In item 2 of the recovery model, it makes reference to a generic higher power but was careful not to identify that higher power.

This is like wanting the power but denying the source. This was intended to be a secular program that recognizes the power of a belief system in combating addictions. This is no doubt a starting point that may have provided relief and recovery for some but its lasting impact is yet to be fully known. So, assuming that you happen to believe that sexual addictions and addictions in general are spiritual issues, then you are finally ready to hear what theologians will have to say about this:

Theological Views on Sexual Addictions

I had earlier made the case that addictions of most, if not all sorts, trace their origins to the thought process of the individual. If someone is having a sexual fantasy towards another person then it is what they are thinking that is driving those sexual fantasies. Both psychologists and psychiatrists agree that the inability to control behavior is behind sexual addictions, but they somehow fail to link those behaviors to thought patterns.

---

[148]   https://www.verywellmind.com/the-twelve-steps-63284

But we can safely conclude that behaviors do not just happen in a vacuum. But where do those thoughts originate? Do thoughts suddenly appear out of thin air? That is exactly what is being suggested by most scientists and here is one such view: *Thoughts come from nowhere and from everywhere! I think both contain an element of truth. Subjectively, our thoughts come from nowhere: they just pop into our heads, or emerge in the form of words leaving our mouths. Objectively, we say that thoughts emerge from neural processes, and that neural processes come from everywhere. What I mean by this is that the forms and dynamics of thought are influenced by everything that has a causal connection with you, your society, and your species.*[149]

This is the thinking of a neuroscientist, Yohan John, and this is the prevailing view amongst most philosophers, psychologists and scientists. The bottom-line is that thoughts have no real origin, or so they say. There is a sense of randomness in the thought processes. "They just pop into our heads," but where did they pop up from, to get into our heads? The simple truth is that no thought can ever exist without an origin; else, it would not be a thought. Without a cause there will be no effect. This seems to fall into the same category as the evolutionary theory which states that the earth suddenly appeared out of thin air, hence the big bang theory. Here is another scientist: *In 2001, Colombian neuroscientist Rodolfo Llinas declared that prediction is the ultimate function of the brain. Such a sentiment was apparent in the earliest form of biological life. Eukaryotes used intention to survive; move toward sustenance, flee from toxicity. Predicting where to harvest and avoid danger,*

---

[149]

https://www.forbes.com/sites/quora/2016/10/21/where-do-our-thoughts-come-from/?sh=5540af322ee2 *he argued, is the foundation of what would evolve into nervous systems and all that followed: emotions, thoughts, consciousness.*[150]

       This scientist seems to be in concurrence with the former but this brings a new twist into the argument. The phrase, "would evolve into nervous systems," is to probably imply that our emotions, thoughts and consciousness came into being through an evolutionary framework. Yohan John said that our thoughts came to being through a random process and Rodolfo Llinas said that they evolved over time. If our thoughts are random and evolved, then our behaviors that proceed from our thoughts are also random and evolved. Just as creation was not random, so our thoughts are not random but are carefully orchestrated. Did you know that thoughts come from the heart? They do not evolve and are not random, either.

The Power of Thought

       Thoughts are the most powerful force in the universe. Every human action ever taken begins with a simple thought. Adolf Hitler set the Second World War into motion with a thought and an idea. The Wright brothers invented the flying machine, an aircraft, with a simple thought and an idea. Every idea begins with a thought. So, the idea that thoughts have a random origin is not even conceivable and possible. Jesus had a very interesting conversation with some Pharisees and scribes in Matthew 15, as they came to Him, asking why His disciples were breaking the tradition of the elders by not washing their hands before they eat.

---

[150]   https://bigthink.com/neuropsych/origin-of-thinking/

Jesus seized this occasion to teach one of the most profound truths in the entire bible. They were concerned about keeping the traditions of the elders but Jesus was concerned about them breaking the commandments of God. They were concerned about outward hand washing but Jesus was concerned about the inward washing of their sin-stained hearts. Here is how it all went down: *Then some Pharisees and scribes came to Jesus from Jerusalem and said, "Why do your disciples break the traditions of the elders? For they do not wash their hands when they eat bread, "* Matthew 15:1. Jesus seized this opportunity to address two very important doctrinal truths: (1)the origin of thought and the sinfulness and (2)the corrupt nature of the human heart.

First the origin of thought: *Peter said to Him, "Explain the parable to us," Jesus said, "Are you also still lacking in understanding? Do you not understand that everything that goes into the mouth passes into the stomach, and is eliminated? But the things that come out of the mouth come from the heart, and those things defile the person. For out of the heart come evil thoughts, murders, acts of adultery, other immoral sexual acts, thefts, false testimonies, and slanderous statements. These are the things that defile the person; but to eat with unwashed hands does not defile the person,* Matthew 15-15-20.

Jesus is certainly not advocating a position that proper hand washing before a meal is unimportant. It would seem like there was the tradition of the elders that had been passed down from several generations that outward cleanliness brought a person close to His God. But Jesus was saying that was not the case at all. The heart is evil and likewise, the thoughts that proceed from it are evil. It expressly says in verse 19 that, "out of the heart comes evil thought," and the text goes on to name those thoughts that come from the heart, and among them, were "murders, acts of adultery, other immoral sexual acts, thefts, false testimonies."

The Greek word "poneroi" has been translated here into English as "evil," and this Greek word means more than bad thoughts, like someone having a bad day at the office. This is where we get our English word "porn," as in "pornography," and this is as bad as it gets. This describes the source of the most debased, deplorable, degrading thoughts that any human being can ever conceive, perceive or utter through their mouth. They all originate from the heart. So when the bible speaks of the "heart", depending on the context, it is mostly not talking about the organ that pumps blood to keep us alive, but it is talking about the seat of our will, thoughts and emotions. This is where thoughts are conceived and decisions are made. This is where decisions are made to commit adultery, commit murder, or become an addict. This is where the battle is lost or won. So we have clearly seen and proven that evil thoughts originate from the heart and since the heart is evil then the thoughts must also be evil. Our second question is whether the condition of the heart is evil or good.

Is the Human Heart Evil or Good?

This is a very important question in the context of the origin of thought and sexual addiction. If you are convinced that evil thoughts originate from the heart, then what is the condition of the heart? Is the heart evil or good? Let's say that the water supply of a very large city comes from a very large reservoir tank that is attached to a river that crosses the city. The city gets all its water from that tank and water inspectors discovered that there was a dead human body in the tank that had decomposed; so what will happen to the rest of the water that flows from that tank? So the logical question to ask is how did the body get into the tank and how did the human heart become evil? And that is a very fair and logical question to ponder!

The question of human nature is central to human existence – central, because many other human problems are tied to a correct understanding of human nature. Answers to many of life's questions, like human greed, selfishness and cooperation are intrinsically linked to human nature. Human suffering, pain, death, and natural disasters cannot be properly understood without a proper understanding of the origin of good, evil and human nature. The view that human beings are inherently good is the prevailing and widely held view, but is that really true?

This view sounds very appealing; after-all, it helps to make us feel good about ourselves and indeed that may even temporarily boost our self-esteem. I have never met anyone who will not want good things said about them. Let's be real! I love good things said about me too! Any negative thing that is said about us would definitely crush our emotions and damage us. To admit otherwise would mean that there is a problem and change is needed; so, to maintain the status quo, it is okay to say that our nature is good. The view that human nature is good is indeed very appealing and interesting but it raises more questions than it answers.

Let's go back to our water tank analogy above. Is it ever possible for the city's water supply tank to supply the city with clean drinkable water and contaminated water from the same tank source simultaneously? Can a good human being commit evil? Think about that and let it sink in. Can a good human being sexually assault children? Can a good human being use an AK-47 machine gun to gun down

30 children at a kindergarten? Can a good human being rob another human being at gunpoint and take their car or possessions and leave them stranded? Goodness can simply be defined as the absence of evil and does anyone really believe that this definition accurately defines human nature? Do you really believe that human beings are good because there is no evil in us? Ponder the implications of your thoughts and answer.

A few years ago, I had a conversation with a young lady in my office while she was with her two year old daughter, and somehow the conversation turned to the issue of human nature, being good or evil, and I somehow had the audacity to tell her that her two year daughter is born with a corrupt and evil nature. As you can properly guess, the conversation went downhill from there! She was exceedingly angry and responded saying, "How dare you say that my child is born with an evil nature," and she said that her daughter is an angel and innocent.

I softly asked her if her daughter has ever been in a room full of toys with other children and she said yes, and I asked if her two year old daughter gladly shares her toys with other kids who don't have any toys and she said absolutely not. So, I said, why is that? I asked her, did you teach your child those skill sets of not sharing? She said, "No!" So I said to her, where did she get them from? Why wasn't she naturally cooperative and sharing with other kids?

This encounter was not really a surprise to me! I have been speaking with people in my office and on the streets about the nature of humans and about 7 out of 10 people who I encounter tell me they are born as good people. I suddenly realized this issue was much bigger than I thought. I took to the streets asking people randomly what they thought of themselves! Were they born with a good or evil nature? The result was identical! I suddenly realized that about 80 percent of the population see themselves as having a good nature. So I suddenly realized that people are desperately sick and don't even know it.

This is not just the prevailing view on the streets but most likely, the prevailing view among academia. Here is a view on human nature by Nigel Barber PhD, posted on psychologytoday.com: *Humans may be inherently good but we assembled a horrifyingly long rap sheet over the past five thousand years, and it's not getting any shorter.*[151]His view asserts that humans are inherently good and contradicts himself again by saying that they have a long history of committing evil. It would be like speaking out of both sides of his mouth. Humans cannot be inherently good and at the same time commit evil deeds. The logic does not simply add up and both cannot be true. It is an either-or and not a both-and proposition. Remember that inherent goodness of a being is the absolute absence of evil in that being.

Here is another view on human nature: *Although this does not definitely solve the puzzle of human nature, it does give us evidence that we may use to solve this puzzle for ourselves and our solutions will likely vary according to how we define "human nature." If human nature is something that we must be born with, then we may be neither good nor bad, cooperative nor selfish. But if human nature is simply the way that we tend to act based on our intuitive and automatic impulses, then it seems that we are an overwhelmingly cooperative species, willing to give for the*

151

https://www.psychologytoday.com/us/contributors/nigel-barber-phd

good of the group even when it comes at our own personal expense. [152]

This author and many others like him struggle to come to terms with true human nature. He concludes that human nature is neither good nor bad and that may seem to imply that there is some neutrality in human nature. Is that a real possibility, that human nature is neutral? So the question that this section is trying to answer goes like this: Is the condition of the human heart evil or good? We have spent quite a considerable amount of time looking at human nature from the human point of view but the simple truth is that humans did not create or make themselves, unless you may happen to believe that humans evolved from some other species over time or suddenly appeared!

If you do not believe this, then there must be a creator who put it altogether. I do not believe that any normal person would want to take a brand new 2023 Mercedes Benz top class to a Ford Fusion dealer for any maintenance advice or some repair malfunction. So humans did not make themselves, so why consult another human in order to understand human nature? Now, only the creator of humans can authoritatively speak about the condition of the human heart because He made the heart. The bible talks about the human heart as being evil, wicked, and the source and origin of wickedness. The human heart, beginning from Genesis to Revelation, is referred to as the source of evil and wickedness and here is Moses speaking: *And God saw that the wickedness of man was great in the earth, and that every imagination of the thoughts of his heart was only evil continually,* Genesis 6:5.

---

[152]

https://www.scientificamerican.com/article/scientists-probe-human-nature-and-discover-we-are-good-after-all/

This was and still is God's assessment of the human nature and human heart, only a short while after the creation of the human race. The Hebrew word that is translated in this verse as "man," is a word that means man as in mankind, not man as in male. God describes human beings as wicked, evil and bad. This is the totality of the human condition from head to feet. There is nothing good in mankind and not only that mankind is bad, wicked and evil, but the heart of man is evil and so are his thoughts and actions.

The text says that "every imagination of the thoughts of his heart was only evil." This verse also links human thoughts as coming from the heart. The best and well minded of any human imagination and thoughts are completely evil and tainted with evil and it was not intermittent but continuous. At this point the human heart is only capable of thinking evil thoughts. This was God speaking through Moses; let's now turn to God's assessment through Jeremiah in a different dispensation: *The heart is more deceitful than all else. And is desperately wicked! Who can know it?* Jeremiah 17:9.

This is probable, a few thousand years after Genesis, and God spoke through another prophet, Jeremiah, about the condition of the human heart, that it's evil, deceitful and desperately wicked. The heart, which in this context represents the whole person, the complete person, is desperately sick and wicked. If the heart, from where all thoughts originate, is evil then by default, the thoughts are evil. An evil heart cannot think clean and good thoughts since the source of it is evil. It is rather no surprise that if you hear someone putting garbage out of their mouth, then it is because it is coming from their heart. If someone curses you out with some bad foul language and later says that they made a mistake and they are sorry, they did not misspeak because they spoke exactly what they believed. An evil heart is incapable of saying good words and a good heart and a transformed heart is incapable of saying evil words. The human heart is a deadly poison and its thoughts are a deadly poison.

Here is the apostle Paul: *as it is written: "There is none righteous, no, not one; no one understands; no one seeks after God. All have turned aside; together they have become worthless; no one does good, not even one. "Their throat is an open grave; "they use their tongue to deceive." "The venom of asps is under their lips." "Their mouths are full of curses and bitterness." "Their feet are swift to shed blood; in their paths are ruin and misery, and the way of peace they have not known." "There is no fear of God before their eyes,"* Romans 3:10-18. It is quite clear that the human heart and human nature are not good. It is evil and corrupt and unless it is transformed and replaced, no good dwells in it.

So if the human heart is evil, then the human thoughts are also evil because the thoughts originate from the heart. Now, if the thoughts are evil, then is there any surprise if the behavior and actions are also evil? Is there any surprise why sexually immoral conduct, like sexual addiction, is so rampant? Sexual addiction is a real societal problem and manifests itself in many forms, including pornography.

Pornography and Sexual Addiction

Pornography is probably affecting more people than anyone is even able to realize and quantify its impact. The amount of people involved in pornography is staggering and jaw dropping. The amount of people involved reveals something about the epidemic of pornography and sexual addiction. But what is pornography? Here is a definition by psychologists: *Pornography, or porn, is any sexually explicit material-written, visual, or otherwise-intended to sexually arouse. The world's largest porn site claims that in 2018, it had a daily average of 92 million unique viewers, the vast majority of them males.*[153]This porn industry is probably the biggest industry on the planet. The majority of all combined website traffic is porn related.

Here are some stats about the impact of porn in the daily lives of people around the globe: *So how many people are on porn sites right now? How many people watch porn? Well, according to top global* traffic *data from Statista, the top 3 porn sites in the world, receive a combined 5.8 billion website visits per month. That means there are about 134,491 new website visits per minute – just on those 3 websites. Plus, website traffic tools suggest that visitors to porn sites tend to spend about 18 minutes on the site each time that they visit. All in all, that means that there are about 2.4 million people on the top 3 porn sites every minute.*[154]These are very disturbing statistics on how pornography has permeated the human race. This is beyond my wildest imagination. Here are some more statistics:

Today, porn sites receive more website traffic in the U.S. than Twitter, Instagram, TikTok, Netflix, Pinterest, and Zoom combined.[3]

According to site data from 2019, in the time it takes you to read this article, Pornhub will have recorded more than 200,000 visits.[4]

---

[153]

https://www.psychologytoday.com/us/basics/pornography
[154]

https://fightthenewdrug.org/by-the-numbers-see-how-many-pe ople-are-watching-porn-today/

Pornhub estimates that in 2019, 12,500 gigabytes of porn were uploaded to the site every minute—enough to fill the memories of every smartphone in the world.[5]

Enough porn was watched in 2016 on this one website that all the data would fill 194,000,000 USB sticks. If you put the USB sticks end to end, they'd wrap all the way around the moon.[6]

According to a 2021 study, 1 out of every 8 porn titles shown to first-time visitors to porn sites described acts of sexual violence.[7]

"Teen" is the most common word used in porn titles.[8]

In 2017 alone, Pornhub got 28.5 *billion* visits. That's almost 1,000 visits a second, or 78.1 million a day—way more than the population of the entire United Kingdom. That number jumped to 2 billion4 site visits in 2019.[9][10]

In 2016, 91,980,225,000 videos were watched on Pornhub. In 2018, that number jumped to more than 109,012,068,000. That's over 14 videos watched for every person on the entire planet.[11][12]

More than 5,824,699,200 hours of porn were watched on Pornhub in 2019 alone. That's equal to almost 665 centuries of content consumed in 1 year, on just one porn site.[13]

"Lesbian," "teen," "stepmom," "mom," and "stepsister" have all topped the charts as some of the most searched terms on the site for the last 6 years, at least.

Technology has changed not only the content of porn, but also *how*, *when*, and *at what age* people begin consuming it. Studies show that most young people are exposed to porn by age 13,[14] and according to a nationally representative survey of U.S. teens, 84.4% of 14-18 year-old males and 57% of 14-18 year-old females have viewed pornography.[15] And for adults, an estimated 91.5% of men and 60.2% of women report that they've consumed porn in the past month.[16]

In analytics released by popular porn site Pornhub a couple of years ago, women are 113% more likely to search the term "hardcore" than men. They are also over 105% more likely to seek out more intense genres of porn like "gangbang" and "rough sex." (Click here to read an article about why that may be.)[155]

So all the evidence and statistics shed light on the extent of sexual addictions as it is amplified through pornography. The fact that 92 % of men and 60 % of women consume porn on a monthly basis is jaw dropping. This is an issue of struggle for everyone, including those in the church, including the clergy. This is a sleeping time bomb that is leaving many casualties in its path. It is a silent killer that kills slowly. Pornography is simply a manifestation of sexual addiction that results in several negative consequences.

Porn destroys real sexual intimacy. The one who is engaged in porn receives his or her sexual satisfaction from porn and may have difficulties maintaining a real and true sexual relationship. They may appear physically but emotionally absent in their marriage or sexual relationship. They have already received their sexual arousal from porn and may appear emotionally absent and uninterested in sex when in the presence of a real sexual partner or spouse. A lot of marriages that end up in divorce cite addiction to porn by a spouse as one of the main reasons. So when divorce happens, you can think of the collateral damage inflicted on children and other family members involved. Porn may be considered a type of solo sex, where a person is having sex

155

https://fightthenewdrug.org/by-the-numbers-see-how-many-people-are-watching-porn-today/

alone but sex was never intended to be enjoyed alone or solo.

This is not God's plan for sex and it has to be enjoyed in the context of a God ordained marital union. If a person is sexually addicted to porn then in all likelihood, they are addicted to other addictive behaviors, like masturbation.

Sexual Addiction of Masturbation

So, what is masturbation? It is the rubbing on or playing with your sexual organs (alone) like penis for the male or vagina for the female for the purpose of achieving arousal and possibly, ejaculation. There is ongoing debate if this is even ethical and acceptable sexual behavior! There is even debate in the psychological communities, questioning whether masturbation is a sexual addiction. Some in those communities see it as a normal sexual activity and here is what some are saying: *While engaging in masturbation regularly does not necessarily mean that you have a problem, any of the following could signify that it's time to reach out for help:*

Masturbation takes up a lot of your time; Your personal or work life is suffering because of masturbation; You choose masturbation over in-person activities (e.g., going home instead of staying at a party, choosing to be alone instead of with a partner); You find yourself engaging in masturbation in public or in places where you would rather not (e.g., a public restroom); You are masturbating when you don't feel like it or when you are not aroused; You masturbate to cope with negative emotions; You find yourself feeling guilty or upset during or after masturbating;

You find yourself thinking about it often.[156]The psychological communities are reluctant to classify masturbation as a compulsive sexual behavior or sexual addiction. They are even more inclined to validate masturbation as a normal and enjoyable behavior. Sex is to be enjoyed in the context of a God ordained sexual union and anything outside of that is a deviation from the creator's design for sex. Solo sex or masturbation by a male or female is a deviation from the original design. Sex is intended to provide a unitary and combined pleasure for the couple and not a solo joy or pleasure for an individual. Masturbation is an egoistic and selfish act meant to fulfill and satisfy the natural human instinct of selfishness. This is all about the individual and not the couple.

The idea of shared pleasure is foreign to the human DNA, which is all about my needs, my pleasure, and how to meet my needs and pleasure. Human beings are not innately altruistic and that concept is foreign to the natural person. It is then no surprise that pornography, masturbation and many other sexually deviant behaviors come naturally, and these tendencies seem extremely difficult to resist as experienced by everyone for that matter, and more so for the natural person. So, we have labored to show that sexual addictions originate from human thoughts, and those evil thoughts originate from an evil heart, and the evil heart is caused by sin that separates the human race from God.

Origin of an Evil Heart

The logical question to ask is how did an evil heart come about if our evil thoughts originate from an evil heart?

156

https://www.verywellmind.com/what-is-masturbation-addiction-5077411

How did the human heart become evil? That is a very logical question and here is the deal: When God created Adam and Eve, they were good and were created in a state of perfection and goodness. There was a time when our original parents, Adam and Eve, were good, perfect, and without defect or sin. They were ethically and morally good and in a state of perfection. Their thoughts were pure and not tainted with evil.

At one point all of God's creation, including humans, were good and without defects. Here is God's declaration: *Then God saw everything that He made, and indeed it was very good. So the evening and the morning were the sixth day,* Genesis 1:31. This is the first and only time in the bible that God said anything good about man. All of God's creation, including mankind, was exceedingly good and free from sin and defect, but something happened! So, God puts mankind to a test and here is what God said: *And the Lord commanded the man, saying, of every tree of the garden you may freely eat: but of the tree of the knowledge of good and evil, you shall not eat of it: for in the day that you eat of it you shall surely die,* Genesis 2:16-17. At this point in the creation order, mankind was presented with the first test with a premise and a promise. The premise was that man was free to eat of every tree of the garden except the tree of the knowledge of good and evil.

And the promise was that a violation of this explicit command would result in death. The death that is in view in this context is not physical but spiritual. This is a death of spiritual separation from God. Disobedience to God results in a separation from God. Every disobedience to God is sin. Sin always separates man from God because God is without sin and cannot sin. If Adam and Eve had simply obeyed God, then sin would not have entered the world and into the heart

245

of man. There would have been no issue with lust, sexual addiction,sexual immorality, adultery, fornication, pornography and the rest. We would have been living in a state of perpetual purity, goodness, and perfection.

Sadly, that was not the case! The tempter, the devil, who had already been cast out of heaven for disobedience, was now on the Earth (Revelation 12:7-9). The tempter, knowing what God had said to Adam, came to Eve and diluted what God said, and in a sense, created doubts in the hearts of Adam and Eve by questioning what God had said. "God did not really mean what He said, did He?,"according to the tempter. Here is what the tempter or devil said to Eve: *"For God knows that when you eat from it your eyes will be opened, and you will be like God, knowing good and evil." When the woman saw that the fruit of the tree was good for food and pleasing to the eye, and also desirable for gaining wisdom, she took some and ate it. She also gave some to her husband, who was with her, and he ate it,* Genesis 3:5-6.

Adam and Eve disobeyed God's explicit command in Genesis 2:17 and the result was that they died and were separated from God spiritually. They did not immediately die physically but were separated from God, and He did not come again to speak with them physically like He did in times past. They lost that moral and natural goodness. Evil came into the world from this point on. The human race from here on was described as evil, corruptand sinful.

Someone may raise an objection saying: but Adam's sin and disobedience had nothing to do with us, and so why are we held responsible for something that we did not do? That is quite an interesting and valid objection! So let's say that Mercedes Benz designed its latest luxury vehicle and there was a design defect in the prototype original design when they had already shipped out over 10 million cars to car dealers across the globe –but because the prototype was defective, the rest of the 10 million cars are also defective.

Adam is the prototype of the human race and if he is defective, corrupt and sinful, then all human beings are corrupt, evil and depraved. Here is the Apostle Paul on this: *Therefore, just as through one man sin entered into the world, and death through sin, and so death spread to all mankind because all sinned,* Romans 5:12. This is the entrance of sin into the world and human race. This is the entrance of sin into the human heart and out of this, comes corrupt and sinful hearts, then corrupt thoughts, and out of those corrupt thoughts come corrupt beliefs and then corrupt beliefs end up in corrupt actions.

Corrupt Beliefs lead to Corrupt Actions

We already demonstrated that thoughts originate from the heart and those thoughts, over time, turn into an entrenched belief system and once that happens, actions flow from that belief. Thoughts may come from information that has been fed into an already evil heart and that may be things like books that we read, people who we follow (influencers) on television, radios, books that we read, or online and other platforms. Your belief system is a prized possession and it needs to be protected and guarded because your life depends on it.

Just as the water tank analogy mentioned earlier, the heart is the reservoir of thoughts from which actions are drawn and decisions are made. The reservoir for water in that large city must be guarded because someone may break in and contaminate or poison the water supply of the city and there will be severe loss of life. In like manner, the human heart must be securely guarded because it is the reservoir of thought. For if or when it is contaminated by evil thoughts, then those thoughts will eventually show up in the person's actions.

Here is some advice from Solomon, the wisest man that ever walked the earth and here is what he said: *Above all else, guard your heart, for everything you do flows from it,* Proverbs 4:23. Solomon considered the matter of guarding your heart as top priority. He began by using the phrase, "above all else," to mean top of the agenda, and the utmost priority in your life is to guard your heart. The reason he gave to guard your heart is that, "for everything you do flows from it." I don't even know of a better way to put this! This verse puts it so plain for the average person to understand. Protect what goes into your heart for it will soon come out in your actions.

So plainly put, that leaves no room for further clarity. So it is extremely critical to protect the information that goes into your heart, like the books you read, the people who you follow, and the online programs that you watch. You will hear that almost all mass shooters were radicalized online and they were following the writings and teachings of somebody. They believed and then they acted on that belief. Being addicted to anything, from alcohol, drugs, food, porn, sex and the list is endless, are based on a belief system and actions are a function of that belief system.

And so, for actions to be altered, good or bad, there must be a change in belief. There is absolutely no reason for anyone to change or alter their behavior if they are convinced that their actions are justified and right. In order to change behavior, the source of thought must be good and clean. So an evil heart cannot bring forth good thoughts, hence good actions. Just as a contaminated water tank has to be replaced before the city can get clean water, so the evil human heart also has to be replaced in order for the human to think good thoughts and hence, perform good actions.

That is exactly what God did; He replaced the human's evil heart with a new heart. He did a heart transplant. God was the first heart transplant surgeon that did a heart transplant with no anesthesia and never lost a patient. Here is what happened: *I will give you a new heart and put a new spirit within you; I will take the heart of stone out of your flesh and give you a heart of flesh,* Ezekiel 36:26. This is the heart that He plans to give to whomever He chooses. And He will not just give a new heart but a new spirit also.

The evil heart that we have will be replaced with a clean heart and a good spirit. This new and good heart will result in good thoughts, and the good thoughts will also result in good actions. So the evil person with an evil heart has been transformed into a good person with a good heart. So the heart of a sexual addict has been transformed into a good heart and the thoughts of porn, masturbation, adultery, fornication and all other sexually deviant thoughts are gone or much reduced, and so are the evil actions and desires. These addictive behaviors tend to cause other problems within the marriage that damage the marital relationship.

Chapter 8

The Problems of Sex within Marriages

We just finished talking about sexual addiction, pornography, and the extent of the need for more sex. You have seen that the world is on fire with all kinds of sexually deviant behaviors and so it's no surprise when marriages are filled with all kinds of problems. Marriage is a union between two unique individuals that need to be carefully and divinely selected to minimize problems. One of the main reasons cited for most no-fault divorces in America is "irreconcilable differences." This is a legally recognized reason for divorce.

This simply means that the couple could not agree on most or on key issues in the marriage. A lot of times, it really means that they could hardly agree on anything and since the legal system anticipates that there would be differences, then there are bound to be problems. These problems can be properly managed and minimized if the foundation of the marriage is strong and secure. By foundation, I am primarily talking about the reason for the marriage. Why did you decide to get married to that person? This is critically important if you intend to minimize, but not necessarily eliminate, problems in your marriage. Why did you get married to that person?

Reasons to get into a Marital Union

This is the most important question to contemplate and carefully answer because most people cannot simply give a straight answer to this question. The simple truth is that most people have no clue why they got into a marriage to that person. Then, is it any surprise why marriages are filled with all kinds of problems? The reason for getting into marriage is like the foundation of a house or the domain name of a website. Everything depends on it. Some people get into a marriage hoping to gain security, and that is their reason for getting into that marriage; in other words, they get married for financial security.

The very interesting part about the whole thing is not revealing the real reason for getting married to the other spouse! The other spouse may have been deceived in thinking and believing that love was the reason, but it probably really wasn't! Even the idea of security may come in different forms and shapes as some are seeking financial security. So long as the person has money that can secure them a large bank account, houses and cars, then that becomes the overarching reason for getting into the marriage. What happens, after a few years into the marriage and then you suddenly realize that you are not as secure as you were made to believe, or your spouse loses everything; then what? The marriage will certainly experience problems and eventually come to an end because the reason is not being accomplished and you are hit with unmet expectations.

Some are seeking security in a partner who will provide and care for them just in case they get sick or are in some kind of crisis. Their entire marital expectation is based on security in the event of a sickness or in some potential crises. So most marriages may be built on deception because both spouses may have hidden different reasons and expectations for getting into a marriage and those reasons may not even be known to the other spouse and vice versa.

No one will openly let a potential spouse know that they are getting married to them for their wealth; some reasons can be hidden or are plainly in the open. Let's face it. What does a seventy year old man who is worth over 10 billion dollars have in common with a thirty year old, young, beautiful and attractive lady? It may be very difficult to find anyone who would believe that there is some other reason for this marriage other than financial security! Some are not so overt but the reason for the marriage is hidden from public view.

Any potential marriage on which the reason is anything other than a genuine reciprocal love for each other is almost bound to fail. You get into a marriage union to give and not to gain. This must be a reciprocal giving on both partners in the marriage, so much such that it may seem like a contest to see who out-gives the other.If anyone gets into a marriage to gain then, that marriage will most likely fail and not last very long. When most people hear of giving, they are somewhat frozen and frightened, and they almost instantly think about money. Giving is way bigger than material possessions and money, and a giving person takes the interest of their partner more importantly than theirs; this is radical, as it is about giving one's self for the interest of their partner.

They put the interest of their spouse before their own. This can only perfectly work if both partners are on the same page so that a partner is not used or taken for granted. This is the picture of a perfect marriage and this is only possible if both hearts are right and regenerated. All greed and selfishness have been eradicated. A giving heart is not possible, nor conceivable, if greed and selfishness permeates the heart of one or both partners.

Honestly speaking, I have been reflecting on the reasons why people get into a marriage, and every night that I go to bed, sometimes, in the middle of the night, at about 2-4 am, a new reason pops up into my mind. I finally stopped counting and concluded that there are an endless number of reasons why people tie the knot. So you can clearly see that if the foundation is unstable then the house will eventually collapse. This is probably one of the central issues that lead to problems in marriages and this opens the gate for many more problems; and when the reason to get into marriage is in question then that will certainly lead to trust issues.

Trust Issues in Marriages

As with the reason why people get married, trust is another foundational pillar in marriages. When I talk about trust in this context, I am referring to a character issue that represents the person. Trust could mean a financial instrument, whereby marital assets are transferred in the event of the death of a spouse. This is not of concern to us in this context. We are talking about the faith, confidence and belief in a person based on their past character and conduct.

Trust is one of the layers upon which any marriage is built. Any hint of no-trust rattles the foundation of the union. Trust is the glue that holds it all together and without it, all falls apart. In a general principle, the functioning of society as a whole, including governments, businesses, banking, and international relations among nations, are all based and built on trust.

So in the marriage context, trust is the cornerstone which holds it all together. There is really no marriage without trust. How can you sleep in a bed with someone you do not trust? How can you have sexual intercourse with someone you don't trust? How can you share a meal with someone you do not trust? I was having a conversation with someone who was into insurance sales a few years ago and he made this statement that made an impression on my heart to this very day, and here is what he said: "I cannot do business with someone with whom I cannot leave my wife with them in my house."

That is a pretty strong statement echoing the importance of trust, that a person was comparing a business relationship with that of him and his wife. Everything that we do each and every moment of our day is based on trust. We live and breathe trust. You put money in the bank because you trust that it will be there when you need it. You go work at your job every day because you trust that at the end of the week or two weeks, you will get a check or money deposited into your bank account. Trust is like drinking water or breathing air. Without trust the entire global banking system will collapse and with it, the entire global economies will come to a halt.

So is it any surprise why there are so many problems in marriages? Trust is at the root of all of it and it is in very short supply, so the marriage problems escalate. Here is God speaking through the Prophet Amos: "*Can two walk together except they be agreed?*"Amos 3:3.This is a very profound verse that goes to the heart of the problems in marriages.

This is a two part proposition: first part is "can two walk together," and the second part is a condition, introduced by the word, "except," meaning that the prerequisite for two people walking together is agreement and this requires trust in that person. You cannot agree with someone that you do not trust. When there is no trust then the married couple basically lives separate lives under the same roof. They are living and sleeping in separate rooms or separate areas of the same house. If young children are involved, then the cost of divorce may be too much to handle, so they manage living under the same roof but live separate lives. This may have been triggered by arguments over money or other issues. Money is one of the biggest issues of problems in marriages.

Money and Problems in Marriages

Arguments over money seem to expose deeper problems in a marital union. On the surface, it may seem like it is all about the money but the problems may be a lot deeper than what they seem. One person may want to save money but the other person may want to spend more. One is a saver and the other is a spender. One of the couples has a very expensive lifestyle and the other is very careful about their spending habits.

They are arguing about who is paying the rent or mortgage, buying groceries, paying for child care, or paying for vacations. There are constant and persistent arguments and disputes over money and material issues. There is no agreement about the family budget and spending priorities. This spells disaster. It is very difficult for a marriage to survive unless these issues are addressed head-on. It may, on the surface, seem like it's all about money, but underneath all of that are hosts of other deep-seated problems. Marriage is a physical and spiritual union between a male and a female. Most couples have a physical union but are not united spiritually. Couples who are united spiritually have a united purpose for their union, knowing that God has joined them together.

They are united in their spending and money management habits. They are united in the raising of

255

children, including how to discipline them. They are united in their love for God. If there is no spiritual unity then there can hardly be physical unity. Most if not all of the problems in marriages are as a result of lack of spiritual unity. This is at the root of problems in most marriages. Here is how God puts it: *For this reason a man shall leave his father and his mother, and be joined to his wife, and they shall become one flesh,* Genesis 2:24.This verse and many like it clearly makes the case for spiritual unity in a marriage union. There are two words here that are the focus of the argument and they are "joined," and "one."

A lot of couples are physically in a marriage but were never spiritually joined, and are not one and cannot function as one because they are not joined spiritually. That is why such marriages are filled with quarrels, fights, insults, selfishness, greed and the likes of it. Here is what God said about the source of quarrels: *What is the source of quarrels and conflicts among you? Is the source not your pleasures that war in your members? You lust and do not have, so you commit murder. And you are envious and cannot obtain, so you fight and quarrel. You do not have, because you do not ask. You ask and do not receive, because you ask with the wrong motives, so that you may spend what you request on your pleasures. You adulteresses, do you not know that friendship with the world is enmity towards God? Therefore whoever wants to be a friend of the world makes himself an enemy of God,* James 4:1-4.

This chapter in James begins by identifying the source of quarrels and conflicts in the society at large but more important to us in the marriage context. Marriages are not quarrel and conflict-free zones but are largely infested with quarrels and conflicts. James seems to identify the source as coming from "war in your members."James does

256

seem to be addressing conflicts and quarrels with others (conflicts without) and at the same time, identifying the source of the conflicts and quarrels as coming from within them. That could mean from within the group or from within each individual person. The point is that there are quarrels and conflicts and there is no peace. There are wars of words and James is simply saying: Look! You can't speak out of both sides of your mouth.

You cannot appear to be for God and at the same time appear to be for the world. We know that because in verse 4 of James chapter 4, he called them," you adulteresses," meaning that they were committing spiritual adultery. They seem to be married to God but yet, they have other husbands, meaning other gods. They want to be married to God and at the same time be married to the world. That is adultery (spiritually) plain and simple, and they cannot have two husbands for either you are married to Jehovah or married to Satan; it is that simple. No adultery is allowed, and James is simply saying that either you are for God or against Him.

You cannot be for both. If you are a friend of the world then by default, you are an enemy of God. This is extremely important in the marriage context and problems in marriages. Fights, quarrels and conflicts are guaranteed to happen when couples are not truly joined and united as one spiritually.The couple must first and foremost be married to God if fights, quarrels and conflicts are to be reduced or eliminated. Not being married to God as their one and only husband, means that they are engaged in spiritual adultery and fornication.

So that when a man is joined to his wife, they do not lose their individual identities and preferences on the physical side of things. The husband may still retain his habit of love for soccer, football, or basketball and the wife may retain her habit of, say, cooking, dancing, swimming, or whatever she enjoys doing on the physical side of things.

A couple that is spiritually joined do not have to discuss if they should pray together or not because that is a settled issue. There is no debate or discussion if they should do a weekly bible study or not. There is no argument of whether they should attend church every Sunday or not together. There is really no debate if they should serve God for the rest of their lives or not. They do not have to debate if they should give money and resources to support and advance God's plan of redemption for mankind.

They may debate the amount, but not if they should support the work of God. This oneness comes with the understanding that God is in absolute control and He owns everything, for we brought nothing into this world and it is certain that we will leave the world with nothing. We were born naked and shall leave the world naked and blessed be His name. These are settled matters and not up for debate or discussion and if any debate should arise about any of these matters, then that is clear evidence that you are not spiritually joined.

So you cannot be spiritually joined as a married couple, if you constantly quarrel, fight, and have conflicts over money and material possessions. Then money may not really be the issue, but it may reveal a much deeper and entrenched spiritual problem. You may not be really united and joined as one. You may be married but spiritually, you are single and God has not truly joined you together, hence the saying: *So they are no longer two, but one flesh. Therefore, what God has joined together, let no one separate,* Matthew 19:6. If this has not truly happened then all kinds of marital problems will persist. So the list of marital problems are endless like I mentioned earlier, and some problems come from not having enough sex.

Not having Enough or Any Sex at All

This may sound like a joke but this is very serious business. Sex deficiency in marriages is a very serious matter. Not having enough sex is bound to make or break a marriage. This is a subject that few would even dare to talk about but this issue is central to the survival of a marriage. A marriage without enough sex is a marriage on life support. Some husbands and wives have been, for years, with no sex, despite living under the same roof. Sex is an innate human need and desire that needs to be fulfilled in the context of marriage, and not having enough of it or none at all is very detrimental to the marriage.

A husband and wife are not a brother and sister and sex is central to their union. This is not the only reason for getting into a marriage but it is no doubt central to it. I remember growing up as a child, hearing instances where a married person (mostly women, sometimes rarely men) would call a family meeting, which meant calling her side of the family and her husband's side of the family, sometimes about 10 to 20 people. The woman would bring a complaint to the family to adjudicate and her complaint would go something like this: "My husband is not giving me sex, and has not given me sex for over two years now!" Now this is the complaint brought before the family to adjudicate! These are not trivial matters but very serious and are to be taken as such. She is yearning for attention from her husband, or vice versa, and not getting it. She or he is frustrated and miserable and they have called a family meeting because they have run out of options with nowhere else to go.

Sex does something to the human psyche that is unexplainable. Have you noticed that the countenance on people's faces change and brighten when they have had good and pleasurable sex? You could sometimes look at a woman or a man and tell if they had enjoyable sex the previous day as soon as they walked into the office. There is an unusual sense of satisfaction that comes through their faces. The way that they walk is different and you can notice an unusual glow on their faces. But on the flip side, you can quickly and easily discern if they have not had sex for a while: they are angry and agitated at strangers or people around them,for apparently no real reason. You can see the frown on their faces. They complain about the slightest thing and are angry over the simplest stuff. Sometimes, you are able to look at someone and recognise that they have not had sex for a while, but sometimes not.

Can you really imagine what happens to a married couple if they go for, say, five years or longer with no sex? This is actually the case for millions of people or couples around the globe. It may look something like the image below!

Image of couples that built resentment against each other[157]

Does this image represent your current marital situation? Are you actually sleeping in separate rooms in the same house? Do you wake up without even saying "good morning"to your spouse, whom you once said you loved? Does each partner cook their own food? Do you communicate through a third party, like the children? Let's be very clear; sex is important but there are many other reasons why sexual intercourse is absent in marriage. As important as sex might be, there are many other factors that lead up to sex that are far more critical and important. Intimacy and romance happen long before sexual intercourse is even contemplated. There is non-sexual intimacy that happens on a daily basis that has nothing to do with sex.

Your spouse is your partner, friend, and confidant. They are the one with whom you share your innermost thoughts and aspirations. The one with whom you share your passions and dreams. Your play and laughing partner. The one with whom you share your pain and suffering, your accomplishments and your failures. Who would you normally call if you suddenly have a car problem on the highway? Or you are in some unexpected crises, who would you call first? Would you call your mom or your spouse first? If your spouse knows that you have genuine love, care and concern for them, it is in this context that sexual intercourse naturally happens.

You will be able to enjoy sex if these things are not true in your marriage. It's almost impossible to have and

---

157

https://www.marriage.com/advice/intimacy/5-reasons-why-ther es-intimacy-missing-in-your-marriage/#:-:text=While%20sex%2 0is%20not%20the,damage%20to%20the%20relationship%2C%2 0ending enjoy sex with your spouse who has not spoken with you in about a month. Suddenly, they show interest in having sex, and you are saying to yourself, "What's up with this? And what are they up to?" It is not enjoyable to have sexual intercourse with your spouse who you know does not care about you as a person,or your interests, and does things to hurt and damage your reputation. So a lack of sex may naturally lead to feelings of rejection as shown below.

Feelings of Rejection as a Result of Lack of Sex

Does the picture below look familiar? Are you going through this right now? Acceptance is a natural human phenomenon and any feelings of rejection goes to the core of our being. We naturally crave love and acceptance and no one enjoys rejection. Any feelings of rejection destroy the person and their ability to function. Rejection tears down the fabric of the marriage and any semblance thereof. It communicates to the other person several non-verbal communications, like: "I don't want you," "I don't love you," and the likes of it. Rejection signals disunity, a separation, a dismantling of the union if at all there ever was one. There is no longer any interest in sexual activity with that spouse. The spouse who feels rejected is withdrawn and secluded. As a result, there is little or no communication between them.

Feelings of rejection and lack of intimacy[158]

      The image above may represent your current situation when you are living with feelings of rejection. Some have suggested that the reasons for these feelings of rejection are due to low self-esteem and physical appearance, and here is one such view: *If you ever think to yourself, "I don't know why my husband/ wife doesn't want to connect with me sexually. I don't know why they're ignoring me. I don't know why they're not relationally available to me. What have I done wrong? And what can I do?" The best way that you can initiate a spark in your marriage is by beginning with you. Let me explain what that means.*

     There was a research study that took 6,000 married couples and measured their self-esteem as a unit. Afterward, they had them work on themselves to become better. As a result, their self-esteem increased. They found there was a direct correlation between a person who would increase their own self-esteem, and the positive effect on the marriage. When you start working on yourself and becoming the best that you can be, it has an amazing positive effect on your relationship. Improving yourself is the best thing you can do to bring your spouse back around. [159]

      The view advocated by this post is quite interesting and helpful, and it is by no means to be ignored, but it may

---

[158]

https://www.marriage.com/advice/intimacy/5-reasons-why-ther es-intimacy-missing-in-your-marriage/#:~:text=While%20sex%2 0is%20not%20the,damage%20to%20the%20relationship%2C%2 0ending

[159]

https://marriagehelper.com/emotionally-and-sexually-rejected-b y-spouse-fxb/

not really get to the root of the issue. It addresses things that make spouses physically attracted to each other. This post, in the second paragraph, says that, "the best way that you can initiate a spark in your marriage is by beginning with you," but did not elaborate on what that means. What does it really mean to begin with you to initiate a spark in the marriage? This is a big deal and a lot of married couples are struggling with just this very question.

How to initiate a spark in their marriage? The marriage is dead and on life support and in desperate need of a revival. The focus of initiating a spark, with the goal of boosting self-esteem, seems to be the way to get a stagnant marriage back on track. So improving self-esteem seems to be the focus and there is really nothing wrong with that; after-all, we are visual beings and what we see and perceive are what we often value the most. So looking at a tall, slim, beautiful, 24 year old girl or a handsome-looking, tall, well dressed young man, drives all kinds of sexual desires from members of the opposite sex and those desires do come regardless of one's marital status.

The sad truth is that outward beauty is very important but outward beauty alone will hardly sustain a marriage. It is appealing to the eyes and seduces you to come and have sex but will hardly sustain a marriage through thick and thin. There are millions of very beautiful women and millions of very handsome looking men who look very attractive from a distance but once they come close, on your bed and you get to know them well, you won't want to have anything to do with them. If you are married to a beautiful or handsome looking person outwardly, and they also have impeccable character, then you have gold in your hands.

As much as I love beauty, I will prefer character anytime over outward beauty. Things like honesty, trustworthiness, integrity, dependability, unselfishness, caring, devotion to God, devotion to your spouse, accountability, fidelity to your spouse, not greedy for money; these are deep seated character traits that will give miles to your marriage. You cannot buy these things with money. You can paint yourself, wear makeup, darken your gray hair, wear hair wigs, paint your face, put on the most expensive clothes on your body, live in the most expensive house, drive the most expensive vehicle and you have but at the same time, not change one iota of your character.

These are all fake things intended to mask your true person and character. These character qualities transcend outward appearances. Outward appearance is like a flower that shines in the morning and fades away in the evening. Remember that you will go to the grave with your character but not with your outward beauty. The character of a person is the true person that is constant and does not change with time but beauty fades like a flower blooming in the morning and fading away when heated by the sun.

Fixing these outward qualities will do very little to fix the feelings of rejection and abandonment, and draw your spouse back to you. It may actually provide some temporary fix that may not be long lasting. The real issue is with the inward beauty and not the outward beauty. This is the beauty that will bring a spark to your marriage. This is the beauty that does not get old! This is the beauty that will stand the test of trials in your marriage. Aspire to acquire such beauty for it is long lasting and eternal.

Here is what Peter said about this kind of inward beauty: *1. Likewise, ye wives, be in subjection to your own husbands; that, if any obey not the word, they also may without the word be won by the conversation of the wives; 2. While they behold your chaste conversation coupled with fear. 3. Whose adorning let it not be that outward adorning of plaiting the hair, and wearing of gold, or of putting on of apparel; 4.But let it be the hidden man of the heart, in that which is not corruptible, even the ornament of a meek and quiet spirit, which is in the sight of God of great price. 5. For after this manner in the old time the holy women also, who trusted God, adorned themselves, being in subjection unto their own husbands: 6. Even as Sara obeyed Abraham, calling him lord: whose daughters ye are, as long as ye do well, and are not afraid with any amazement. 7. Likewise, ye husbands, dwell with them according to knowledge, giving honor unto the wife, as unto the weaker vessel, and as being heirs together of the grace of life; that your prayers be not hindered,1 Peter 3:-7.*

This is a classic picture of the beauty of a woman inside-out as opposed to outside-in. This is a very difficult situation in which the woman finds herself. She is married, most likely, to a man who does not yet have a new and transformed heart like she does. God, speaking through Peter, is saying that she is to be subject to her own husband. This is a pretty tough assignment to obey someone who has no regard for the things of God. They may be married but living completely separate lives. I am not by any means advocating that any woman should stay in an abusive marital relationship, but only that you simply obey scriptures and God will grant you wisdom to know what to do at any given moment and situation.

The key ingredient of change here is the woman's conduct and character, and the goal is that the man may be won or converted without a word. The woman's conduct and character will do the talking for her. The word, "conversation," is used in verses 1 and 2 as translated in the King James Version (KJV) of the bible. This Greek word should have been better translated as "manner of life," "behavior," "conduct," for the average English reader to fully understand its meaning. Nothing against outward beauty and makeup, but verses 3 and 4 contrast outward beauty and inward beauty, and that inward beauty is of great price in the sight of God, and also remember that your attitude will determine your altitude. Only those with good character will have doors open for them in life and in marriage.

This is the most important beauty that any woman or man should strive to achieve. So verse 5 makes an application back to Sara and how she obeyed and was subject to Abraham, calling him "lord." I am not suggesting that you go around calling your husband "lord," but remember that what you say sometimes is of little importance, but it is what you do that matters. Some women may say something like, "I'm not calling him lord ever." Do not get hung up on calling him (your husband) lord! It's not that big of a deal if you do or don't! If you struggle with this, then this may be revealing something about the condition of your heart.

A heart that is completely yielded to God, will likely not find any contradiction.You may call your husband "lord," without calling him "lord," that is, in your behavior and conduct towards him, you may be calling him lord, without verbally calling him lord. Remember what Jesus said: *Not everyone who says to me "Lord, Lord," shall enter the kingdom of heaven, but he who does the will of my Father who is in heaven,* Matthew 7:21. The point is that calling your husband "lord," means absolutely nothing if it does not come from a transformed heart, followed by transformed conduct and character to back it up. This kind of marriage is bound to enjoy non-sexual and sexual intimacy to the fullest extent. There is no feeling of rejection and abandonment in this kind of marriage. This is a dream marriage for many and God is ready to make it happen for you if you would simply ask Him. But for others, the feelings of rejection and abandonment may affect other areas of their marriage, including Erectile Dysfunction(ED).

Erectile Dysfunction (ED) and Problems in Marriages

Sex has been identified as central to the functioning of a marriage and any reduction or complete lack thereof may have dire ramifications for the healthy functioning and future of the marriage. But first of all, what is erectile dysfunction?According to the Mayo clinic, "erectile dysfunction (impotence) is the inability to get and keep an erection firm enough for sex."[160]The male penis simply fails to erect and maintain erection long and firm enough to engage in sexual intercourse with a female (wife).

This is an issue of catastrophic proportion for both the man and the woman. Sex is central and pivotal to a marriage's survival and the absence of it would mean severe consequences. Not being able to perform sexually destroys the confidence and manhood of the man. Some may even find their existence on the earth useless and may even lead to other emotional and psychological issues, like fear, anxiety, loneliness, rejection, abandonment and even suicidal ideation. All hopes for the marriage are dashed if the man is unable to have and maintain an erection and ultimately, perform sexual intercourse.

---

[160]

https://www.mayoclinic.org/diseases-conditions/erectile-dysfunction/symptoms-causes/syc-20355776

The man is rendered impotent, powerless, confused and not knowing what to do. Shame is also added to the equation as the man may be ashamed and embarrassed to even seek medical attention or tell anyone else for that matter. The man may try to keep it a secret but his wife or mate may not be so inclined. The knowledge of this information getting to people outside the marriage will be devastating to the man. He may withdraw from social and family gatherings, because of the knowledge that his wife or mate has spread the information into the community and everyone knows about it. I have been in a gathering and overheard a married woman mockingly talking about the size of her husband's penis with friends.

She openly talked about the size and length of her husband's penis with her friends and acquaintances as they all laughed together. And she said something like this: "His penis is so short and tiny, and not even able to penetrate me well. I need a man with a long and sizable penis so that I can feel it going into me. With him, I feel nothing and I think, it is a joke."This is simply the case of the size and length of his penis, and I wonder what she or any of the other women would have said if there was no erection at all?I supposed that it would have been a real disaster!

As a matter of fact there was a case of a married woman ridiculing her husband in public for lack of erection and being unable to perform in the bed. She said something like this to her husband in a public gathering: "Are you even able to sex a woman? Look at you? Your penis cannot even rise! It lies down like a dead dog!" This is what this woman said to her husband, in public, and in the hearing of many, and what a public ridicule of her husband! This may simply not be an isolated incident but is likely a common occurrence.

So how common is erectile dysfunction? Here are some statistics from some healthcare professionals: *Approximately one in 10 adult males will* suffer *from ED on a long-term basis. Many men do experience occasional failure to achieve erection, which can occur for a variety of reasons, such as drinking too much alcohol, stress, relationship problems, or from being extremely tired. The failure to get an erection less than 20% of the time is not unusual and typically does not require treatment. However, the failure to achieve an erection more than 50% of the time generally means that there is a problem and treatment is required. ED does not have to be part of getting older. While it is true that some older men may need more stimulation, they should still be able to achieve an erection and enjoy intercourse.*[161]

These problems may be even more severe than the study will show since the study only records those who engage the healthcare system, like a hospital. The actual gravity of the problem may never be actually known since many men may never report or engage the healthcare system because of the shame and stigma associated with such revelation. They may prefer to seek alternative remedies as opposed to engaging the healthcare system. But what are some root causes of erectile dysfunction? Here are some listed by some healthcare professionals:

ED can be caused by a number of factors, including:

Vascular disease: Blood supply to the penis can become blocked or narrowed as a result of vascular

---

[161]

https://my.clevelandclinic.org/health/diseases/10035-erectile-dysfunction

disease such as atherosclerosis (hardening of the arteries).

Neurological disorders (such as multiple sclerosis): Nerves that send impulses to the penis can become damaged from stroke, diabetes, or other causes.

Psychological states: These include stress, <u>depression</u>, lack of stimulus from the brain and performance anxiety.

Trauma: An injury could contribute to symptoms of ED.

Chronic illness, certain medications, and a condition called Peyronie's disease can also cause ED. Operations for the prostate, bladder, and colon cancer may also be contributing factors.[162]

These factors have been recognized by the healthcare profession to potentially lead to ED but some identify other non-medical factors like stress, relationship problems or being extremely tired as potentially causing ED also. This is quite interesting because if someone is having marital problems so much that they even sleep in separate rooms, then it may be normal to encounter problems with erection in such situations because the desire and love for that person is diminished or nonexistent and as a result, it becomes difficult to get aroused and get an erection. Now if these issues are not timely addressed then they may lead to other marital problems like infidelity.

162

https://my.clevelandclinic.org/health/diseases/10035-erectile-dysfunction

Infidelity in Marriages

Marital infidelity is one of the leading causes of divorce today. As a matter of fact, this is the leading cause of divorce in America and the world at large.The temptation to have and engage in sex with someone other than your spouse is very strong, powerful, and millions of couples simply lack the ability to withstand such a force. This is like the force of a tornado that is ravaging everything in its path. Infidelity leaves many hearts completely shattered, broken and devastated, and it is sometimes difficult to quantify the emotional and physical toll that it leaves behind. Infidelity is a betrayal of trust that may be very difficult to mend even if forgiveness is granted. It is a wound that may never heal!This is a betrayal of loyalty that goes to the soul of the person and that is why very few marriages survive acts of infidelity.

The simple truth is that this is the human struggle and any honest human being would admit battling impure, sexual thoughts and the struggle or battle is acting on those thoughts to become infidelity. You cannot control what thoughts come through your mind but you may be able to control what you do with those thoughts. Sex is pleasurable but it is also through sex that many lives come to ruin and disaster.Sexual thought is like a drug that overpowers all of our rational human thoughts, and people completely lose any semblance of rational thinking. It is as being drunk with alcohol or some other controlled substance like marijuana or cocaine that impedes right thinking and judgment. Why would a man or woman suddenly abandon their marital home, get on a plane, and fly across the world, to go and meet some stranger who they met on the internet just to have sex, leaving wife and children behind, crying? Men and women would leave behind hungry children for such an adventure. This is insane but that is the power of sexual insanity.

I often advise teenagers as early as middle school, to abstain from sexual intercourse until they meet their future husband or wife, and I will also tell them never to have sexual intercourse, even with the person who they intend to get married to. The reason is simple: The person whom you plan to get married to, is the single and most important decision that you will ever make in your life and once you have sexual intercourse with that person before the decision is made, then you lose any ability to see any potential pitfalls about your potential mate. All you can see is life in paradise with that person and any advice to the contrary is immediately dismissed. They have taken over your mind and you sleep, eat and dream about them.

Others, like parents and family, may see and warn you about that person not being the right match for you, but you cannot see with them because you are drugged up with sexual fantasies about them. You are now thinking with your penis or vagina and not with your brain. Such advice is hardly taken seriously by most young people until they reap the consequences of their decisions, years later. Young people would often respond to me like this: "Abstaining from sex! Really! Who really does that? That is old school!" Is it any wonder that we are where we are as a society and culture? So we can safely conclude that infidelity in marriages is a deeply rooted generational, cultural but ultimately, a spiritual issue.

How can parents teach their children about infidelity if they themselves are not faithful to their spouse? Herschel Walker recently lost his U.S senate race for the state of Georgia and here is what his son, Christian Walker said about his dad: "You're not a 'family man' when you left us to bang a bunch of women, threatened to kill us, and had us move over 6 times in 6 months, running from your violence," Christian Walker wrote of his father on Twitter.[163] According to the son, his father was involved in repeated cases of infidelity and as a result, they suffered as children from no fault of their own.

This is certainly the case for millions of children around the globe. But how bad is the Issue of infidelity? Here are some factors given as reasons for infidelity: *Why do people cheat? A variety of factors can bring out types of affairs. A study of 495 people revealed eight key reasons: anger, low self-esteem, lack of love, low commitment, need for variety, neglect, sexual desire, and circumstances. It's important to understand that these reasons arise within the cheater and are not the responsibility of the betrayed partner. Upwards of 40% of married couples are affected by infidelity. Frustration in marriage is one common trigger; the cheater may make several attempts to solve problems to no avail. Maybe they had second thoughts about getting married or they are jealous over the attention given to a new baby and neither partner had the skill set to communicate these feelings.*[164]These are certainly issues that may trigger causes of cheating or infidelity but I am not so sure that these issues rise to the level as to be the cause of infidelity. You may have heard a saying coined by venerable

163

https://www.nytimes.com/2022/10/06/us/herschel-walker-son-christian.html
164

https://www.verywellmind.com/why-married-people-cheat-2300656

father Patrick Peyton, which says: "A family that prays together stays together."[165]

I may not necessarily agree with father Patrick Peyton's belief system about praying the rosary, but I will agree with this statement as it stands. I see this as a statement of spiritual connectivity between couples. People are physically married but have no spiritual connectivity. They live completely separate lives. Other than having sex, they have nothing in common. A marriage cannot be sustained if the only time that they come together is for sex.

Sex is the climax but many things should lead to that. Lack of spiritual connectivity will eventually lead to a host of other problems, including cheating or infidelity. If you are spiritually connected to your spouse and want the very best for your spouse, praying for them when you are away from them, then it may be almost unthinkable to look at another man or woman who is not your spouse with lustful intent. Yes, you may think lustfully, but you are less likely to act on those thoughts because you are connected first to God, then to your spouse. Your horizontal connection will depend on your vertical connection. If you are vertically connected to God, then the likelihood for infidelity is not completely eliminated but greatly reduced.

So the reason, in my humble opinion, for all marital problems, is the spiritual un-connectedness of couples. They have practically nothing in common spiritually. Marriage is first and foremost a spiritual union. There is no mission for marriage without being spiritually connected. You can ask most married couples this simple question: "What is the

---

165

https://onepeterfive.com/the-family-that-prays-together-stays-to
gether-but-why/

mission for your marriage?" They may say something like,"What are you talking about?" They have no clue as to why they are together! They are not joined as one flesh. They are physically joined but not spiritually joined, and this may lead to other sexual problems where sex becomes a commodity.

Chapter 9

Sex as a Commodity

It may be very difficult to believe that sex is used as a commodity but that is sadly the case. When we talk of commodities, then we often think of exchanging money to get sex in return, but the idea of exchanging sex may have broader implications. Sometimes, in the marriage context, sex is given or withheld based on the other partner performing or stopping certain actions to get it in return. But on a broader side of things, exchanging money for sex is the ultimate use of sex as a commodity.

This too is also debatable because some would argue that if sex is considered to be a commodity then that leads to normalization of the behavior but is that really the case? Those who oppose the view that sex is a commodity would likely view any commercialization of sex as sin. Then the broader question would be, is prostitution a work or a sin? Those who see it as work and a means of employment would seek to pass laws to decriminalize prostitution, and those who view it as a sin would seek to pass laws to keep the women and men off the streets and hotels.

The facts are that this is an economy and like any other economic activity, there is a demand and a supply side. The only reason why any economic activity would ever thrive is because there is demand. No economic activity would ever survive without demand for its product. If there is supply but no demand, then there is no economic activity. If there wasn't such a demand for sex, then women and men would not be out there selling their bodies.

Tangible money is not the only medium of exchange as sex has been used from time immemorial to gain favors and access. Maybe it is not regularly happening in America, but in most developing countries around the world, a college or university female student may sometimes offer sex to a university lecturer in order to receive a passing grade in her exam and it sounds unrealistic but these are facts. Some have offered sexual favors to gain access to employment or move up the corporate ladder, and the demand seems to outpace its supply and there is simply no shortage anytime soon. The debate about the commercialization of sex has mostly been about the women or females selling their bodies as a means of employment to gain income to support their family, but little is often said about the men who create the demand for such an economy!

The behavior of men seems to have been normalized by society at large,and those of the women criminalized, what a tragedy!Here is the state of commercialization of sex: *While prostitution has become a relatively common practice throughout North America, the majority of prostitutes are female and as a result of this, significantly less research has been conducted on male prostitution, and much of the business remains enigmatic. Male prostitution can be defined as the act of providing sexual services in exchange for payment. It has been estimated that of the 40-42 million prostitutes in the world, 8-8.42 million of them are men. Homosexuality plays a defining role in this lucrative business enterprise, as females rarely choose to pay men for sex, causing other men to become the most common customers.*[166]

166

https://wiki.ubc.ca/Male_Prostitution_in_North_America#:-:text=M ale%20prostitution%20can%20be%20defined,million%20of%20th em%20are%20men.

As you can tell from this Wikipedia entry, sex is an extremely powerful global force and the commercialization of it is just another evidence of the power that sex exerts on people's lives. Prostitution has been widely believed to be a female dominated industry but as you can tell from the statistics, there are literally millions of male prostitutes around the world. This is a sad state of affairs for the world if this many men are selling their bodies for sex to other men who are willing and eager to pay for it. This is unbelievable,and the world has gotten to such a very dark and sick place.

Here is the state of affairs in Canada as it relates to prostitution: *Although prostitution for both males and females is considered legal in Canada, there is a unique set of laws which makes the act of legally selling one's body for money nearly impossible. In June of 2014, the government introduced Bill C-36. This declared that it is legal to sell sexual services, but it is illegal to purchase sexual services. Additionally, it prohibits the promotion and advertising of others' sexual services. The goal for this is to decrease the demand for prostitution. Yet, Bill c-36 has faced significant backlash as some critics believe these stricter guidelines prevent prostitutes from certain safety procedures, such as screening clients before meeting them.* [167] This is a skillfully crafted law that tries to please opponents and advocates of prostitution. The law seems to say that it is legal to sell sex and at the same time illegal to buy sex. The lawmakers recognized that the reason that there is prostitution is because there is the demand for it and so making the demand illegal will eventually curtail or eliminate the supply.

---

[167]

https://wiki.ubc.ca/Male_Prostitution_in_North_America#:-:text=M ale%20prostitution%20can%20be%20defined,million%20of%20th em%20are%20men.

This is a very interesting thought process in the minds of Canadian lawmakers but not sure what effect,if any,it is having on the prostitution economy. But it shows a tremendous amount of effort on their part to use the only tool that they have available to try and solve a major societal crisis. They clearly identified part of the problem but the solution is clearly light years away.

Here is the state of prostitution in the United State of America: *Under the 13th Amendment of the US Constitution, prostitution is illegal in the USA, except for nine counties in the state of Nevada. Prostitution is considered a form of human trafficking, and the penalties for being charged with it vary from state to state. While male prostitution in Nevada is still uncommon due to a past law that required a cervical exam to be performed in order for a prostitute to be employed in a brothel, in 2010, the Shady Lady Range hired the USA's first male gigolo. However, in 2014, the Shady Lady Ranch was shut down. State laws in Nevada require that prostitutes working in brothels commit to monthly STI testing, and the use of condoms is mandatory.*[168] These Nevada lawmakers clearly saw the dangers of STDs to the human population by requiring monthly STDs testing in order to work as a prostitute.

Prostitution is considered a crime in the USA; yet, this has not deterred people who want to engage in this illicit and dangerous profession. Moral conduct can hardly be regulated through the passage of laws,and rarely is anyone prosecuted for breaking these laws. We commend any government for their efforts in addressing this global

---

[168]

https://wiki.ubc.ca/Male_Prostitution_in_North_America#:-:text=M ale%20prostitution%20can%20be%20defined,million%20of%20th em%20are%20men.

epidemic but the issue is way bigger than any governmental effort. This single issue has the potential to destroy billions of lives for generations to come. The lasting effects of sex and prostitution can hardly be quantified and may be beyond any human computation to quantify. The human toll is greater than the loss of lives from all wars ever fought, combined. The effects of sex, pornography and prostitution have the potential to wipe out the entire human civilization as we know it. Let's look at some of the destruction that prostitution is leaving in its path:

Prostitution & Mental Health

Sex is the most sacred activity on the planet after your relationship with your creator. It is designed to be such an activity that is to be performed with careful thought and consideration. It is not to be performed with just anybody but with a carefully selected and ordained partner. So performing sex with just about anyone with the most money is more dangerous than drinking poison. This destroys the sacredness of the activity. Sex for money has the potential to destroy the self-esteem of the person engaging in prostitution. It is not a profession that anyone can really be proud of. I am not aware of any parent who would proudly announce, "My daughter or son is a prostitute," because this brings shame and disgust to the parents, family, friends and to the person. The life of a prostitute is most likely filled with a host of emotional issues like anxiety, fear, loneliness, aloneness, stress, depression, and then suicidal ideation.

Here is an article posted about the emotional state of some prostitutes: *Many prostitutes extinguish their emotions while they are with customers. At least that is the case for Roberta Victor, a prostitute who was interviewed in Working by Studs Terkel. At the outset of her interview,*

Victor claims that "The role one plays when hustling has nothing to do with who you are." However, by the end of the interview, she states that, "You become your job. I became what I did. I became a hustler. I became cold, I became hard, I became turned off, I became numb. Even when I wasn't hustling, I was a hustler. I also don't think it's terribly different from somebody who works on the assembly line forty hours a week and comes home cut off, numb, dehumanized.

People aren't built to switch on and off like a water faucet." Victor seems unaware of the fact that she contradicts herself by stating that she becomes her job [a prostitute] when before she said that she is a different person when she works. Her mindset and analytical process has changed enormously. What factors affected her mindset, from her being able to separate her work from her identity to her thinking that she has become a hustler? What are the psychological and physical effects of prostitution on a prostitute? What factors lead prostitutes to have such a mindset? Is there a way to decrease the effect prostitution has on a prostitute's mental and physical state?[169]

So, this was an interview and subsequent analysis by the interviewer on the emotional state of a prostitute. In this instance, the person finds a way to cope and either conceal their true emotions or accepts it as a way of life. In this instance, such a person may use denial as a coping mechanism. The numbing of her true feelings and emotions become a way to cope. To accept that there is nothing

---

[169]

https://edubirdie.com/examples/psychological-and-physical-effe cts-of-prostitution-on-the-prostitute/#:-:text=Prostitution%20has %20many%20psychological%20effects,and%20the%20introducti on%20to%20drugs.

wrong about being a prostitute and suppress any negative emotions becomes a way to cope. Here is the same author above and what he had to say: *Prostitution has many psychological effects, which include PTSD, anxiety, depression, somatization and stigmatization. The physical effects include the high risk of STDs, sexual and physical violence, and the introduction of drugs.*[170] This is an emotionally dangerous activity to be engaged in, with catastrophic consequences. It is quite disturbing that the effects and risks associated with prostitution, includes; "somatization." This is my first interaction with this term and it is quite scary to say the least.

This is a term given to a medical condition that doctors simply do not know what it is and what caused it. Let's say that you are very sick and doctors are unable to identify the source of your illness, so they just throw out a word: "somatization." This word may have multiple meanings and definitions depending on who you are talking to. It is defined this way in a psychiatry dictionary: *The production of recurrent and multiple medical symptoms with no discernible organic cause.*

Here is another definition, most likely from the psychological community: *Somatization is the expression of psychological or emotional factors that manifest as physical (somatic) symptoms. For example, stress can cause some people to develop headaches, chest pain, back pain, nausea or fatigue. Disorders where somatization manifests ranges from somatic symptom* disorder

---

170

https://edubirdie.com/examples/psychological-and-physical-effe cts-of-prostitution-on-the-prostitute/#:~:text=Prostitution%20has %20many%20psychological%20effects,and%20the%20introducti on%20to%20drugs.

(previously called somatization disorder) to malingering. People with these disorders always focus on their physical problems, meaning they often seek physical solutions.[171]

So, could the idea of somatization involve people getting sick from working as a prostitute and leading to medical diagnosis? Getting injected with sperm by multiple and unknown numbers of people whom the prostitute knows nothing about. The mixture of all kinds of STDs, from AIDS to gonorrhea, all injected into the same vagina and the men who just left carry that same infection to their wives, husbands or to the next sexual encounter. So it is quite clear from many studies that prostitutes exhibit a host of emotional issues from their profession.

They work and live in constant fear, anxiety, and aloneness. Imagine having sexual intercourse with three men per night and that is about ninety men a month. They may not or never remember the names of any of them. They are completely detached from any of them. They are very alone and lonely since they are not emotionally attached to any. They have plenty of sex but no emotional attachment. Fear, loneliness and anxiety will soon progress to depression and suicidal ideation. Emotional issues are not all that they have to face on a daily basis; STDs are big issues.

Prostitution & STDs

STDs or sexually transmitted diseases are wreaking havoc in the general population; then just imagine what is potentially happening in the prostitution community. STDs are diseases that are transmitted through sexual intercourse,

---

[171]

https://www.psychologytoday.com/us/blog/strictly-casual/20141 0/do-sex-workers-have-more-mental-health-problems either heterosexual or homosexual. The situation and prevalence of STDs in the general population is pretty bleak and this may be a cause for concern in the Prostitution population.

Here is the Center for Disease Control (CDC's) assessment: A *2021 CDC analysis provides the clearest picture to date of how common and costly sexually transmitted infections (STIs)are in the United States. CDC's latest estimates indicate that 20% of the U.S population- approximately one in five people- had an STI on any given day in 2017, and STDs acquired that year cost the American healthcare system nearly $16 billion in direct medical costs alone. CDC's analysis included eight common STIs, four of which are treated and cured if diagnosed early: chlamydia, gonorrhea, syphilis, and trichomoniasis.*

Also included in the analysis are four sexually transmitted viruses: human papillomavirus (HPV), herpes simplex virus type 2 (HSV-2), human immunodeficiency virus (HIV), and hepatitis B virus HBV.[172] According to the same CDC's report, there are nearly 68 million infections yearly and nearly 46% of all new STIs in the country occur among young people (ages 15-24). This is the situation with STDs and STIs in the general population and statistics in the prostitution population is somewhat scanty but it is evidently clear what the situation really is.

Married people have sex with a prostitute, get infected with an STD, and bring it home and they get their spouse infected. It does not even have to be sex with a

---

172

https://www.cdc.gov/nchhstp/newsroom/fact-sheets/std/STI-Inc idence-Prevalence-Cost-Factsheet.html#:-:text=CDC's%20latest% 20estimates%20indicate%20that,in%20direct%20medical%20cos ts%20alone.

prostitute; it could simply be, having sex with a co-worker who already had an STD from some other source. Remember that 68 million Americans or more are current STD carriers. The CDC's figures are modest in my opinion. I have to believe without any hard evidence that the STD infection rate in the general population is upward of 90 %. So getting involved in prostitution of any kind, heterosexual or homosexual, is a death sentence. It is like going on a suicide mission because you have a 90% chance of getting infected with some form of an STD. Sex is important but not so important that I will give my life in exchange for it.

That is why I often tell young girls (mostly) to study hard and get highly educated, so that they would not have to resort to selling their God-given body for income or exchange their bodies to gain favors from any man. This is true for men also, but mostly girls. I told a young girl once that there are four ways that a young girl can get out of poverty: (1) inherit a lot of money from her parents (2) win the power ball lottery (3) sell drugs or cocaine to earn income (4) study hard in school and get highly educated, become a lawyer, doctor, or pharmacist, or run for public office and become President of the United States of America.

Option 1 is highly unlikely because not too many girls or boys have wealthy parents. Option 2 is also very highly unlikely because it may be easier to get struck by lightning than to win the power ball lottery. Option 3, Selling drugs or cocaine may seem to provide some short term benefit, but nothing fulfilling and long lasting and you are more likely to end up overdosed, dead, or in a lengthy prison sentence than enjoy anything from that. What do you think about option 4?Your body is very precious in the eyes of God and it is never to be used for sexual immorality, including prostitution.

Prostitution, harlotry, and STDs continue to impact societies in ways that are beyond our comprehension. People are well aware of the dangers associated with having sexual intercourse with a harlot, prostitute, or any unlawful sexual activities, yet they are nonetheless drawn to their doom. You would think that people would reflect on the millions of people who have died from all kinds of STDs, including AIDS, and that will be enough to deter people from such behavior.

People are simply unable and unwilling to stop as the force is irresistible. This inner and powerful force that draws the human race is seemingly beyond any human capacity to see the danger and stop. Imagine a man inserting his penis into the vagina of a harlot or prostitute, with no protection. This is very dangerous as it is like sticking your tongue into a toilet and licking feces. No right-thinking person should do such a thing, and yet millions are plunging to their destruction in the name of pleasure.

You have no idea what the other person is carrying in their body that is ready to be shared and transmitted into you. The desire to have sex overrides the desire to think and save your life.The focus in this chapter has been on harlots or prostitutes,but it is equally dangerous for a man or woman to engage in such sexual activities with anyone who is not their spouse.

This one decision may just be the one that ends your life as you are likely to contract some form of STD, including but not limited to AIDS. Don't forget that about 90% of adults in the country and around the world, have some form of STD and that means, you have a 90% chance of contracting some form of STD just by having sexual intercourse with someone other than your spouse. Think about it before you engage in your next sexual adventure.

Get tested for STDs, you and your spouse, and abstain from sexual intercourse between you and anyone other than your spouse, so you may be STD free for good. But if you are a harlot or prostitute then my prayer for you is, "May God enable you to abandon that lifestyle." Fall on your knees and beg God for the ability and He is ready and willing if you only ask Him before it's too late, because many have died early. He is ready to forgive and to cleanse you from all unrighteousness and set you free from the penalty, power and presence of sin.

Prostitution, Violence & Early Death

The risk of attracting some form of STDs as a harlot or prostitute is about 99.9999 % but this is only one of many risks associated with the profession of prostitution. Like many other professions, this is also pretty risky and downright dangerous to say the least.Just imagine the risk of inviting someone who they know absolutely nothing about for the purpose of undressing before them and having sex to be paid in return.

This could be a rapist, serial killer, child molester and so on, but she has no clue who that person is. This is scary and dangerous stuff. Girls and women are killed and their families may never know what happened to them and may never hear from them again. This is a profession full of violence and saturated with fear. They are constantly fearful and afraid of who may harm them and take advantage of them. Men often take advantage of them because they are often defenseless and powerless.

Some are beaten, forced into actions against their will and volition, and this makes my stomach sick. Here is part of an article posted on Psychiatry Times about sexual violence: *The experiences of a woman who prostituted primarily in strip clubs, but also in massage, escort and street prostitution, are typical (Farley et al, 2003). In strip club prostitution, she was sexually harassed and assaulted. Stripping required her to smilingly accommodate customers' verbal abuse. Customers grabbed and pinched her legs, arms, breasts, buttocks and crotch, sometimes resulting in bruises and scratches. Customers squeezed her breasts until she was in severe pain, and they humiliated her by ejaculating on her face. Customers and pimps physically brutalized her.*

She was severely bruised from beatings and frequently had black eyes. Pimps pulled her hair as a means of control and torture. She was repeatedly beaten on the head with closed fists, sometimes resulting in unconsciousness. From these beatings, her ear-drum was damaged, and her jaw was dislocated and remains so many years later. She was cut with knives. She was burned with cigarettes by customers who smoked while raping her. She was gang-raped and she was also raped individually by at least 20 men at different times in her life.

These rapes by Johns and pimps sometimes resulted in internal bleeding. Yet this woman described the psychological pain of prostitution as far worse than the physical violence. She explained that prostitution "is internally damaging. You become in your own mind what these people do and say with you" (Farley et al. 2003). Almost two decades earlier, Norwegian researchers noted that women in prostitution were treated like commodities into which men masturbate, causing immense psychological harm to the person acting as the receptacle (Hoigard and Finstad, 1986).[173]

The picture painted by this article sickens me to my stomach and this looks like something that was produced in a movie theater but this is fact and not fiction. This kind of sexual violence is actually happening across America and the globe. Women and girls, made in the image of God, are being sexually ridiculed and humiliated by men with a debased mind. This is pure sexual slavery. This is beyond criminal and is simply inhumane animal behavior.

A person made in the image of God is brought so low, ridiculed, humiliated by depraved, debased, by destructive men who seek their own self-satisfaction and glorification at the expense of another valued human being who is worthy of honor and adoration. But this is not only a dangerous line of work in terms of the amount of daily violence, but sex workers regularly pay the ultimate price with their lives.

It is very easy for a girl or woman to be killed, working as a prostitute than the non-prostitute female population and here is an abstract from the NIH's National Library of Medicine: *It has been estimated that women involved in street prostitution are 60 to 100 times more likely to be murdered than are non-prostitute females. In addition, homicides of prostitutes are notoriously difficult to investigate and as such, many cases remain unsolved. Despite these large risk factors, little literature exists on homicides of prostitutes, and there is a lack of basic statistics and knowledge regarding this very specific group*

173

https://www.psychiatrictimes.com/view/prostitution-sexual-violence

that could possibly help key investigators. The aim of the current study is to conduct an exploratory study to explore the key characteristics of this group and how they differ from other subgroups of homicide. Forty-six cases of U.K. prostitute homicides are analyzed and compared to 59 male offender-female victim non-sexual homicide cases and 17 male offender-female victim sexual homicide cases. [174]

It may be safe to conclude that the business of prostitution is in some way, following the business model of organized crime because in some cases, they may be intertwined, meaning that organized crime rings are sometimes mixed with prostitution, making homicides of prostitutes harder to solve. The lives and potentials of a lot of young people get cut short way too early. They are either killed from some acquired STD, drug overdose or physical violence.

Here is a glimpse of the state of violence and death associated with prostitution recorded by crime museum: *In 2005, Markoff met McAllister while they were volunteering at the hospital. Both were students at SUNY and soon became college sweethearts. Markoff graduated in just three years with a bachelor's degree in biology and was accepted into Boston University's School of Medicine. McAllister had also planned on attending medical school, but was not accepted by the school she wanted to attend, the couple moved to Boston and Megan put her plans on hold.In 2008,Markoff and McAllister were engaged, and set their wedding date for August 14, 2009. McAllister kept herself busy with wedding planning, while Markoff attended*

---

[174]   https://pubmed.ncbi.nlm.nih.gov/18319375/

medical school and frequented casinos – racking up over $130,000 in debt.

In April 2009, Boston police were investigating two separate attacks on women who had advertised erotic services online and had planned to meet their "client" at a luxury hotel. On April 10, 2009, 29-year-old Trisha Leffler, an escort, was gagged, bound, and robbed at gunpoint at a Westin hotel by a man who responded to an ad she had placed on Craigslist. Four days later, Julissa Brisman was found murdered in the doorway of her Marriott hotel room. It appeared that she had been trying to fight off her attacker, when she was shot multiple times.

She had placed an ad on Craigslist offering erotic massage services and had scheduled an appointment to meet a man named "Andy" at her hotel room. Police believed the same attacker was linked to the attempted robbery of Cynthia Melton, an exotic dancer offering lap dance services. Markoff had scheduled an appointment to meet her at a Holiday Inn hotel in Rhode Island through the usage of a disposable TracFone cell phone. The three incidents were similar in that the motive appeared to be robbery, that attacks were on women offering sexual services, the dates were close together, and two of the women had been bound with plastic cords. Through all of this, Markoff's fiancée remained in the dark believing that he was "beautiful inside and out."[175]

This may not be a unique case because a lot of people, on the male side who are involved with prostitutes, are also married. They may manage, for a little while, to live

[175]

https://www.crimescenecleanup.com/prostitution-death-statistics/

multiple lives but it will soon catch up with them. A prostitute is not going to rent a hotel room at Marriott to have sex with a poor person. The high end prostitutes maintain a well-connected male clientele. These are business people, lawyers, doctors, and politicians. The desire for sex and to pay for it, is not determined by someone's economic status. This is the desire and longing of the human heart regardless of one's position in life and this desire for sex fuels the need to supply and young girls and women are murdered in the process. This demand for sex and the need to supply it has opened up a host of other sex crimes, including sex trafficking.

Prostitution & Sex Trafficking

Sex trafficking is a very complex and emotionally broad subject that may require volumes of writings to actually get into the heart of the issue. We may only whet your appetite by getting into the elementary issues with sex trafficking. This may also be called sex slavery because millions of girls are lured into prostitution through sex trafficking. This is a global underground economy that is flourishing underneath the watchful eyes of global law enforcement. Desperate young girls are lured into prostitution under the guise of a prosperous and better life. It is very dangerous to be desperate in any given situation because desperation means that they are running out of options. When anyone is desperate then it may mean that there are no good options available (so they may think and conclude). Desperate people do desperate things.

Imagine a young beautiful college or university graduate in some third world country, say, in Africa, South America or Asia, that has completed her education and there are no employment opportunities. She has tried for years to apply for employment but no success. She may be the first of ten children in her family and her parents, with very limited resources, and have done all that they could in sponsoring their first child. In some of those cultures, it is expected that it is now the responsibility of the first child to take over the responsibility of providing for her parents and siblings so they are under a lot of pressure.

Oh, but there is one problem! She is willing but not able. She has no employment and no income. They are living in complete poverty. They are living in a house of about 20 people, and the house has about two bedrooms, no indoor plumbing, no electricity, using an outhouse as a toilet. This is abject poverty, to put it mildly. This is simply no excuse to become a prostitute but this is the situation in which many of these girls find themselves. Her family may even lack enough daily food to feed 20 people. The level of desperation is beyond the pale.

So, it is in this context that she suddenly hears of an opportunity to work in, say,Europe, Dubai, or some other Western country. She is promised to be paid about 1500 Euros a month or $1800 a month in Dubai. She is promised free housing and feeding but there is one catch! She may have been told that she will be working as a "customer service specialist," or something similar but she may not even know what that really means and she may be too afraid to ask, for fear of losing the opportunity. Not until she boards the plane and touches down and she is taken to her place of residence; then, within days, it begins to sink in, after she receives her work assignments. They will seize her passport and she has no money to return to her home country even if she wanted to do so.

This is somewhat of a picture for most young girls in some of these countries but there are others who remain in

294

their countries who also choose prostitution, regardless of their economic status. They see their mother, grandmother, great grandmother, sisters and friends doing prostitution, and it was natural to do it because everyone around them is a prostitute. Now, the situation in North America and Europe is a little different.

The girls who are born in these countries are living in completely different economic circumstances and yet some still chose prostitution. This is an extremely complicated subject with varying situational reasons why girls are lured into such a profession. The level of desperation is hardly as abject as in most developing countries, yet, many girls still chose the path of prostitution. Even in these wealthy countries, sex traffickers still exist to lure girls into prostitution, deceiving them with the idea of a better life.

Here are some real life stories of sex trafficking and prostitution: *In California, Sara is eighteen and has to leave her foster home; she is offered training to be a waitress working on cruise ships. She accepts, but is sold to sex traffickers by Diane.*

In India, young teen Amba is partying with her friends when a guy she'd rejected tries to hit on her again. He is thrown out. On her way back home, he throws acid on her and her friend. Her friend is facially disfigured and Amba's hand is scarred. Then he forces Amba to be sold into sex slavery. Sara and Amba both wind up together in a Texas brothel with Mali, from Nigeria, and are raped repeatedly. Mali tells them to do what they can to survive, and not fight back. Amba, hopeless, listens, but Sara resists and is beaten and drugged.

Amba gets pregnant and Simon (Sean Patrick Flanery), the owner of the brothel, finds out and makes her take pills to have an abortion. She loses a lot of blood and Mali pleads with Simon to call a doctor. He does, and Sara discreetly begs the doctor for some sleeping pills "for her friend." He relents. Sara plots with Amba and Mali to escape. She tells them that Simon is going away with the rest of his men for the night, and only Max, one of the guards, will be left. Sara says that they could catch a train nearby.

Mali agrees, but Amba, still depressed over her abortion, says that she won't leave. She thinks her family would be too ashamed of her when they find out what she's been doing. Sara puts in the sleeping pills in Max's drink, and once he's asleep, she sneaks out with Mali. Amba changes her mind and goes with them. Sara grabs the keys to the front gate from Max, but he awakens and chokes her. Mali hits him and knocks him out, and the three girls run. They get to the train station, but are too late; the train has already left. Mali trips and injures her ankle. Meanwhile, Simon has found out that they had escaped and runs back.

Gameboy, another guard, searches the station, which is also a truck stop, and hears Mali's yells of pain. Mali tells Amba and Sara to run away, and they finally do, reluctant to leave her. Mali is captured and Sara and Amba run and hide in a truck. They were taken to a bus station, where they bought two tickets. They get in the bus and see Simon, who has tracked them there and is searching the buses. They duck and hide and manage to evade him. Sara is reunited with her younger sister and Amba calls her family, who are overjoyed to hear from her. Simon and Diane are arrested, along with everyone else involved in trafficking. As for Mali, she is shown with a group of prostitutes, holding one of them and crying as the one she was holding is taken away.[176]

---

[176]   https://en.wikipedia.org/wiki/Trafficked

This is the sad state of affairs in the world of sex trafficking. This is happening, sometimes in broad daylight, and under the watchful eyes of law enforcement. Girls are trapped in a circle of captivity and violence and are pleading for help. The issue of sex trafficking is also widely misunderstood and many even question its existence. Girls are being lured all around the world as I am writing, within the guise and promise of a better life. But what really is sex trafficking?

Below is the image of a brothel in the state of Nevada, where legal prostitution is practiced.

Image of a brothel in Nevada, USA[177]

What is sex trafficking?

Here are some key statistics to ponder: *In 2019, the National Center for Missing & Exploited Children (NCMEC) estimated that 1 in 6 endangered runaways reported to them were likely sex trafficking victims.*

The International Labor Organization and Walk Free Foundation, in partnership with IOM, estimated that there are 4.8 million people trapped in forced sexual exploitation globally. In the United States, the Trafficking Victims Protection Act of 2000 (TVPA), as amended by the Justice for Victims of Trafficking Act of 2015 (JVTA), defines sex trafficking as "recruiting, harboring, transporting, providing, obtaining, patronizing or soliciting of an individual through the means of force, fraud, or coercion for the purpose of

---

[177]

https://www.businessinsider.com/legal-prostitution-in-nevada-photos-of-brothels-marc-mcandrews *commercial sex." However, it is not necessary to demonstrate force, fraud, or coercion in sex trafficking cases involving children under the age of 18. The term "commercial sex act" is defined as "any sex act on account of which anything of value is given to or received from any person" (22 U.S.C. 7102). Sex trafficking may be distinguished from other forms of commercial sex by applying the Action + Means + Purpose Model.*

Human trafficking occurs when a trafficker takes any one of the enumerated actions, and then employs the means of force, fraud, or coercion for the purpose of compelling the victim to provide commercial sex acts. At a minimum, one element from each column must be present to establish a potential situation of sex trafficking. The presence of force, fraud, or coercion indicates that the victim has not consented of his or her free will. In addition, minors under the age of 18 engaging in commercial sex are considered victims of human trafficking regardless of the use of force, fraud, or coercion. [178]

There is clearly no doubt that prostitution and sex trafficking are posing a severe threat to the lives and futures of our young girls. Many are sucked into this with the deception and expectation of having a seemingly better life, and yet their lives are shattered or prematurely cut short. Young girls are forced, coerced, defrauded of their precious bodies, only to return, if they do return, with broken lives. But what is really at the root of prostitution and sex trafficking?

---

[178] https://humantraffickinghotline.org/type-trafficking/sex-trafficking

What Pushes People into Prostitution & Sex Trafficking?

These are no doubt very bad and terrible crimes committed against humanity but what really drives people to such a level of degradation? What really drives men and women to force and coerce young girls into prostitution and what even causes some girls to choose a life of prostitution? This is quite a complicated subject, as there are all kinds of ideas as to the root cause of this. Some may think and say that the environment in which people have grown up may have exposed them to such behavior patterns. There is certainly some level of truth to that, and the thinking is that if someone's mother is a prostitute, then they are likely to follow prostitution as a career path and if someone's father or mother is a sex trafficker, then they may well likely follow that path also. Yet, others have argued that coercion and poverty are at the root of prostitution and here is one such argument:

These feminists argue that, in most cases, prostitution is not a conscious and calculated choice. They say that most women who become prostitutes, do so because they were forced or coerced by a pimp or by human trafficking, or, when it is an independent decision, it is generally the result of extreme poverty and lack of opportunity, or of serious underlying problems, such as drug addiction, past trauma (such as child sexual abuse), and other unfortunate circumstances.

These feminists point out that women from the lowest socio-economic classes -impoverished women, women with a low level of education, women from the most disadvantaged racial and ethnic minorities – are overrepresented in prostitution all over the world; as stated by Catherine MacKinnon: "If prostitution is a free choice, why are women with the fewest choices the ones most often found doing it?" A large percentage of prostitutes polled in one study of 475 people involved in prostitution reported that they were in a difficult period of their lives and most wanted to leave the occupation. Mackinnon argues, "In prostitution, women have sex with men they would never otherwise have sex with. The money thus acts as a form of force, not as a measure of consent. It acts like physical force does in rape."

Some anti-prostitution scholars hold that true consent in prostitution is not possible. Barbara Sullivan says: "In the academic literature on prostitution, there are very few authors who argue that valid consent to prostitution is possible. Most suggest that consent to prostitution is impossible, or at least unlikely." Most authors suggest that consent to prostitution is deeply problematic, if not impossible. For radical feminists, this is because prostitution is always a coercive sexual practice. Others simply suggest that economic coercion makes the sexual consent of sex workers highly problematic, if not impossible."

 Finally, abolitionists believe no person can be said to truly consent to their own oppression, and no people should have the right to the oppression of others. In the words of Kathleen Barry, consent is not a "good dividing rod as to the existence of oppression, and consent to violation is a fact of oppression. Oppression cannot effectively be gauged to the degree of consent, since even in slavery, there was some consent, if consent is defined as inability to see any alternative." [179]

179
https://en.wikipedia.org/wiki/Feminist_views_on_prostitution#:~:t

This is quite a fascinating take and twist on the reasons for prostitution, where feminists and others argue that poverty and coercion are the primary reasons why women turn to prostitution as a last resort. They argue passionately that when money becomes a motivating factor to engage in sex, then there is no consent. This is quite an intriguing way to look at consent. The argument is that when money or something of value is present in the context of the prostitute's poor economic circumstances, then they are motivated by money and are rendered powerless and without the ability to truly consent.

The idea of "consent" is agreeing or granting permission for some action to take place. Both consenting parties must be in agreement, without any fraud, force or coercion. They must be over the age of 18 and not under the influence of any controlled substance, marijuana, alcohol, drugs, or any such substance that impairs thinking and judgment. There are about 8.4 million male prostitutes in the world and I am not sure if they are also coerced into prostitution. This includes every race and color and is hardly limited to economic coercion.

There are very poor girls around the world who will hardly sell their bodies for sex and there are women with regular 9 to 5 jobs who also sell their bodies for sex. It is no wonder that prostitution is called "the oldest profession in the world." The fundamental issue here is taking responsibility for any human action. The one paying for the prostitute is no doubt enabling her action but hardly causing her actions. The one providing the sex also has culpability. They are equally guilty of a deplorable immoral act.

---

ext=They%20say%20that%20most%20women,addiction%2C%20
past%20trauma%20(such%20as

Using coercion as a defense for the woman's actions, is seeking to relieve the woman from any culpability. Neither can a male use coercion as a defense for their action and decision to get into prostitution. Economic conditions, like poverty and socio-economic factors, may act as proximate causes but not the actual causes of prostitution. If this were the case then hardly would anyone be held responsible for their actions. The idea of coercion, if any at all, could be applicable to girls in some third world countries but why would any girl in America claim coercion and poverty as the cause for her becoming a prostitute? This is a country filled with opportunities if only they are willing and able to see it and make use of it.

There is really no justification for a girl in America to use poverty and economic-coercion as reasons for engaging in prostitution. The bible has a lot to say about prostitution that will blow up your mind. It is then no surprise that prostitution is called the oldest profession and here is some of what the bible has to say:

1. Deuteronomy 23:17 None of the daughters of Israel shall be a cult prostitute, and none of the sons of Israel shall be a cult prostitute.

3. Leviticus 19:29 Do not defile your daughter by making her a prostitute, or the land will be filled with prostitution and wickedness.

4. Leviticus 21:9 If a priest's daughter defiles herself by becoming a prostitute, she also defiles her father's holiness, and she must be burned to death.

5. Deuteronomy 23:17 No Israelite, whether man or woman, may become a temple prostitute.

One with a prostitute!

6. 1 Corinthians 6:15-16 Don't you realize that your bodies are actually parts of Christ? Should a man take his body, which is part of Christ, and join it to a prostitute? Never! And don't you realize that if a man joins himself to a prostitute, he becomes one body with her? For the Scriptures say, "The two are united into one."

Sexual immorality

7. 1 Corinthians 6:18 Flee fornication. Every sin that a man doeth is without the body; but he that committeth fornication sinneth against his own body.

8. Galatians 5:19 Now the works of the flesh are obvious: sexual immorality, impurity, depravity.

9. 1 Thessalonians 4:3-4 It is God's will that you keep away from sexual sin as a mark of your devotion to him. Each of you should know that finding a husband or wife for yourself is to be done in a holy and honorable way.

Beware!

10. Proverbs 22:14 The mouth of an adulterous woman is a deep pit; a man who is under the LORD's wrath falls into it.

11. Proverbs 23:27-28 For a prostitute is like a deep pit; a harlot is like a narrow well. Indeed, she lies in wait like a robber, and increases the unfaithful among men.

12. Proverbs 2:15-16 Whose paths are crooked and who are devious in their ways. Wisdom will save you also from the adulterous woman, from the wayward woman with her seductive words.

13. Proverbs 5:3-5 For the lips of the adulterous woman drip honey, and her seductive words are smoother than olive oil, but in the end she is bitter as wormwood, sharp as a

two-edged sword. Her feet go down to death; her steps lead straight to the grave.

God does not accept prostitution money.

14. Deuteronomy 23:18 When you are bringing an offering to fulfill a vow, you must not bring to the house of the Lord your God any offering from the earnings of a prostitute, whether a man or a woman, for both are detestable to the Lord your God.

15. Proverbs 10:2 Tainted wealth has no lasting value, but right living can save your life.

I will let the bible speak for itself concerning these matters of deep importance to our individual lives and our global communities. It is quite clear that prostitution or harlotry is sinful conduct that proceeds from a sinful heart. God said, "Do not defile your daughter by making her a prostitute, or the land will be filled with prostitution and wickedness," Leviticus 19:29. Prostitution, adultery, fornication, homosexuality, and all other forms of sexually immoral conducts cause the land to be filled with wickedness.

Sin is any transgression of God's law and that includes all sin, like lying, stealing, gossiping, and jealousy; these are all sins but there is something quite different with sexual sin. When we lie or don't tell the whole truth, we lie to them and it is affecting them. When we steal from someone, we take what belongs to them. We covet or want what someone else has then all these kinds of sins are external to us and our bodies and that is why sexual sin and sexual immorality is different, because while it is equally a sin,it is placed in a category of its own, in that, it is a sin against our own bodies. This is very profound and critically important to understand the extent and impact of sexual sin. There is nothing like it!

There is something about sexual sin that we cannot fully comprehend in our feeble minds. The rashness in which God deals with sexual sin looks somewhat different from how He deals with other types of sin when an infraction does occur, and He has prescribed the remedy for any such infraction. Here is what God said in one case: "If a priest's daughter defiles herself by becoming a prostitute, she also defiles her father's holiness, and she must be burned to death," Leviticus 21:9. If the daughter of a priest becomes a prostitute, then death will be the only remedy for such a seemingly minor infraction.

God takes sexual sin seriously and all sexual sin is against the body of the person committing sexual immorality. Here is what God said about that: Every sin that a man does is outside the body; but he who commits sexual immorality, sins against his own body,1 Corinthians 6:18. This text places sexual immorality in a class of its own. Every other sin is outside the body but sexual immorality, which is a general term for any sex activity that deviates from the standards set by God. Genesis 2:24 is the standard and any deviation would be classified as sexual immorality. So how do we get out of this mess? What is the solution?

Solution to Sexual Immorality

While sexual sin may be in a class of its own, all sins are essentially the same. They all end up with the same consequences. All sin separates man from God and all sin results in death, which is a spiritual separation (spiritual death) between man and God. Every disobedience to what God has said is sin. It is that simple. "Sin is transgression of the law," 1 John 3:4. God has a standard for holiness and no

306

one meets the standards set forth by God. It doesn't really matter if you are a prostitute, pimp or president of a country. There is one thing that is common to all mankind.

All are sinners and sin separates us from God. The ground is level at the cross. It does not matter what you have done and where you have been. It does not matter how you start the race but how you finish. God is able to completely wipe out your past and give you a brand new beginning. But you have to know and believe certain things about yourself. You have to know and believe that you are a sinner. This is the foremost and foundational truth. You are not a sinner because you commit sinful acts like prostitution; you are a sinner because you were born a sinner from your mother's womb. Prostitution is only a sin that you commit because you are a sinner.

Without prostitution or other sexually immoral acts, you will remain a sinner. Separate who you are from what you do. We sin because we are sinners. We are not sinners because we sin. Society tries to elevate or look down on a certain class of people as either sinners or righteous based on what they do. If someone is a priest or a pastor as opposed to being a prostitute or a pimp, then society would likely pass judgment that the pastor and the priest are likely to end up in heaven but it is not quite that simple.

The most famous prostitute in the bible is a woman called, "Rehab," and here is her story: "By faith the harlot Rehab did not perish with those who did not believe when she had received the spies with peace," Hebrews 11:31. This harlot or prostitute appeared in the genealogy of Jesus in Matthew 1:5. This is an amazing story of the grace of God and redemption. God is not a respecter of persons. If you happen to be a harlot or prostitute then remember that there is hope. And if you are not a prostitute but the president of a country, then there is hope for you too. With God's help, you have to know, believe and acknowledge your true condition. No one goes to see a doctor unless they are sick and know that they are sick.

Sin is a sickness that separates the human race from God. Here is what God said about this: "But your iniquities have separated you from your God; your sins have hidden His face from you, so that He will not hear," Isaiah 59:2. Sin is the wall of separation between man and God. This separation is also called death, (Ephesians 2:1) which means that man or mankind is physically alive but spiritually dead and separated from God in this life and may someday become eternally separated from God if they die without hope.

Here is what God said again: "For the wages of sin is death but the gift of God is eternal life in Christ Jesus our Lord," Romans 6:23. When you work for a company, you earn weekly or monthly wages for the work done and in like manner, death or separation from God is wages for sinning against God. The second part of this verse talks about eternal life, which is contrasted from the former part, which talks about death. This eternal life is a gift from God to you. This is the solution to the sin issue. The removal of sin so that you can be brought into God's presence. Sin is the barrier and obstacle.

Sin keeps God out of your life but the shed blood of Christ reconciles you back to God, for without the shedding of blood there is no forgiveness of sin, Hebrews 9:22. The key step here is to admit your true condition. God says that you are a sinner and the question is, "Do you agree with God's assessment of you or do you disagree with God? Do you think that God is wrong in calling you a sinner? Most people really believe that they are good people but what do you believe about yourself?"All have sinned and fall short of the glory of God, Romans 3:25. The word,"all,"means all inclusive to mean everyone, including you, have sinned, no exceptions. We are all in very bad shape and we cannot get out. All you have to do is to agree with God and here is what God says: "Because, if you confess with your mouth that Jesus is Lord and believe in your heart that God raised Him from the dead, you will be saved. For with the heart one believes and is justified, and with the mouth one confesses and is saved," Romans 10:9-10. The Greek word that is translated here into English as "confess," has the idea of agreeing with God or being of the same mind with God about what He says about any given matter. Agreeing with God that you are sinner and also agreeing that He is Lord, meaning that He is God, in fleshly or human form.

And also believing that He was crucified, buried and on the third day, He rose triumphantly out of the grave. If you truly believe this then you have eternal life. You have passed from spiritual death to eternal life and never to be eternally separated from your creator again. But to those who reject the invitation from God and continue on a self-destructive path, then certain destruction awaits them. Here is what God said through the writer of Hebrews: "How can we escape if we neglect so great a salvation?" Hebrews 2:3. This is a rhetorical question and with the answer embedded in the question itself. Some may choose to continue on a path of other destructive behaviors, like unwanted sex.

Chapter 10

The Destructive Power of Unwanted Sex

Unwanted sex has the power to destroy a person's core being. Sex is the most intimate activity between a man and a woman, and such activity is only pleasurable and enjoyable when there is mutual consent. Forced or unwanted sex invades and destroys the person. It is very hard to believe, but unwanted and forced sex is actually happening every single day in your house or your neighborhood. This is not some fringe idea; it is actually happening every single day. Unwanted sex happens in many forms, and you may often hear of unwanted or forced sex due to intoxication on college campuses.

Some make headline news but others don't and in either case, it is happening across America and the globe.Cases of rape, incest and many other forms of unwanted sex are happening in or near you right now.

Unwanted Sex in Marriages

Here is an analysis about unwanted sex: *Through analysis of 41 interviews with women who had experienced some form of unwanted sex in a marital or long-term relationship, the author identified five types of acquiescence to such unwanted sex. One type of acquiescence involved occasions when the women initially did not want sex but began to enjoy it after a few minutes. In the second* type of acquiescence, the women neither desired nor enjoyed the sex but *considered it their wifely duty. The third type of acquiescence occurred when the women consented to the sex just to avoid the partner's verbal or nonverbal abuse. The fourth type of acquiescence differed from the third type in that the women acquiesced out of fear that they would be seriously physically harmed if they did not comply; and the fifth type of acquiescence was due to the women having been previously abused by the partner for refusing to have sex. After identifying these types of acquiescence, the paper discusses the conditions under which women adopt a given type. This research extends Finkelhor and Yllo's nonphysical types of coercion to better understand the contexts in which women experience unwanted sex in marriage.*

The author argues that the processes and consequences of "giving in" to unwanted sex with an intimate person have not been given much scholarly attention as other forms of forced sex that have traditionally been identified as rape.[180]So this article analyzes unwanted sex in the context of a marital union. This may sometimes fall outside the traditional understanding of unwanted or forced sex. This understanding may raise more questions than answers. It may raise some ethical and philosophical questions. Could things like consent be applicable in a marriage context? What about coercion, and is that also happening in a marriage context? Could a husband or wife be charged with rape? These are tough questions to think and ponder!

How do you really know that your spouse does not want sex? Because, in practice, they may hardly verbally tell you that they do not want sex at that moment. You may sense that they do not want it based on body chemistry and

---

180

https://www.ojp.gov/ncjrs/virtual-library/abstracts/rape-acquiescence-ways-which-women-give-unwanted-sex-their-husbands language but not from any audible voice with certainty, like, "Don't touch me, I don't want any sex." Nothing with that kind of clarity was ever communicated but the other spouse is expected to know and do what is expected. I could be wrong, but again, I could be 100% correct! Most husbands do not normally walk up to their wives, sit on the bed or in the bedroom and say something like, "Do you want to have sex now?" and then just sit there and wait for some kind of response, like, "Yes," or "No."

This seems to be what is expected but it is hardly the way that it usually happens. There is some level of spontaneity in these things that is not clear cut. Things just simply happen and get out of control. What if one of the partners is red hot and in desperate need for sexual intercourse, but the other is withdrawn and has no such desire? The one who is red hot is still expected to exercise self-control over their raging testosterone.

The very idea of unwanted or forced sex in the marital context is extremely difficult and downright impossible to police. I am not even sure if a thing like that exists in a good marriage. Sex is often used as a weapon or a bargaining chip to settle scores from other areas of disagreements. The issue of unwanted, forced sex, coercion, or rape should never even be mentioned in a harmonious marital union. Even the slightest thought of such an idea only reveals that the marriage has other bigger problems to resolve. There are genuine periods in a marriage when one partner may not be in the mood for sex and the other partner should be able to understand and bear with one another for a time. If you are a follower of Jesus Christ, then sex is not to be withheld from your partner except with mutual consent for a time, until both of you return to normalcy. One of the partners may be ill, tired, and physically exhausted, and not ready to undergo the rigor of intense sexual activity and the other should graciously understand and accept that. No need to force or coerce your partner into unwanted sexual activity. You have to bear with and understand your partner, hoping that it is not a prolonged period, like months of always refusing to have sex.

Here is what God said through the Apostle Paul: "The wife does not have power over her own body, but the husband does, And likewise the husband does not have power over his own body, but the wife does. Do not deprive one another except with consent for a time, that you may give yourselves to fasting and prayer; and come together again so that Satan does not tempt you because of your lack of self-control," 1 Corinthians 7:4-5. The issue of forced or unwanted sex should never be occurring in God ordained marriages but who knows, maybe it's happening! Unwanted sex continues to pose problems outside the normal marital settings, like cases of unwanted sex due to intoxication.

Unwanted Sex due to Intoxication

Unwanted sex due to intoxication is very likely, especially on college or university campuses across the globe. Some sleeping pill is likely slipped into a drink by a male partner in order to have the female intoxicated and incapacitated for the purpose of taking control over her body, so that they can engage in unconsented sex. It's very scary to think that this may potentially happen when you send your daughter to any university around the world to study and get an education. Young men, mostly, who are unable to gain consent from a lady, would turn to other crude and unlawful means to gain sex.

This is simply rape and it is criminal. So how wide-spread is this problem? Is it really a serious concern? College campuses are sometimes like a war zone, from idle boys harassing girls in hallways and classrooms,to throwing verbal insults, to physically grabbing them. Girls are sometimes living in constant fear on campuses. They are afraid to walk from the library late at night to go to their dormitories, afraid of being sexually assaulted by a male student. A college campus is supposed to be a place of excitement, curiosity and adventure, yet, for a lot of female students, it is a place of dread, fear, anxiety and sometimes, depression. Constantly in fear of unwanted sexual advances and when booze is introduced into the mix then other sexual crimes, like rape, assault and ultimately murder, will soon follow.

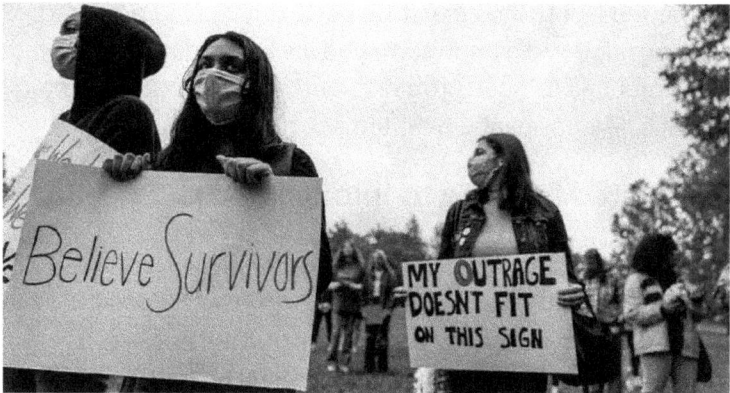

College students protesting against sexual violence[181]

The pictures above tell it all. People do not simply get involved in campus demonstrations until it becomes

[181]

https://www.apa.org/monitor/2022/04/news-campus-sexual-assault

personal for them. Either they themselves have been personally affected or someone that they know has been impacted. Going to campus parties, either in a club or a birthday party at a friend's house, is sometimes risky, because that is where a sexual admirer will slip something into your drink that you left on the table to go to the bathroom.

That may be the same person who will carry you home in their car once you are intoxicated and passed out. Then they proceed to rape you as they please. This is a criminal act against human beings made in the image of God. Here is a study on the effects of intoxication and unwanted sex: The study found that for people of all genders, unwanted intoxicated sex was associated with higher likelihood of experiencing forced sex, being diagnosed with a sexually transmitted disease, or drug use. For women it was associated with increased risk of pregnancy termination and heavy drinking. For men it was also associated with tobacco smoking, increased psychological distress and poor general health.

Dr. Carter said drinking was a big part of Australian culture – with one in four men and one in 10 women drinking at risky levels – and a lot of young people used drugs at parties, music festivals and clubs. However, she said the perception of great sex when drunk or high was not reality.

"So often people think about alcohol and other drugs in terms of enhancing our experiences with sex – increasing arousal, desire, attraction, curiosity, courage and pleasure," she said. "But drunk, consensual sex is in fact more often rated as unwanted and less pleasurable compared with

sober, consensual sex, and also most sexual assault is attributed to being too drunk or high to consent."[82]

Being under the influence of alcohol or any other substance that impairs one's decision making faculties has ruined the lives of victims of unwanted sex and perpetrators alike. Young girls have ended up with all kinds of emotional trauma as a result of unwanted sex. For some, it is unwanted pregnancies that may end up in murder of the unborn child through abortion. For others, it is shame, and a violation of their human dignity. Yet others are abandoned with feelings of emptiness, worthlessness, and suicidal ideation. This is rape, pure and simple, but not all rapes are associated with alcohol intoxication,

Unwanted Sex due to Rape

Rape is the most humiliating thing that can ever happen to a person. It denies the person basic human dignity. It violates their body against their consent and it is very damaging mentally and psychologically. People are rendered helpless and hopeless. Why would a human-being do this to another? By raping another! This is what animals do in the wild and yet humans are reduced to such a low level of degradation. No one has the right to coerce, force, intimidate, or threaten another human-being to give over their body to you for your sexual pleasure and gratification. Their body is not yours and not to be abused for your sexual pleasure and gratification. Rape is more common than most people even seem to realize.

182

https://www.smh.com.au/lifestyle/life-and-relationships/consent -and-wanting-are-not-the-same-research-reveals-extent-of-un wanted-sex-while-intoxicated-20201121-p56gn2.html#:~:text=On e%20in%20six%20women%20and,associated%20with%20poor %20health%20outcomes

A lot of rapes are done by people who are sober and not influenced by any intoxicating substance. They are awake, alert, and know what they are doing or about to do. They want sex and have determined that they will get it, with or without the consent of the person. The power to have this sex has so overpowered them that they are incapable of any rational thinking and decision making. They are incapable of seriously considering all the ramifications of their potential actions. The power to have this sex has overridden the power of self-control. They are incapable of seeing that they are destroying another human-being, yet they are responsible for their actions.

The decision to rape anyone is not only sinful but can be live-altering for the victim and rapist. The rapist should think about the victim as someone else raping your own daughter, sister or mother. How would that affect you if your best friend raped your daughter, sister or mother? How will that sit with you? Think about that for a second! Here is a snap shot on the global situation on rape: Also, many countries' laws against sexual assault are insufficient, inconsistent, or not regularly enforced. This can leave the victim convinced that getting law enforcement involved will do no good, and in some cases could actually make things worse instead of better.

Whatever the reason for a victim's silence, the effect is that rape goes grossly underreported in many countries. It is estimated that approximately 35% of women worldwide have experienced sexual harassment in their lifetime. However, in most countries with data available on rape (including the U.S.), fewer than 40% of those women seek help—and fewer than 10% seek assistance from law enforcement. As a result, most rapists escape punishment. In the U.S., for instance, it is estimated that only 9% of rapists are prosecuted, and only 3% spend time in prison. 97% of rapists walk free.[183]

These statistics reveal that approximately 35% of women worldwide have experienced some form of sexual harassment. This also depends on what is classified as sexual harassment. It is very difficult to find any woman or girl, anywhere in the world, who would not testify of being sexually harassed sometime in their lives. If the definition of harassment does not include rape then the moment that any woman or girl leaves their home, they are constantly faced with harassment on a consistent basis. The percentage of those being harassed is much higher since most girls or women would likely not report most cases of harassment. Here are some stats on rape in America:

Every 68 seconds another American is sexually assaulted.

1 out of every 6 American women has been the victim of an attempted or completed rape in her life time (14.8% completed, 2.8% attempted)

About 3% of American men - or 1 in 33- have experienced an attempted or completed rape in their lifetime.

From 2009-2013, Child Protective Service agencies substantiated or found strong evidence to indicate that 63,000 children a year were victims of sexual abuse.

A majority of child victims are 12-17. Of victims under the age of 18: 34% of victims of sexual assault and rape are under 12 and 66% of sexual assault and rape are age 12-17.[184]

183

https://worldpopulationreview.com/country-rankings/rape-statist ics-by-country

[184]https://www.rainn.org/statistics/scope-problem#:~:text=Every%
2068%20seconds%20another%20American%20is%20sexually%2

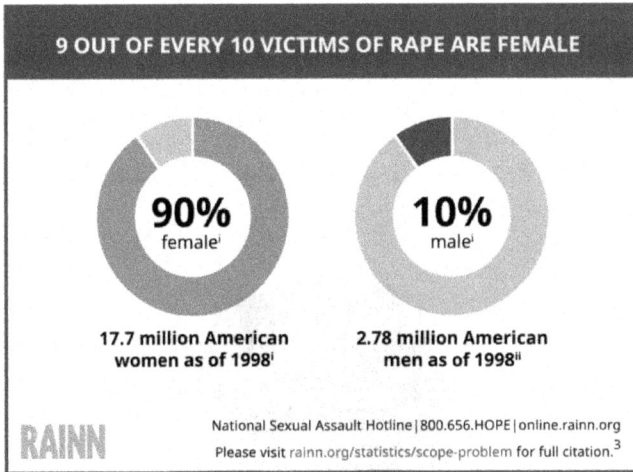

9 OUT OF EVERY 10 VICTIMS OF RAPE ARE FEMALE

90%
female[i]

10%
male[i]

17.7 million American women as of 1998[i]

2.78 million American men as of 1998[ii]

RAINN

National Sexual Assault Hotline | 800.656.HOPE | online.rainn.org

Please visit rainn.org/statistics/scope-problem for full citation.[3]

Rape stats [185]

As you can tell from these stats, the state of unwanted or forced sex through rape is pretty bleak. It is really a sad state of affairs but some little known facts have emerged from these stats. Men also report cases of rape by women. That is not a widely known fact because it may even be ridiculed and considered laughable by many who may scorn at the validity of such a possibility. How does that even happen, that a woman would rape a man? Some would say things like, how does she force him to get an erection? What is really going on? How does she force herself on him

Oassaulted.&text=1%20out%20of%20every%206,completed%2C%202.8%25%20
attempted).&text=About%203%25%20of%20American%20men,completed%20rape%20in%20the%20 lifetime.
[185]https://www.rainn.org/statistics/scope-problem#:~:text=Every%2068%20seconds%20another%20American%20is%20sexually%20assaulted.&text=1%20out%20of%20every%206,completed%2C%202.8%25%20
attempted).&text=About%203%25%20of%20American%20men,completed%20rape%20in%20the%20 lifetime.

if he objects? These are very interesting objections to ponder and think about!

Rape of Men by Women

This sounds very much like a fairy tale but it is actually happening, that women would attempt or complete rapes on men. Women are raping men at an unconceivable rate and here is the image of a rape victim below.

Image of a rape victim [186]

So rape of men by women is actually more common than society is even made aware of. Most men may even feel too ashamed to report that they were raped by a woman. The image above clearly shows the shame and disgust that a man may feel and experience after going through an attempted or completed rape. Here is a report on rape of men:

---

[186]

https://www.scientificamerican.com/article/sexual-victimization-by-women-is-more-common-than-previously-known/

In 2014, we published a study on the sexual victimization of men, finding that men were much more likely to be victims of sexual abuse than was thought. To understand who was committing the abuse, we next analyzed four surveys conducted by the Bureau of Justice Statistics (BJS) and the Centers for Disease Control and Prevention (CDC) to glean an overall picture of how frequently women were committing sexual victimization.

The results were surprising. For example, the CDC's nationally representative *data* revealed that over one year, men and women were equally likely to experience non consensual sex, and most male victims reported female perpetrators. Over their lifetime, 79 percent of men who were "made to penetrate" someone else (a form of rape, in the view of most researchers) reported female

perpetrators. Likewise, most men who experienced sexual coercion and unwanted sexual contact had female perpetrators.[187]

This is quite a disturbing trend that rape and all other forms of sexual assaults are not limited to gender but is a human problem. It is a problem of the human heart that is bent on committing evil no matter what. Women also are in desperate need for sexual pleasure and are willing to do anything in their power to get it, and rape if necessary. They want it and they want it now, with or without the consent of the male! The cases of women in their mid-twenties or early thirties have often made the headline news for raping young boys, ages 14-17.

These are often middle or high school teachers who coerce boys who are placed under their care and control for academic instruction. The reason that these women seek to

187

https://www.scientificamerican.com/article/sexual-victimization-by-women-is-more-common-than-previously-known/

do this is the same reason that men who are teachers in middle or high school would seek to rape underage girls placed under their care and control. These sexual crimes are happening on a daily basis all across the globe. Here is a rape case involving a coach and a female student: A one-time Oklahoma high school teacher and track coach allegedly raped a teenage student at his home in 2019, says authorities.

On Friday, Brandon Neal, 34, of Bixby, who resigned from Broken Arrow High School, turned himself in to police on an arrest warrant charging him with second-degree rape and sexual battery, court records show.

Authorities allege Neal and the unidentified student began a month-long sexual relationship in December of 2019 after they saw each other at The Body Masters Fitness gym in Bixby, according to the affidavit of probable cause, KMRG reports. [188]

The amount of cases of rape on middle, high school and college campuses is alarming to say the least. Your daughter or son has a very high probability of being raped by someone placed in authority over them, like a coach, teacher or administrator. This is more likely in middle and high school, where the students are minors. Here is a rape case of a 16 year old teenage boy by 26 year old female teacher:

---

[188]

https://people.com/crime/okla-teacher-allegedly-raped-student-in-his-home-while-wife-and-daughter-were-out-of-town/

Teacher Andee Lantz has been charged with raping a 16 year-old student. Pictures: Carnegie High School/ Caddo County Jail)[189]

This is how it happened:

A 26 year-old teacher took a 16 year-old boy to her house – then raped him, police say. Andee Lantz had sex with her alleged victim on two or three occasions, and also sent him a nude photo of herself, it is claimed.

Lantz, a former teacher at Carnegie High School in Caddo County, Oklahoma, was charged with rape earlier this month, and appeared in court last Wednesday. She is said to have been confronted about rumors of an inappropriate relationship with the boy in mid-November.

Both Lantz and the youngster are said to have initially denied the claims. But Lantz later began to open up and admitted she'd groomed the boy after riding around in a car with him after a homecoming game, it is alleged.

She is said to have told investigators that the boy 'leaned in and kissed her and it went from there.' Lantz brought the

---

[189]

https://metro.co.uk/2020/12/28/teacher-26-took-boy-16-to-her-house-and-raped-him-13817349/

youngster back to her house, for the first of multiple rapes she now stands accused of inflicting on him.[190]

These cases of rape are mind-blowing to say the least. The power to commit such or any other crimes or sin,for that matter, overwhelms any ability for any rational and logical thinking person. These are cases of minor children, whose lives are forever changed by people placed in their lives to provide guidance and instruction, and they dropped the ball.The lives of these rape perpetrators are also altered and destroyed forever. They will spend years in jail after destroying their lives, that of their families, and their children, not to think of the cost to society, emotional, psychological, financial and otherwise. All the years that they had invested in educating themselves in becoming a teacher, down the drain and gone. The power to have sex takes over any semblance of logic and rational thinking.This is the power of sex, the irresistible force.

But the idea of rape is as old as men have been on the earth. Rape is not a novel idea, for it has been going on as long as mankind has been on the earth. Here is a typical rape case in the bible. Potiphar's wife tried to seduce and rape Joseph. Potiphar was a high ranking political person, whose wife tried to seduce Joseph who was sold as slave to her husband. This is how it all went down:"[7] *And it came to pass after these things that his master's wife cast longing eyes on Joseph, and she said, "Lie with me.* [8] *But he refused and said to his master's wife, "Look, my master does not know what is with me in the house, and he has committed all that he has to my hand.* [9] *There is no one* greater *in this house than I, nor has he kept back anything from me but you, because you are his wife. How then can I do this great wickedness, and sin against God?"* [10] *So it was, as she spoke to Joseph day by day, that he did not heed her, to lie*

190

https://metro.co.uk/2020/12/28/teacher-26-took-boy-16-to-her-house-and-raped-him-13817349/

324

with her or to be with her. [11] But it happened about this time, when Joseph went into the house to do his work, and none of the men of the house was inside, [12] that she caught him by his garment, saying, "Lie with me." But he left his garment in her hand, and fled and ran outside, Genesis 39:7-12.

Verse 7 says that Potiphar's wife had her eyes on Joseph, and she plainly asked him in verse 7 to have sex with her and he categorically and flatly refused. She began by asking him to commit adultery with her and when that did not work, she came up with plan B. The young man, Joseph, probably recounted how his brothers tried to kill him because of jealousy and when that did not work, they sold him into slavery to traders going to Egypt. Now, by the grace of God, he was serving in a very high ranking Egyptian officer's home.

Now, the devil was again at work, passing through the woman and trying to get him to commit adultery. Joseph recognized that if the sin of adultery was to be committed, it would be a sin against God. Joseph recognized how God had kept and protected him all this while and asked how he could possibly do such a wicked deed. Having sex with the wife of his boss will be like going on a suicide mission. Not only was it a sin against God, but it would also mean a death sentence for him in the human court. So when she was unsuccessful in getting him for adultery, she now proceeded to rape as the next option. She failed to gain consent then she proceeded to force, coerce and rape. This too is the power of sex, the irresistible force.

The text in verse 10 says, "She spoke to Joseph day by day," probably meaning she was nagging him every single day about the same thing. This was a hostile work environment. Once her husband was out of the house, she probably followed Joseph around all day asking for sex and when Joseph would not give in, she had enough of the games that Joseph was playing and she moved into action to get her desires met, with or without consent. Since she failed to get consent, she now moved to rape as the only viable

325

option. She made sure that no one was in the house but the two of them, and she grabbed him as he ran out, leaving his shirt in her hand. Then she turned around and accused him of rape, and showed his shirt in her hand as evidence to her husband when he returned. Rapists sometimes do not begin as rapists.

They may initially try to seek consent and when that fails, they may move to rape and if that fails, then they may call the police and the victim may become the rapist and if that fails then other crimes, including murder, may follow. A sexual pervert will not stop until their aim and goal is achieved. But Joseph did a very brave thing that most men in the same situation would fail to do. When faced with sexual temptation, Joseph ran for his dear life. He did not sit around to toy with it, but he ran. He got out of there in a hurry. So when you are faced with such a great temptation, run! Run,run, and run, because the temptation will eat you alive. Most rapist may never stop until they get what they want while others may proceed to yet other forms of unwanted sex, including incest

Unwanted Sex by Incest

All sexual sins and crimes are terrible and sickening but incest is the lowest of the low. How can a human being descend to such a very low level of degradation? This kind of sin is beyond the pale. This is beyond animal behavior. Incestuous relationships have been happening as long as humans have populated the earth but what really is incest or an incestuous sexual relationship?

Here are some ideas about incest: Incest is human sexual activity between family members or close relatives. This typically includes sexual activity between people in consanguinity (blood relations), and sometimes those related by affinity (marriage or stepfamily), adoption, or lineage. It is strictly forbidden and considered immoral in most societies, and can lead to an increased risk of genetic disorders in children.A common justification for prohibiting incest is to avoid inbreeding, a collection of genetic disorders suffered by the children of parents with a close genetic relationship. Such children are at greater risk of congenital disorders, death, and developmental and physical disability, and that risk is proportional to their parents' coefficient of relationship- a measure of how closely the parents are related genetically.[191]This definition above prohibits any sexual activity between close relatives. It is quite interesting that some genetic disorders are associated with sexual activities with close relatives. Imagine the possibility of sexual activity between parent and child or vice versa.

 This is sexual perversion that is beyond my comprehension, that a man or woman would have sexual intercourse with the child that they gave birth to. Humans have been reduced to beyond the level of animals. Or a brother and a sister who were born of the same mother, having sexual intercourse and even getting married. Humans have been acting like this for as long as humans have been on the earth.

Here is what is happening in other cultures: In some societies, such as those of Ancient Egypt, brother-sister, father-daughter, mother-son, cousin-cousin, aunt-nephew, uncle-niece and other combinations of relations within a royal family were married as a means of perpetuating the royal lineage. Some societies have different views about what constitutes illegal or immoral incest. For example, in Samoa, marriage between a brother and an older sister was allowed, while marriage between a brother and a younger

---

191   https://en.wikipedia.org/wiki/Incest

sister was declared as unethical. However sexual relations with a first-degree relative (meaning a parent, sibling or child) are almost universally forbidden.[192]

Like it is mentioned in the Wikipedia entry, greed is driving some of these incestuous activities and marriages. The idea behind some of these is that if a man or woman is married into a family of wealth or royalty, then upon death, the royal line or wealth is transferred outside of the original royal family. Such royal or wealthy families concluded that incest was the only plausible solution to the dilemma. In these cases, royal lineages and money are the driving forces behind the decision making but in other cases, royal purity is driving the decision. Someone from the royal line would not want to marry someone who is not from the royal line. In their drive to protect the royal purity, marrying someone outside the royal line would potentially pollute the royal line. Meaning someone may potentially become king, queen, or royalty who was not part of the royal line. So they instituted incest to maintain perpetuity of the royal lineage. These are cases where money, wealth and power are the driving forces for incest. Here is an image below of Egyptian King marrying his half-sister:

---

[192]   https://en.wikipedia.org/wiki/Incest

Egyptian King, Tutankhamun married his half-sister, Ankhesenamun [193]

All the sexually deviant desires under the sun have always existed and been perpetrated by mankind which has made some sections of the population to conclude that these actions may have been sanctioned by God; after all, it is in the bible, right! Some may raise questions like, how was the world populated; if Adam only had two sons, Cain and Abel, then where did their wives come from, especially Cain's wife, since he was the older of the two? And those are fair and logical objections!

Who was Cain's Wife?

The identity of Cain's wife and how God populated the earth through Adam and Eve has raised all kinds of questions and speculations. Some have made this a classic case of incest. According to the biblical record, Adam and his wife Eve had two sons, Cain and Abel, and later Seth.No

---

[193]   https://en.wikipedia.org/wiki/Incest

other children or sisters are mentioned, so then how did Cain procreate? There are seemingly only two possible solutions to this apparent dilemma: Either Cain had children with his mother (highly unlikely), or Adam and Eve gave birth to girls who are not listed in the biblical record. Some have even suggested that Cain may have met his wife in the land of Nod, where he fled after killing his brother, Abel.

Other sources outside the bible have other suggestions as to the identity of Cain's wife. One such source is the"book of Jubilees". This book was rejected as part of the accepted books included in the biblical canon. Here are some facts about the "book of Jubilees:"*The book of jubilees sometimes called, Lesser Genesis (Leptogenesis), is an ancient Jewish religious work of 50 chapters (1341 verses), considered Canonical by the Ethiopian Orthodox Church as well as Beta Israel (Ethiopian Jews), where it is known as the book of Divisions.* [194]

This book, which was not accepted as part of the biblical canon, mentioned and identified a lady named "Awan" as a sister of Cain, whom he took as wife and here is the quote: *Jubilee makes an incestuous reference regarding the son of Adam and Eve, Cain, and his wife, in chapter iv (1-12) (Cain and Abel). It mentions that Cain took his sister Awan to be his wife and Enoch was their child.*[195] The question that immediately pops up in my mind is one of biblical inerrancy. Is the bible without error and can it be trusted as the infallible word of God?

The book of Jubilees was completed in its final form at about 100 BC, according to britannica.com[196] and so this

194   https://en.wikipedia.org/wiki/Book_of_Jubilees
195   https://en.wikipedia.org/wiki/Book_of_Jubilees
196   https://www.britannica.com/topic/Book-of-Jubilees

would make the writing of the Pentateuch by Moses and the giving of the Law at Mount Sinai thousands of years older than the book of Jubilees. How did they come up with the identity of the wife of Cain? The biblical record does not explicitly tell us. How and where did the writers of that book get that name which Moses did not tell us? The idea that Cain was married to one of his sisters is a likely possibility because most often, God would only mention characters in the genealogy who are part of the biblical narrative that God is conveying in the immediate context, and to us by extension.

Adam and Eve could have possibly had other sons and daughters other than Cain and Abel, and the rest were most likely not part of the biblical narrative and they were left out, although not necessarily ignored. This is what was said about what Jesus wrote: "And many other signs truly Jesus did in the presence of His disciples, which are not written in this book: But these are written, that you might believe that Jesus is the Christ, the Son of God; and that believing, you might have life through His name," John 20:30-31. Jesus went on to say in that very text that if all that He did was recorded, the books of the world would not be able to contain them. So it is very likely that Cain married his sister even though the bible does not mention that he had any sisters. In the genealogy from Adam to Noah in Genesis 5, no women are mentioned but that does not mean that there were no women or that they were not important.

The family lineage was often continued through men and more important was that the lineage was often continued through God's plan of redemption of mankind. God included 4 women in Matthew's genealogy in Matthew chapter 1. The genealogy in Genesis 5:1 went from Adam to Seth and bypassed Cain. God's plan of redemption was through Seth and Cain was not even mentioned. Abel was already murdered by Cain. And in Genesis 5:28, it mentioned that Lamech begat a son, and in verse 29, it identified the son of Lamech as Noah but in verse 30, it said that Lamech begat a son and daughters. The bottomline is that God will only mention any character that is important for the narrative in that context, and omit – not ignore – what is not necessary.

Some would conclude that Cain married his sister, which was an incestuous marriage, and that could give grounds to justify incestuous marriages or sexual relationships today, in their opinion. Some would argue that if this truly happened and it is in the bible then it must be okay, really? This truly happened, but it does not give grounds for incestuous sexual relationships of any kind today. God allowed incest temporarily, it does not mean that He okayed or approved of it. He allowed it for a limited amount of time to fulfill His divine prerogatives.

He had given a command to Adam and Eve to multiply and fill the earth with people. Then, how else were they to obey God's command if they were only two of them upon the earth? How else would their children help in that endeavor unless a brother and a sister by blood were to get married? Once the earth was populated over thousands of years, then very extended cousins and nieces that are several generations apart could get married and it would not be considered incestuous because the blood line would become so diluted that there would be no closeness to the original bloodline.

And there was no law against incest during that time because everyone would potentially be a law breaker since the only person available to be your wife was related to you by blood directly. It really made no sense to pass any incest laws then, because 100% of the people would break the law. The prohibition against incest was not given until Leviticus 18:6-18, when the earth was well populated. Incest was not a sin then because there was no law against it. That did not mean that it was okay, but only that God did not hold it against the people because there was no law. Here is what God said through the Apostle Paul: "For the law brings wrath, but where there is no law there is no transgression," Romans 4:15.

So let's say that your state suddenly passed a new law against speeding over 50 miles per hour on some highway that is going to take effect January 1, 2023. You find yourself driving 70 miles per hour on the same highway on December 10th, 2022. Even though your action is bad, you are not a law breaker because there is no law against it when you committed that act, and so was the case with incest committed before the institution of the law in Leviticus 18. So anyone involved in incest, and other sexual immorality or any sin for that matter is clearly a law breaker in need of repentance and without which, sex becomes an irresistible and uncontrollable passion of love.

Chapter 11

The Power of Love and Sex

Love and sex are arguably the most powerful forces in the universe, and their effects have far reaching consequences. Love is probably the most powerful force in the universe. People get into all kinds of unhealthy emotional states simply because they feel unloved and unwanted. People are in desperate search for love and for someone, anyone, to love and care about them. Love is one of those attributes of God that has been planted into the human DNA. Millions of people around the world are facing all kinds of emotional issues simply because they do not feel loved.

People are fearful, stressed, lonely, anxious, and depressed. Sex and love attract and draw people together such that they become inseparable, and that power is finally evidenced in the marriage union between a man and woman. This power of love is invincible, yet so potent that it grabs the human soul and spirit. The power is unexplainable and unstoppable. Love is considered to be one of the most important human emotions, and yet the least understood and most misunderstood.

Is love a feeling? Is love biological? Is love cultural? Love is like breathing air or drinking water to a human! A life without love is catastrophic to put it mildly and it is detrimental to the human psyche. All kinds of songs and music have been composed for love. Love is like eating food and drinking water, we perish without it. But what is really the mystery behind love? People spend their entire time on earth searching for love and most die empty without finding it. Love seems elusive; it seems, as soon as you get closer, it gets further away. Humans need to love and be loved.

All kinds of ideas have been advanced to define love but what is love? Here are some ideas about love from the psychological community: Love is a set of emotions and behaviors characterized by intimacy, passion, and commitment. It involves care, closeness, protectiveness, attraction, affection, and trust. Love can vary in intensity and can change over time. It is associated with a range of positive emotions, including happiness, excitement, life satisfaction, and euphoria, but it can also result in negative emotions such as jealousy and stress.1

When it comes to love, some people would say it is one of the most important *human emotions*. Yet despite being one of the most studied behaviors, it is still the least understood. For example, researchers debate whether love is a biological or cultural phenomenon.

Love is most likely influenced by both biology and culture. Although hormones and biology are important, the way we express and experience love is also influenced by our personal conceptions of love.[197]

What is Love?

As I said earlier, love is probably the most complex subject on the planet and that is why you may ask ten people to define love and you may just get ten different responses. Everybody wants love but hardly anyone knows what love is. The quote above defines love as," a set of emotions and behaviors characterized by intimacy, passion, and commitment." So the view here is that love is "a set of

---

[197]   https://www.verywellmind.com/what-is-love-2795343

emotions and behaviors," and this is their basic definition of love and as a derivative of that, comes intimacy, passion, and commitment. Here is a definition of love by one dictionary: noun a profoundly tender, passionate affection for another person.A feeling of warm personal attachment or deep affection, as for a parent, child, or friend. sexual passion or desire.[198]

Love is defined here as a "feeling of warm personal attachment or deep affection." The key takeaway from this definition is that love is a feeling. The former definition says love is an "emotion." The societal understanding of love is that it is emotional. Love is understood in emotional terms. This definition rightly identifies "deep affection, for a parent, child, friend and sexual passion or desire," as love. The lumping of a diverse category of relationships under a singular category has done little to help in our English understanding of love.

Another aspect is that love is widely understood to be a stative verb. These are verbs that describe a state or a condition of being rather than dynamic verbs that describe an action. This understanding of love has done irreparable damage to a vast majority of the populous. It is widely believed, from the laity to academia, that love is an emotion and a feeling of some sort. It is all about how I feel and whether it makes me feel good. Whether love is used as a noun or a verb in English, its meaning is often emotional and feelings-oriented. But is that really the case? The idea of love being a feeling or emotion is actually foreign to the bible. Love is most often portrayed in a dynamic sense rather than a stative.

---

[198]   https://www.dictionary.com/browse/love

Love is an action, and before we get into love being an action, let's get into the different kinds of love. The word love, in English,is understood in the general and generic sense and only the context would shed some light into what they are actually talking about. There is a saying that the Greeks have a word for everything and that saying is largely true, since love is no exception. The Greeks have at least four different words that are translated as love into our English language. Here are the four kinds of love:

Storge -Love due to family ties

This word identifies love based on family ties, parent-child love, or sibling-love; this bond flows naturally, with no strings attached. You were born in the same family and you know that they are your parent, sibling, uncle, aunt, cousin. Here is how Wikipedia puts it:

Storge (storgē, Greek: στοργή) is *liking someone through the fondness of familiarity, family members or people who relate in familiar ways that have otherwise found themselves bonded by chance. An example is the natural love and affection of a parent for their child. It is described as the most natural, emotive, and widely diffused of loves: It is natural in that it is present without coercion, emotive because it is the result of fondness due to familiarity, and most widely diffused because it pays the least attention to those characteristics deemed "valuable" or worthy of love and, as a result, is able to transcend most discriminating factors. Lewis describes it as a dependency-based love which risks extinction if the needs cease to be met.*

Affection, for Lewis, included both Need-love and Gift-love. He considered it responsible for $\frac{9}{10}$ of all solid and lasting human happiness.[8]

However, affection's strength is also what makes it vulnerable. Affection has the appearance of being "built-in" or "ready-made", says Lewis, and as a result, people come to expect it irrespective of their behavior and its natural consequences.[9] Both in its Need and its Gift form, affection then is liable to "go bad", and to be corrupted by such forces as jealousy, ambivalence and smothering.[199] You are born into this love relationship and there isn't much that you can do to alter this natural bond. Another kind of love is philia.

Philia - Love among friends

This is the kind of love that is among friends and people with no blood or sexual ties. This kind of love grows out of companionship. Sometimes, the bond among friends is stronger than the love among blood relatives. You may often hear that a good friend is better than a bad brother or sister. To really call someone a friend who is not related to you by blood is deep. This is more than a casual acquaintance. This is someone who has been tested and trusted. This is someone who is dependable. This is someone who defends your interests in your absence. A brother or sister is a love by blood but a friend is a love by choice. That is why a friend may be there for you through thick and thin but a blood brother or sister may abandon you.

Here is a quote about a close friend: "A man that hath friends must show himself friendly: and there is a friend that sticks closer than a brother,"Proverbs 18:24. Friendship is a very powerful force and to call anyone a friend is powerful. This friend who sticks closer than a brother may happen in this life but the ultimate friend who sticks closer than any

---

[199]   https://en.wikipedia.org/wiki/The_Four_Loves

brother is Jesus Christ, Himself. Jesus Christ is the ultimate friend. A friend who will never forsake you. A friend forever.

Here is another quote: *A friend loves at all times, And a brother is born for adversity,* Proverbs 17:17. This verse talks about a kind of friend who loves at all times. This kind of friendship will never let you down and he is there besides you, in good and bad times. This is a friend whom you can call at 2 AM in the morning and he will happily come to your assistance. While there are friends like that who walk the earth, this kind of friendship can only be completely fulfilled in Christ Jesus. Even our trusted childhood friend may turn on us at some point. Maybe your friend becomes jealous because of your success.

Jesus is the only true friend who can truly love at all times. The key word in the text is "all," and only Jesus has the ability to fulfill this verse. No human friend has the ability and capacity to love 100 percent of the time. The next part of the verse says that, "a brother is born for adversity," and what does this really mean? Some think that this verse means that a brother will stick with brother during tough times and adversity but I doubt this to be the case! If that were true then it will directly contradict Proverbs 18:24, which says that a friend sticks closer than a brother. We have to consider the genre of literature that is involved here! We are dealing with Hebrew poetry and not prose. And in poetry, the second poetic line restates the first poetic line with a sharper focus. So a brother, being born for adversity, is actually restating "a friend loves at all times," with a sharper emphasis.

You cannot read this passage like you are reading prose but if you do then you will end up with an erroneous understanding of the passage. Jesus's own brothers were against Him and the bible is filled with many such stories and some in our own lives as well. A brother who is born for adversity is restating the bond between friends who love at all times.

A friend who loves at all times is born for adversity and will never abandon his friend in troubled times. So that is exactly why they are born for adversity. Hear what Jesus said: *"This is My commandment, that you love one another, just as I have loved you. Greater love has no one than this, that a person will lay down his life for his friends. You are My friends if you do what I command you.No longer do I call you slaves, for the slave does not know what his master is doing; but I have called you friends, because all things that I have heard from My Father I have made known to you, John 15:12-15.*

This is what it means that a brother is born for adversity, he suffers for his friends. This was all fulfilled in Jesus Christ, who is the Friend of Friends and the Friend of all Friends. He is the friend who sticks closer than a brother. He is the friend who loves at all times. He is the brother who is born for adversity. Jesus likens the one who obeys Him as His friend. A friend signifies closeness and a bond. A true friend would hardly do anything to hurt you but a brother or sister, just might. A true friend definitely sticks closer than a brother. This section is dealing with the love among friends, which is philia love. philia is a noun and phileo is the verb form. But in this verse above, where it says: "Greater love has no one than this, that a person would will lay down his life for his friends," John 15:13. The Greek word that is used in this text for love is "agape," which is not the love among friends. This is sacrificial and unconditional love.

This is radical love that the world cannot comprehend. This is the perfection of love. This is the apex of love. There is no greater love. People have gone to the highest mountains in the world in search for love and could find none greater;

some have ventured into the deepest ocean below, in search of love and could find none greater, others have traveled to every city in the world, hunting down love and could find none greater, yet still others have had sex with over a 1000 partners, desperately searching for love and could find none greater. Solomon, the wisest man who ever lived, had over 800 wives and 300 concubines, yet he was still searching. Your search is over! Search no more! Stop searching!

Still looking for love? Fall in love with Jesus! I will hear people say, "I have fallen in love," and I will say to myself, "what do they really mean?" but I guess, what they may really mean is "infatuation," and someone has taken over their mind. They are unable to sleep, think and function. The thoughts about the other person have taken control of their mind. Get infatuated with Jesus Christ and let Him be the love of your life, for greater love has no one than this, that a person would lay down his life for his friends. But sex is used synonymous with love and that leads us to the next kind of love, eros.

Eros-Erotic Love

Eros is the Greek word for love that is demonstrated through the passion of sex and from this word, we get our English word, erotic. So through this word, sex has become synonymous with love. You may often hear phrases like, "I made love with that person," to mean that they had sexual intercourse with that person. Here is one definition of eros:

Of the four Greek terms that describe love in the bible, eros is probably the most familiar today. It's easy to make the connection between eros and our modern word, "erotic." And there are certainly similarities between those two terms- as well as a few differences. Eros is the Greek term that describes romantic or sexual love. The term portrays the idea of passion and intensity of feeling. The word was originally connected with the goddess Eros of Greek mythology. The meaning of eros is slightly different from our term "erotic," because we often associate "erotic" with ideas or practices that are naughty or inappropriate. That wasn't the case with eros. Instead, eros describes the healthy, common expressions of physical love. In the Scriptures, eros primarily **refers to** those expressions of love carried out between a husband and wife.[200]

Eros was actually sexual activity in the context of a God ordained marital union but that understanding has shifted to mean mostly sexual activity outside the context of marriage. Unfortunately, the idea of eros or erotic is being almost exclusively used to refer to explicit sexual acts or activities. You may hear of terms like erotic dances and here is how a Wikipedia entry defines it: An ***erotic dance*** *is a **dance** that provides erotic entertainment and whose objective is the stimulation of **erotic** or **sexual** thoughts or **actions** in viewers. Erotic dance is one of several major dance categories based on purpose, such as **ceremonial, competitive, performance** and **social dance**.*

The erotic dancer's *clothing* is often minimal, and may be gradually decreased or eliminated altogether. In some areas of the United States where exposure of *nipples* or *genitalia* is illegal, a dancer may wear *pasties* and *g-strings* to stay within the law.[201] So anything eros or erotic is now mostly understood to mean sexual excitement, entertainment, and pleasure. People long for such pleasure and entertainment and will do just about anything to get it. Eros was so misused around biblical times by the pagan culture that the Greek

---

200

https://www.learnreligions.com/what-is-eros-love-700682
201   https://en.wikipedia.org/wiki/Erotic_dance

word, eros doesn't even appear in the entire NewTestament. The idea of erotic love is no doubt found in the Old Testament Song of Solomon. Eros is not inherently evil if the erotic sex is performed in the context of a God ordained marital union. Any

marriage that is built on eros and constant sexual arousal is doomed to fail. Eros is important but a marriage can only be sustained through another kind of love, agape.

Agape -Unconditional Love

This is the ultimate kind of love and it is radical. This is love with no strings attached and seeks nothing in return. This kind of love originates with God and is not found in humans unless infused by God. This is sacrificial love and it originates only with God. This is unilateral and unconditional love that God alone possesses and bestows upon undeserving sinners as He pleases. This kind of love is foreign to the human DNA and can only be imputed by God. All other kinds of love are naturally experienced by humans except this. Humans are naturally void of Agape love except it be imputed to them. The very idea of unconditional love is not available to humans. We, by nature, show love and affection to friends and families as they, in the same measure, show affection to us. We are naturally only able to love those who love us and this is conditional love.

This is all conditional. So agape love radically invades the human species according to the will of God. So what really is agape love? This is the kind of love that puts the interest of others ahead of yours; this is the kind of love that compels us to have compassion on people who have done us harm; this is the kind of love that is bestowed by Christ upon undeserving, disobedient, rebellious sinners as us. The Son of God went to the cross to sacrifice His life because of agape. He loved the world (elect) and sent His Son to atone for their sin. We, the human race, have a tendency and capacity to love only those that love us and that would be storge or phileo, but not agape.

And the kind of love that we naturally exercise towards one another would be "phileo," love among friends, or "storge," love among family members. The origin of agape kind of love is from God and as humans, we are incapable of giving that kind of love because we are not born with it. Here is what Jesus said: *You have heard that it has been said, you shall love your neighbor, and hate your enemy, But I say unto you, Love your enemies, bless them that curse you, do good to them that hate you, pray for them which despitefully use you, and persecute you,* Matthew 5:43-44. The Lord moved from a natural love, which is a love for your neighbor, to a love for people who treat you well, like friends

344

and family, would qualify as neighbors. These are people who would reciprocate love.

This is a very friendly environment to express love. The easiest thing to do is to express love to people who express love back to you. Jesus was expressly restating what was said in the Old Testament when He said, "you have heard it said," and He moved to giving of a new law, since He was the ultimate law giver, when He said, "But I say," "you shall love your enemies." He essentially raised the bar and gave a new law that raised the bar. This raises the bar from possibility to impossibility. We are not capable of loving whoever we identify as enemies. This is a radical love that has to be imputed to us. This is really mission impossible. We are commanded to do something that we, in our natural state, lack the desire and ability to do.

We hardly have the desire and capacity to truly love our neighbor, talk less of loving our enemies? We are further told to bless them that curse us, really? This is not possible in our natural state. Doing good to those who hate you is quite amazing and interesting. God has to impute into the heart these abilities for them to be realized. So what then is the source of this kind of love? Where did it come from? How are we told to do something that we simply lack the capacity to do?

God is Love

This is an amazing definition of love by simply stating that God is love. It is just that simple. Here is what the Apostle John said: [7] Beloved, let us love one another, for love is from God, and whoever loves has been born of God and knows God. [8] Anyone who does not love does not know God, because God is love. [9] In this the love of God was made manifest among us, that God sent his only Son into the world, so that we might live through him. [10] In this is love, not that we have loved God but that he loved us and sent his Son to be the propitiation for our sins. [11] Beloved, if God so loved us, we also ought to love one another. [12] No one has ever seen God; if we love one another, God abides in us and his love is perfected in us, 1 John 4:7-12.

This verse identifies the source of love as from God and the source of this agape, sacrificial kind of love is from God and we do not naturally possess it and it goes on at the end of verse 7 to say that anyone who loves has been born of God and knows God. Unless someone has been justified and regenerated, they are incapable of loving. So then the capacity and ability to love (agape kind of love) is imputed to the elect at the moment of justification. So with justification also come new abilities, including love. Agape kind of love is more evidence that we truly know Him as love, which is also a fruit of the Spirit.

Then it goes to say in verse 8 that a loveless life is evidence of an unregenerate heart. A life without love is evidence of not being a follower of Jesus Christ. If someone finds trouble loving their enemy, finds trouble doing good to those who hate their guts then it may be because they are not born again, born from above or saved. This kind of radical love must show up in your life if you claim to know God. And the verse ends with a philosophical argument: "because God is love."

It is simply saying that since God is love, then in order to love, you must be connected or attached to the source of love, who is God. If anyone is not connected to God, they cannot have the ability and capacity to love because they are not hooked to the source and power, which is love. One of God's essential attributes is love and He imputes that attribute to mankind as He pleases. So an unregenerate person is not able to obey God's command to love their enemies, simply because God's love is not in them and they therefore lack any such ability to obey. So the saying, "God is love," implies God's DNA is love. The saying that God is love is made up of two nouns, God, love and the verb, "is," separating them. If this were a mathematical equation then it would be God equals love, or God = love. God and love would be considered equal sides of the equation. Love is not used here as an adjective that is descriptive or describing something about God. But the word is a noun stating and not describing who God is. Understanding love is somewhat elusive to many; Love is active and not passive.

Love is an action taken for the benefit of someone else who is undeserving and unable to recompense the action taken. Love is always looking for an opportunity to do good, seeking nothing in return. Here is love in action: *In this the love of God was made manifest among us, that God sent His only Son so that we may live through Him*, 1 John 4:9.This is love in action and this verse is like John 3:16, where the love of God prompted Him to give His son. And in verse 10 in the verse above it says that the only reason that we love God is because He first loved us. God is the first cause and without Him loving us, we are incapable of loving Him. And love covers sin.

Love Covers Sin

One of the easiest ways to disarm your enemy is to love them. I understand that this may sound counter intuitive but it is the truth. I am not advocating that anyone should enable sinful conduct, but something miraculous happens when we give love to someone who is expecting hate and revenge. They are flabbergasted, to say the least. I have personally experienced doing good to someone who had treated me very unkindly, and their reaction was unbelievable. They were expecting me to return evil for evil but I returned evil with good, and love is what will compel anyone to return evil with good. Here is what the apostle Peter said: *Above all, love each other deeply, because love covers over a multitude of sins,* 1 Peter 4:8. The love of God is a disarming force that stops further sin dead in its tracks.

Let's say that someone insults you and you insult them in return. Then the person gets angry and comes to your home and vandalizes your car that was parked outside your driveway. You also get angry and tell him, "I will be right back;" now you are really heated, as you are driving back to your house, ten minutes away, doing 90 miles per hour in a 40 miles per hour zone and get stopped and ticketed by the police for wreck- less driving. Now you return with your loaded 45 millimeter handgun and the person's head is blown off. You happen to be a resident of Virginia or Texas and you are charged and tried for murder. The jury finds you guilty and you are sentenced to death. Now, you are taken into custody, put on death row, awaiting execution. You leave behind 6 children and a wife for someone else to enjoy your wife; you leave behind parents and siblings, and a host of other family members. Now, this sounds pretty much like fiction but it is actually happening all across America and the globe.

Now, imagine the emotional and financial toll that this decision has brought upon this person, and his innocent children, wife and family. The emotional and financial toll cannot really be quantified. You cannot put a price on children growing up without their dad! But all these could have been avoided if one party to the dispute showed love instead of retaliation. You return evil with good. If they insult you to your face then in return, find something kind to do to them, and the Spirit of God will certainly reveal to you what you should do and that will blow their mind. Remember that you can only do this if God's love is in your heart. You can only give what you have and you cannot do good if good is not in your heart. Here is what Paul said: *[17] Never repay evil for evil to anyone. Respect what is right in the sight of all people. [18] If possible, so far as it depends on you, be at peace with all people. [1]*

Never take your own revenge, beloved, but leave room for the wrath of God, for it is written: "VENGEANCE IS MINE, I WILL REPAY," says the Lord. [20] "BUT IF YOUR ENEMY IS HUNGRY, FEED HIM; IF HE IS THIRSTY, GIVE HIM A DRINK; FOR IN SO DOING YOU WILL HEAP BURNING COALS ON HIS HEAD." [21] Do not be overcome by evil, but overcome evil with good, Romans 12:17-21. We live in a world that is constantly being bombarded by evil but the injunction here is to overcome evil with good. The word"love," is not in this text above but love is all over the text. The primary motivation for doing good is love, without which, we cannot do any lasting good. Love is at the root of any unconditional act of good ever taken by any human being and that love is imputed and not natural love. And I will also include the love that a husband has for his wife.

Husband's Love for his Wife-Agape love

You may often hear a husband talk about loving his wife but if you were to probe further to find out what they really mean by love, you may find that they may have something completely different in mind. Even in marriages, love is mostly understood to mean eros or erotic. It is definitely true that eros or romantic love is very important in a marriage but a marriage needs more than eros to sustain it. Eros is emotional and fluctuating and may hardly sustain the marriage during challenging times. So love (agape) in a marriage is very challenging but God commands that agape be part of a marriage. Even for those who are regenerate, real agape love is a constant challenge.

Husbands are commanded to love (agape) their wives and this is not erotically but unconditionally and sacrificially. When most men hear the word love, they immediately think erotic and so this agape kind of love is foreign to men. So God is asking men to do something that men are not naturally equipped to do. This is a radical, out of this world kind of love. No wonder marriages have all kinds of problems sometimes, because men simply fall-short of this radical kind of love. Here is what the apostle Paul said concerning this kind of love: *Husbands, love your wives just as Christ loved the church and gave himself up for her*, Ephesians 5:25. Husbands are here commanded to love (agape) their wives.

This is imperative and not optional. Not something that should happen if husbands feel like loving; not something that husbands should do after she has cooked a good meal; not something that he should do after a good night on the bed together and in the arms of each other; not something that he should do if she is acting right and doing all the right things. This love should continue unabated even when she refuses to give you sex; this love should continue unhitched even when she refuses to cook for you; this love should continue unhindered even when she insults you to your face and insults her in-laws. You may be calling me crazy at this point and calling me all kinds of names.

You may be saying to me at this point, "Hey dude, you don't know my situation and this woman is really crazy," and you may even be saying to me, "Hey dude, you don't know what you are talking about," and I kind of get it! I kind of get where you are coming from! You just made my case for me and that is the whole point. We simply do not have the ability and capacity to love the unlovable. We are commanded to do something that is outside our ability to obey. That is why it is easier to go to the moon than to love the unlovable. After the command to love your wife, the next part of the verse says, "Just as Christ loves the church." Wow! Are you kidding me? This is a very tall order! The standard of the husband's love for his wife is measured against Christ's love for His church.

It is then no surprise that just about every man fails to meet the standard that has been set by Christ. Love is demonstrated by action. The proof that Christ loved His bride, the church, was that He gave up Himself for her so husbands are also to give up themselves for their wives, (maybe not literally but at least, figuratively). You may often hear a man say to his wife, "Hey babe, I love you." Now, what does that really mean? This is love, sex, and marriage in action. This is the power of love and sex. The irresistible force. Sex is an integral part of the expression of love but real love transcends sex. So let us not get anxious, weary and hopeless when we find ourselves unable to love like we should, for Christ is our hope and He will fill our cup when we run dry.

Chapter 12

The Power of Hope

So is there any hope for mankind in the midst of a world that is engulfed in uncontrollable sexual desires and other kinds of sins? Sexual immorality is ravaging the world, damaging lives and leaving a trail of blood in its path. Sex and sexual thoughts have taken over the minds of people. Things look pretty bleak, thinking about the millions of babies who have been murdered through abortion. The millions of people who have died after contracting all kinds of STDs.

The marriages that have been destroyed through acts of adultery and the number of innocent children impacted through no fault of theirs. The perverted ideas about sex and its after effects. The effects of pornography and uncontrollable sexual desires and its after effects on families and communities. The total and complete departure from God's plan and desire for sex and its after effects.

Sex is not a game and the human body is not to be used primarily for pleasure. Pleasure is a by-product of sex and not the foundational purpose thereof. Unfortunately, pleasure is the driving force behind the majority of sexual decisions and impulses. Sex is broken and needs to be restored. Sex has become a commodity and boys, girls, men and women are selling their bodies in exchange for income. This is not the plan of God for sex yet millions are on this path. Sexual addiction is taking the world as a storm and so what is the possible solution? Should we just throw in the towel?

Millions of people sincerely desire to be freed from any type of addiction, be it sexual or otherwise. They are in desperate need to get out from under the power of despair and addiction. They are lost and simply do not know how and where to start. They are hopeless and addiction has placed a grip on them. Addiction of any-kind, places someone in bondage and under the control of whatever that person is addicted to. Their addiction brings them to a state of utter despair.

Even the ability to recognize that you are in trouble is a good starting point. That means that you hate your situation and are desiring a change. This is true for addiction and equally true for anyone living in sin of any kind. Admitting that you are in trouble and in need of help and hope is the best thing that can ever happen. This is the beginning of hope and the healing process. Hope is the vehicle that keeps you going when you don't feel like going for another day. When there is no hope,it is like a car that runs out of gasoline by the side of the road.

Here is some experience with hopelessness posted on psychologytoday.com,:My first November as a professional writer wasn't an easy one. My only client failed to pay his bill, I was receiving more rejections than assignments, my arthritis was flaring and my cat got $1,200-worth-of-vet-bills sick. I didn't know how I was going to make my house payment and my stomach was upset. I stopped sleeping. But, I never stopped hoping. I believed that I could make this writing business work, and I set to work making that happen.[202] Hopelessness is faced

202

https://www.psychologytoday.com/us/blog/imperfect-spirituality/201902/why-hope-matters

and experienced every day by people in all kinds of situations.

Financial crises, health crises, emotional crises and the list is somewhat endless that can trigger hopelessness. Just about anyone who is having suicidal ideation, attempted or completed suicide, is not necessarily because they want to die but it is mostly because they have lost the hope to live. They have successfully convinced themselves that no one cares about them, that they have no value and no one will really miss them when they are gone. This may not be true but they have wrestled with these beliefs and convinced themselves to be true.

According to psychologists, hope helps us fight for another day and don't give-up. Here is some of their comments: Research indicates that hope can help us manage stress and anxiety and cope with adversity. It contributes to our well-being and happiness and motivates positive action. Hopeful people believe they can influence their goals, that their efforts can have a positive impact. They are also more likely to make healthy choices to eat better, exercise, or do the other things that will help them move towards what they are hoping for.

Then, other positive emotions such as courage and confidence (self-efficacy) and happiness also emerge. They become our coping strategy, these emotions are crucial in helping us survive. They allow us to take a wider view of life, and become more creative in our approach and problem solving, and retain our optimism.

Hope isn't delusional. It isn't denial. It doesn't ignore the real challenges, details of the diagnosis, or dwindling money in the checking account. It is not woo-woo thinking.[203] This is the kind of hope that depends on us to pull ourselves out of any given situation in which we find ourselves. This is a subjective kind of hope. There may come times in our lives when this kind of hope may simply fail us. So hope cannot work alone but works in conjunction with its sibling, faith. Hope is not a stand alone concept but works hand-in-hand with faith and they are like twin-brothers. If you see one then you will see the other around the corner.

Hope and Faith Connection

Hope without faith is dead. Hope is intricately tied and interwoven with faith. Hope is about future events that have not yet occurred and faith has to be incorporated into hope for hope to be materialized. Here is how the writer of the book of Hebrews defines faith: *Now faith is the certainty of things* hoped *for, a proof of things not seen,* Hebrews 11:1. This is actually diving into the supernatural and some people may initially have difficulty grabbing this concept. If you truly believe something about God then it's like it has already happened. Faith actualizes hope and makes it real and tangible.

Faith makes hope tangible. If you truly have faith then it has already happened and that is hope. You do not hope for what you see already but faith makes hope real. Here is what is said by the writer of Hebrews again: *But without faith it is impossible to please Him, for he who comes to God must believe that He is, and that He is a rewarder of those who diligently seek Him,* Hebrews 11:6. When you believe in a future event because God said it then that is real

---

203

https://www.psychologytoday.com/us/blog/imperfect-spirituality/201902/why-hope-matters

and tangible hope. It has already happened just because God said it. That is why hope in the context of the hope-faith-connection is critically important. This is objective hope as opposed to subjective hope. This is not a wishful thinking kind of hope. There is just one problem! This special kind of hope is only available to those who are part of God's family.

The world is experiencing plenty of hopelessness but only those who are in God's family are experiencing real peace. So you may ask a simple question, "How can I experience real peace, joy and hope?" That is a very sober and interesting question! How do we become part of God's family if we were originally and naturally not part of His family? Let's say that you were to contact Jeff Bezos, the owner and founder of Amazon and the wealthiest person on earth and say to him that you wanted to be part of his family and he may think that you may be mentally unstable. He did not give birth to you and how can you possibly be asking to be part of his family? There are only two ways in which you could become part of Jeff Bezos's family. (1) He had sexual intercourse with a woman, (or his wife) and out of that sexual union, you were born or (2) you were adopted into his family.

It does not matter if you were his natural born child or his adopted child, you have equal rights to inherit all his assets equally as the natural born child. Adoption brings you to equal status as the natural born child. Jeff Bezos has a net worth of about 105 billion dollars and I mean billions with a (B). You stand a chance to inherit a portion of that if he will only sovereignly make a decision to elect and adopt you as one of his children. This decision is completely his to make and you cannot bribe, coerce or influence him into making his adoption decision.

The goal of adoption is primarily, to bring hope to a life. To give hope where there is hopelessness. To give meaning and purpose to a life. Why would someone board a plane and travel to a foreign country to adopt a one year old baby? Hope should be the driving force behind such a decision. The adopted baby has no control or say in the decision. The decision was made by the adopter to choose or elect this child out of billions of hopeless children in the world. God wants to adopt you out of billions of sinners, hopeless and sexual perverts in the world. God's adoption process begins with Him electing or choosing you for adoption and you have no control in the process for you are passive in the process.

God Elects You for Adoption into His Family

For adoption into God's family to occur, election has to happen first. There is ongoing debate about man's election by God and man's freedom of the "will"to either join God's family or reject to join God's family on our own terms. Imagine a one year old baby having to make a decision to allow themselves to be adopted or to reject the adoption altogether. The person doing the adoption has all the power and the one being adopted has no power at-all in the process of election and adoption. This is a sample portrait of election and salvation.

But who are really the elect? The elect are those whom God had hand-picked from eternity past and He also granted them the faith to believe in Him for salvation. These are also those whom He will bring to glory. Here is what God said about those whom He had chosen:"According as he hath chosen us in him before the foundation of the world, that we should be holy and without blame before him in

357

love," Ephesians 1:4. Election is totally and completely an act of God without any human participation and involvement. The text says that God chose or elected us (the elect) in Him (meaning in Christ). The location of our election was in Christ. The elect were placed in Christ. The elect were taken out of the world and placed in Christ. Now we are told where it happens, the location and that is in Christ, but when did it all happen? When were the elect placed in Christ? Did it happen when they joined a local church? Did it happen when they got baptized? Did it happen at some church event after someone preached and made an altar call?

This is quite an interesting and puzzling question! The text above gives us a clue! It says that the elect were placed in Christ "before the foundation of the world." Wow! This is quite amazing! If you are one of God's elect, then know that God elected and set you apart for Him and placed you in Christ before the creation of all things. And because it is a work of God, then you can never lose your salvation. Christ will take you into heaven, and you will be with Him forever, guaranteed, and this is genuine hope, not some wishful thinking.

No one knows who the elect are, but we are commanded to preach Christ to all the nations because faith comes by hearing and hearing by the word of God, Romans 10:17. So then, what is the purpose of God in electing some? Removal of sin is the primary purpose for election. God is assembling people from every nation, tribe and tongue to be with Him in heaven forever, and those whom He elects must be holy and blameless. Sinful people cannot inhabit heaven. No one enters heaven in their sinful state. No one ventures into God's presence unless they are holy. Thus the saying: Blessed are the pure in heart for they shall see God, Matthew 5:8. Holiness is a prerequisite to see and enter God's presence and only those whose sins have been atoned for will see God.

The one being adopted is passive in the adoption process. Election by God to be adopted into His family is probably the most humbling teaching in all of the bible. Election takes away any iota of human pride to have earned the right to be part of God's family. Here are a few things that God says about election: " You did not choose Me but I chose you, and appointed you that you would go and bear fruit and that your fruit would remain, so that what you ask of the Father in My name He may give to you," John 15:16. This is probably the clearest text on election in all of scripture. This kind of text settles all debate for those who are really seeking this truth. Let's face it! How clear can it get?

This, in-your-face kind of text! "You did not choose Me but I chose you," and you may think that a text so clear as this will settle all debates between the freewill of man and God's election plan, but it has not moved some skeptics even an inch. Election is not just a doctrine for some theological debate in some seminary classroom but it is at the center of hope. There is no hope without election. God did not abandon His rebellious creatures but actually elected some to be with Him in all eternity. Hope that there isn't any confusion as to the meaning of the word "choose," mentioned in the text above, because it could have equally been translated as "elect," and this choosing or election is entirely an act of God without any human input or consideration. God never consulted with mankind to see how they felt and if they would like to be chosen. God did not take a poll to see those who would like to be chosen.

Without this action taken by God, then mankind would have remained in a state of perpetual hopelessness.

So why did God choose you for adoption? Is God looking for people to be with? Is He alone and needs company? Certainly not and may it never be! So what is going on? This verse did only talk about election but about something else. Here is what it said: "I chose you and appointed you," and the idea of appointing has to do with "to set, put, place, establish, ordain," [204]So God did not only choose you but also established and ordained you, meaning, setting you apart from everyone else. Making you special to Him.

Remember that the elect are the bride of Christ, and they must be properly adorned for the groom. The doctrine of election is very consistent with several other Bible teachings, like the groom always elects or chooses his bride. And the groom sets the bride apart from all others. So it is practically normal that after the groom chooses his bride, He sets her apart and gets her ready for the wedding ceremony, but in the interval, the bride has to be productive in bringing others to the wedding feast.

So the purpose for God electing and ordaining the elect is laid down in the next part of the verse, which says,"You would go and bear fruit, and that your fruit would remain." So not only are election and ordaining acts of God completely but there is a purpose behind the election. God has a plan and a purpose for your life. He elected you for the purpose of going and bearing fruit. He did not elect you to sit but to go. God does not elect sitters but goers. If you have been truly elected, then there should be a hunger and thirst after righteousness in your spirit and heart, Matthew 5:6. Are you hungry and thirsty for things of God? A hopeful person is hungry and thirsty for the things of God. What are you hungry and thirsty for? The elect are goers and not sitters,

[204]   https://biblehub.com/thayers/5087.htm

and here is what God said about the elect: "Go into all the world and preach the gospel to all creation," Mark 16:15. This is an intentional going, with a purpose. God told the elect where to go! "into all the world," and what to do as they go; "preach the gospel." The elect will bear fruit in at least two ways: (1) going into all the world and preaching the gospel (2) Hungering and thirsting for righteousness. Those whom God elects are always goers and never sitters. The life of the elect is saturated with bearing fruit and doing the will of God.

That is their raison d'être. Here is another text about the elect as goers and not sitters: "Go therefore and make disciples of all nations; Teaching them to observe all that I have commanded you. And behold I am with you always, to the end of age," Matthew 28:19,20. The elect of God are to be fruit bearers and this text is no different. As the elect goes about their daily lives, they are to incorporate two things in their fruit-bearing mission: (1) making disciples of all nations and (2) teaching them to keep God's commands, and the result of election will be that God will never abandon the elect.

This is not a job or duty for some pastor or theologian but the purpose and mission of each and every elect of God. The elect are always forward-looking and never backward-looking. They are not truly citizens of any earthly nation because they are aliens and foreigners, for their citizenship is in heaven, Philippians 3:20-21. They look not to comfort and consolation from any earthly city but eagerly look forward to the city not built with hands and whose builder and maker is God, Hebrews 11:10. The elect are never alone, for they are comforted in this life as they eagerly await the life to come. This is the hope of the elect, and this is your hope.

The Elect are Never Alone

One of the problems encountered by anyone living a life outside the will of God, is loneliness. This is a major problem in the lives of millions of people. Most are living lives void of meaning and purpose. Loneliness affects more people than all cancers combined. All other emotional issues like fear, stress, anxiety, depression and suicidal ideation are tied to loneliness. But the elect are exempted from the amount and level of loneliness that the rest of mankind faces. Here is a word of hope and comfort from God to the elect: And behold I am with you always, even to the end of the age, Matthew 28:20B. God promises to be with His elect always. There is never a time that God is not with His elect and this is a comforting promise. He promised to never leave nor abandon them, Hebrews 13:5-6. Family and friends may and will forsake you but God promised never to leave nor abandon His elect. And God's love for His elect is unending, and nothing is able to separate the elect from God. The elect are safe and secure in the hands of God.

Nothing can Separate the Elect from God

The relationship between the elect and God is eternally secured. They cannot fall from grace or lose their salvation. Not even death is able to separate the elect from God. Here is what God said: [33] Who shall lay anything to the charge of God's elect? It is God that justifieth.

[34] Who is he that condemneth? It is Christ that died, yea rather, that is risen again, who is even at the right hand of God, who also maketh intercession for us.

[35] Who shall separate us from the love of Christ? shall tribulation, or distress, or persecution, or famine, or nakedness, or peril, or sword?

[36] As it is written, For thy sake we are killed all the daylong; we are accounted as sheep for the slaughter.

[37] Nay, in all these things we are more than conquerors through him that loved us, Romans 8:33-37. Meditate on verse 35 that confirms that God's love for His elect is safe and secure, and can never be broken.

The Elect are Secure in the Hands of God

You may often hear teachings like you can lose your salvation unless you work hard to keep it. Such teachings are foreign to the bible. If God elected you for salvation then that can never be lost but if somehow you accepted Christ out of your own free will then you might really think that you are saved then again, maybe you are, only God knows. Here is what God said about the assurance of salvation and the security of the elect: "[28] I give them eternal life, and they shall never perish; no one will snatch them out of my hand. [29] My Father, who has given them to me, is greater than all[a]; no one can snatch them out of my Father's hand. [30] I and the Father are one," John 10:28-30. This is the hope of the elect and their salvation is safe and secure in the hands of God. They have been justified and declared not guilty by Christ and the verdict cannot be undone. The blood has already been sacrificed and the work of atonement is complete. No need for the blood to be sacrificed again. It is getting clearer from so much evidence that the love of Christ is focused on His elect as they are the ones whom He justified.

Christ Justifies the Elect

Justification is another act of God in the election process that brings the sinner into a right standing with God. This is a necessary judicious action that God takes to declare the sinner not guilty, righteous, just. This one act by God brings the sinner into communion and fellowship with God. He takes the act of justification to declare a guilty person as not guilty because their sin has been propitiated by Christ. This is like being charged with a crime of murder in some jurisdiction and all the evidence presented in the court of law points to your guilt. Here are the presiding officials in this courtroom: God, the Father is sitting as the presiding judge over this case, Satan, who is also called the god of this world, (2 Corinthians 4:4), is also in the courtroom and acting as the state prosecutor, state attorney, and his job is to present the evidence against the elect that they deserve death.

They deserve the death penalty and deserve to be condemned and hanged. That is why Satan or the Devil is also called the accuser of the brethren (Revelation 12:10). He represents the governmental system of the world and before anyone is saved, they are and operate under the dominion of Satan. Hardly would anyone entertain the idea that they are actually under the dominion of the Devil, but that is truly the case. All human beings can only be in one of two locations. Either, they are "in Christ," meaning that they are saved, or they are in the world and in the dominion of Satan, who just happens to be the god of this world. There are no neutral locations of existence. There are no fence sitters. If you are not for God then by default, you are against Him, (Matthew 12:30). Hardly, would anyone openly admit that they are against God but they may not enthusiastically admit to be for God either and that makes them to be against God.

If anyone is not sure of their location then they are most likely under the dominion of Satan. Be sure of your location. I am not talking about your GPS location but your location with Christ. Are you standing with Christ or with

Satan? So, back to the courtroom where Satan and his team of lawyers are making the case and bringing accusations and charges against the elect saying that they have committed crimes worthy of death. For anyone's position or location to change, they must be justified. They must be removed from under Satan's dominion and transferred into Christ's. Here is what God said: "For He rescued us from the domain of darkness, and transferred us into the Kingdom of His beloved Son," Colossians 1:13.The elect are rescued from the dominion of Darkness or Satan and transported or transferred into that of Christ through the act of justification.

This is an amazing and instantaneous change of location and position. Before the elect were transferred, they were under Satan's dominion and they were actually hostile towards and enemies of God and the things of God.They had no interest or desire for the things of God. Here is how God describes everyone who is under the dominion of Satan, including the elect, before they were rescued by God and removed from under the control of the Devil: "Because the mind set on the flesh is hostile towards God; for it does not subject itself to the law of God, for it is not even able to do so," Romans 8:7.Then something miraculous suddenly happened! There was a radical transformation of the mind and heart of the elect.

Then back to the courtroom where Satan and his team of lawyers are making closing arguments before God against the elect. But in that courtroom where God Himself was the presiding judge, there was someone in the courtroom standing and acting as a defense attorney. Jesus Christ was in the box for the defense alone and acting as counsel for the defense of the elect. While in the box for the state, was the chief prosecutor, Satan and a host of attorneys making the case for the government. After a lengthy prosecution, the evidence presented, eyewitness account, video presentation, and audio presentation. A jury of 12 were also seated to weigh the evidence presented and pass judgment.

Then God called the jury foreman to know if they have arrived at a verdict, and he replied, "yes your honor," and God said, "You may now read the verdict to the court," and "he said, guilty as charged Your honor," and then God called upon he prison officials to take the prisoners away for condemnation and death sentence in eternal separation from God. But before the prison officials were to carry them away, the defense attorney (Jesus the Christ) stepped forward and said, "Your honor, I just have one motion for the court to consider," and God said, "

You have the floor," and He made this motion to the court: " I will take their penalty, and I will suffer in their place, I will die for them." Then God asked the prosecuting attorney, Satan, saying"Are there any objections? Satan was silent! Then God responded, "Motion granted." Then God hit the gavel on the bench and said,"Court is adjourned! Hence the saying: "For He made Him who knew no sin to be sin for us, that we might become the righteousness of God in Him," 2 Corinthians ;21.

The result of this is that the elect are no longer enemies of God and here is what God said: "Therefore, since we have been justified by faith, we have peace with God through our Lord, Jesus Christ," Romans 5:1.This verse talks about four parts of justification; (1) the act of justification; (2) the means of justification (3) the result of justification; (4) the vehicle of justification. Let's begin with the act of justification: This is wholly and completely a divine action taken to declare the sinner not guilty, just, clean and free from sin. The word, "been," in the English, that is right before justification, indicates that the verb, "justify," is in the passive voice, meaning that a third party is doing the act of justification. And when that third party is not mentioned in the immediate context, this is considered a divine passive. Theologians call this a divine passive. Whenever there is a verb in the passive voice and no subject in the immediate context, acting on that verb, God Himself is considered the subject.

This is an argument from linguistics and grammar that God is the subject of justification. Here is a question raised by Paul concerning Justification: "Who will bring any charge against God's elect, It is God who justifies," Romans 8:33. This argument from the "analogy of faith," makes the point vividly clear that only God can justify. The idea of "analogy of faith," is used to interpret scripture with scripture. The text says that the elect are justified "by faith," and the word "by," signifies the means or method of justification. "By," links or is the bridge between justification and faith. Belief leads to justification,which leads to righteousness.

Faith or belief is the beginning of hope. The most important ingredient in hope is faith. Here is what is said of Abraham concerning faith: What does the scripture say? "Abraham believed God, and it was credited to him as righteousness," Romans 4:3. This may somehow sound a little confusing! How does faith and election work? This is also a very interesting question! The text above said that "Abraham believed or had faith in God," and the result was that righteousness was credited to Abraham's account. This faith or belief is the means of justification. Here is what is said about belief: *9 That if you confess with your mouth the Lord Jesus, and shall believe in your heart that God hath raised him from the dead, thou shall be saved.*

10 For with the heart man believeth unto righteousness; and with the mouth confession is made unto salvation. Roman

10:9-10. Justification is synonymous with being saved. This faith is not subjective faith in yourself but is an objective faith in your creator. The idea of confession means to see things from God's perspective and not from ours. It means to be in agreement with God about whatever He has said about any given matter. Confessing the Lord Jesus means believing in His deity. There must be a sincere faith or believe in your heart of hearts that Jesus Christ is God in the flesh. Without such a belief there is no salvation and no hope for you or mankind. Jesus Christ is not just a good teacher, prophet, miracle worker but He is far more than that.

The world was created by and through Him. Without Him, nothing was made that was made and in Him, all the fullness of God dwells. He is 100% God and 100% man at the same time. He has no beginning of days nor end of life. He will judge all mankind at His soon coming. This is what the Apostle Paul meant by "confess with your mouth the Lord Jesus," and there is a second fact about Jesus Christ that we must be in agreement to get saved: "shall believe in your heart," and the location of that belief is in your heart. Not believe in your head but in your heart. The heart is the center of thought and decision. This is the center of man, the heart.

This belief leads to a transformation. So what facts are to be believed? "That God has raised Him from the dead." No one is going to get saved without believing that God raised Jesus Christ from the dead. This is central to justification. This is the SINE QUA NON of justification. So two facts about Jesus Christ must be believed to get saved: (1) Jesus Christ is God in the flesh and (2) God raised Jesus Christ from the dead. The result of believing these two facts is mentioned at the end of Romans 10:9 above: "You shall be saved." Notice that the text did not say, "You might be saved," but emphatically proclaimed, "you shall be saved." Wow!

This is real hope for mankind. The entire Christian faith hangs on these two doctrines. The doctrine of resurrection is so central to the message of the gospel that Paul dedicated all of 1 Corinthians 15, explaining it. Our faith depends on it and our hope also depends on it. This is the central message of hope in the bible. Unfortunately, a lot of people who say that they are Christians have been taught a concept of Christianity that is alien to the bible. Most say that they have faith in Jesus for this life alone. They believe in Jesus to provide for them in this life alone.

They believe in Jesus for good health, money in the bank, someone to meet their material needs in this life alone. Here is what Paul said about this kind of hope: "If in this life only we have hope in Christ, we are of all men most miserable," 1 Corinthians 15:19. Paul is making the case that if our hope is in this life alone then we among men are most miserable. We are not animals that just live, eat and die tomorrow. We have an eternal soul that will live with God or be absent from God. Then the result of justification is peace with God. Peace with God is a scarce commodity and people are searching for peace in all the wrong places. People are in pieces for there is no peace. No peace for the wicked!

The world is full of turmoil, conflict ridden and people are in desperate need of peace. People are not looking for more money but are in desperate need of peace. So how can they find this kind of peace? There is no peace in fentanyl! There is no peace in opioids! There is no peace in marijuana! There is no peace in weeds! There is no peace in ganja! There is no peace in more sex! There is no peace in drugs! There is no peace in alcohol! There is no peace in material obsession! There is no peace in your home! There is no peace with your wife! There is no peace with your children! There is no peace with your siblings! No peace with your boss on your Job! The world is on fire! No peace between Russia and Ukraine! No peace between Israel and Palestine! No peace between Democrats and Republicans in congress or in this country! Like Rodney King once said: " Can we all just get along!"So then where can peace be found?

Here is what God said about peace: "There is no peace for the wicked,"says the Lord, Isaiah 48:22. God said that there is peace available, then He qualifies it, " but not for the wicked." Someone may say something like, "but who are the wicked?" because "I am not a wicked person." The standards are set by God and He alone determines who the wicked are? Here is something else that God said about the wicked: Even from birth, the wicked go astray; from the womb they are wayward, spreading lies, Isaiah 58:3. The bottom line is that we are all born in a state of wickedness from the womb and from all of us who are born wicked, God elected to redeem some. There is no peace for anyone who is not in Christ Jesus because anyone who is in Christ is a new creation, 2 Corinthians 5:17.

Even all the peace accords in the world will never bring any lasting peace. Think of the historic peace accord, called the "camp David accord," signed on September 17th 1978 and facilitated by American President Jimmy Carter and signed by Egyptian President Anwar Sadat and Israeli Prime minister Menachen Begin. The stated goal of this accord was to usher in lasting peace in the Middle East. It was hailed as the last beacon of hope for the Middle East. And we are now forty five years later, and there is no semblance of peace. There will be no peace on the earth among men or mankind until and unless there is peace with the Prince of Peace. There can be no true horizontal peace until there is true vertical peace. Here is a message from the Prince of Peace: "These things I have spoken to you that in Me you may have peace, In this world, you will have trouble; but be of good cheer, I have overcome the world,"John 16:33.

The Prince of Peace is the only one who can say, "be still," and waves in the ocean become still. He also has the power to calm the storms in your life. He can say, "be still," and the storms of your life become quiet and peaceful. He can bring calm out of chaos in your life. He can calm your marital storms, your financial storms, your relational storms, your mental storms and the list is endless. He can bring purpose and meaning to your life. He can bring peace out of the pieces of your life. But how does this peace get to us? What is the vehicle through which we get that peace?

The last part of Justification at the end of Romans 5:1, says that, " we have peace with God through our Lord Jesus Christ," and the key word in the last part of the verse is "through," describing the vehicle through which our peace is appropriated. The means through that which we get that peace. There is no other name under heaven through which man might be saved, Acts 412. He is the name above all names. There is no redemption through Buda or Mohamed or any other prophet or mediator. For there is only one mediator between God and man, the Man, Christ Jesus, 1 Timothy 2:5. There are not many ways to get to God, but one. This is very exclusive and not inclusive. He Himself said that, " I am the way, the truth and the life, for no one comes to the Father except through Me," John 14:6. Here again, we find that magic word, "through," me. He is also called, " the gate," John 10:9,"the door," John 10:7. The bottom line is that He is the only way to God and not one of many ways. So then those whom He justifies, He also adopts into His family as His dear children.

Adoption of the Elect by God

Adoption is one of those very humbling teachings in the bible that renders those who are adopted humbled and helpless. Humans will like to become prideful, how they have the freedom to choose and believe in Christ for salvation. The freewill of man is irreconcilable to the doctrines of election and adoption. Mankind, in its natural state, lacks the capacity and/or will to exercise free-will in choosing a Holy God. Mankind is dead in its trespasses and sins and that deadness extends to man's total being, including his will. Proponents of the freedom of the will also claim to have support from the bible for their position. Here is one of such verses that is often used in support of the free will of man in choosing God for salvation:"For God so loved the world, that He gave His only begotten Son, that whosoever believes in Him should not perish but have eternal life, "John 3:16.

This verse simply says that God, "in this manner," loved the world. The word, "world," in this verse has been understood to mean, "universal," "global," and if this is truly the case then no one should be sent to hell. If "world," in this context is taken to mean "universal," then Christ died on the cross and atoned for the sin of every single person that has ever been born, including, Idi Amin of Uganda, Adolf Hitler of Germany, Saddam Hussein of Iraq, Mussolini of Italy, Bin Laden of Saudi Arabia and many more. These people were bad but no one else on the globe is any better than them in terms of God's view of sin. If the word, "world," means universal in John 3:16 then no one will be in hell. No serious bible student would believe that no one would be in hell but that is actually the case if Christ died for all of the world. This is what is called "universalism," if no one will be in hell. The word, "world," has a limited and universal use and meaning.

372

You may hear a phrase like, "the world of sport,"(limited use)and this clearly does not mean everyone in the world but only those concerned with sports. But when we say that everyone in the world needs to breathe air to be alive then this is universal and no one is exempt (universal use). Another point of confusion in this verse is the word, "whosoever," and this has been widely understood to mean the ability to choose. This verse has been widely used to support the freewill of man to choose God for salvation but is it really the case? Let's look at the word, "whosoever," and how it has been understood; this word has been translated from the Greek word, "pas," which is translated as, "all, each, every, any, whole, everyone, all things, everything."[205]This Greek word, "pas," could not possibly be translated as "whosoever," and this single translation error probably by the King James Version of the bible has led millions if not billions of people astray.

This translation of the Greek word "pas," as "whosoever," probably, first made its way into the 1611 translation of the King James Version of the Bible and has made its way into about 99 percent of bible translations ever since 1611. Other translations have simply followed the King James Version instead of doing their own translation directly from the original Greek text.Here is a translation from the Tyndale Bible translated in 1526-1530: "For God so loveth the worlde yt he hath geven his only sonne that none that beleve in him shuld perisshe: but should have everlastinge lyfe, John 3:16.[206]This is the English of 1526 and so do not be

205

https://www.biblestudytools.com/lexicons/greek/nas/pas.html
206

http://oldebible.com/tyndale-bible/john-3.asp#:~:text=John%203%3A16%20For%20God,through%20him%20might%20be%20saved.

concerned about the spelling of words. This is the translation by William Tyndale in 1526, directly from the Greek text. Interestingly, Tyndale uses the word, "none," where the King James Version uses the word, "whosoever," and this is quite fascinating and interesting.

Even though the Greek word, "pas," is never translated as "none," the Tyndale translators rightly choose a word that fits the meaning and context of the passage. "None that believes in Him should perish," and "All or everyone who believes in Him shall never perish," means exactly the same thing. This is the right and only way to translate this text from Greek into English. The word, "whosoever," seems to introduce ability into the meaning of the text. All who believe shall have eternal life but the text does not in any way imply that all who believe have the ability to do so. The word,"whosoever," has done irreparable damage to the meaning of this beloved text, John 3:16, and this is the most widely quoted verse in all the bible, even among unbelievers and also the most widely misunderstood verse.

Tyndale got it right and King James got it wrong. This verse should better be understood like this: "For God thus or in this manner, loved the elect, that He gave His only begotten Son, that none that believe in Him shall perish, but shall have eternal life." This is my translation of the text. God's love is for the elect (limited world) and not for the world (universal world). The elect are adopted into the family of God and not everyone is being adopted. Here is another verse that is also widely used to support the freewill of man to choose God and universal atonement: **The Lord is not slow about His promise, as some count slowness, but is patient toward you, not willing for any to perish, but for all to come to repentance, 2 Peter 3:9.**

This verse and others like it have been used as proof text for universalism, meaning "all men or mankind will be saved," and is that what this verse is actually teaching? The idea of not willing that any should perish, but for all to come to repentance, would seem to support the idea that it is up to man to choose God for salvation; but is that really the case? Who are really the "any," and the, "all,"? Who is God not desiring that they should perish, but come to repentance? In the context of this verse in 2 Peter 3:9, Peter was writing to answer those who had thoughts about Christ's second coming. The doubters were saying that nothing has changed since the creation of the world and there is no reason to believe that Christ is coming back at all. Peter wrote and said that God's view of time is not as man views time. If Christ had come back, say two thousand years ago, then millions of the elect who were not yet born would have perished. So until all the elect hear the gospel and come to faith, then the end shall come.

So when the text says, "not willing that any should perish," it must be talking about the elect who are still to be born and come to faith. There are still unborn now and today who are elect and in this sense, God does not desire that any of them should perish but that all of the elect, not all of the world (universal all) as opposed to (limited all, the elect) should come to repentance. Until the last elect hears the gospel and comes to faith, then the end shall come. Here is what Matthew said about the end: "And this gospel of the kingdom shall be preached in all the world for a witness unto all nations; and then shall the end come". Matthew 24:14. Christ cannot return until all (universal all) have heard the gospel message as a witness against them, so they are without excuse and all (limited all), the elect have come to faith then the end shall come.

So, election cannot be separated from adoption as they both render the sinner at the mercy and grace of God, unable to make any choice towards a Holy God. Adoption is a sober act of God that humbles the sinner. No one whom I know has ever worked to get themselves adopted. The one being adopted has no choice to make in the process and it is entirely up to the one doing the adopting. The one being adopted is passive in the adoption process and so are the elect passive in their salvation. God, through Christ, did all the work. Here is how we were adopted into the family of God: "Having predestined us unto the adoption of children by Jesus Christ to himself, according to the good pleasure of his will," Ephesians 1:5. The verse before this says that we were chosen and placed in Christ from the foundation of the world and after that the elect were predestinated.

Election and predestination are like identical twin brothers, because if you see one appear, then know that the other is around the corner. Election is based on predestination but what does it really mean to predestinate? The Greek word, "proorizo," from where we get our English word, "predestination," simply means, "to predetermine, decide beforehand, to foreordain, appoint beforehand."[207]I understand that this is not a subject that is popular with mankind, but the word means that God predetermined who He will elect to adopt into His family. God is God and He made and created us and it was not us making or creating Him.

Who are we to question His actions and motives? How can the thing made question his or her maker? Can the thing created, question his maker, saying, "Why did you make me like this?" He predetermines beforehand those who will believe and put their faith in Him, and these are those

[207]   https://biblehub.com/thayers/4309.htm

that He adopts into His family. All these acts of God are indeed humbling, to say the least! Think of election, predestination, and now, adoption. Now, it is one thing to be adopted by a human family but it is a different ball game to be adopted by the maker of all the earth. This is so overwhelming that God would adopt anyone! The idea of God adopting us would imply that we were fatherless (spiritually) and hopeless. Hardly would anyone adopt a child who has parents and the parents want their child. Usually, adopted children are orphans or abandoned and rejected by their parents. God would certainly not adopt us if we had a father or mother, would He?

We are fatherless and in desperate need of adoption. This word that is translated in this text as adoption is quite fascinating! The Greek word is "huiothesian," which literally means, "divine adoption as sons," and this is a loaded phrase that explains this one Greek word. This is different from any form of human adoption ever undertaken. Maybe you are without an earthly father today, or you never knew your earthly father or they abandoned you as an infant; God is ready to adopt you into His family. He wants to be your Daddy, or Dada. Hear what He said: "A father to the fatherless, a defender of widows, Is God in His holy dwelling," Psalm 68:5. God will not leave us as orphans, running the streets, homeless, cold and naked. His love for the elect is infinite and there is no end to it. Here are a few verses to ponder as it concerns orphans and fatherlessness:

Pure and undefiled religion in the sight of *our* God and Father is this: to visit orphans and widows in their distress *and* to keep oneself unstained [a]by the world, James 1:27.

He executes justice for the orphan and the widow, and shows His love for the stranger by giving him food and clothing, Deuteronomy 10:18.

I will not leave you as orphans; I am coming to you, John 14:18.

Learn to do good;
Seek justice,
Rebuke the oppressor,
Obtain justice for the orphan,
Plead for the widow's case, Isaiah 1:17.

So meditate and reflect on these verses, knowing that we are all (universally) spiritual orphans. Without the heavenly Father, we are fatherless orphans. You may have a very good earthly father but without the heavenly Father, we are without hope. Our adoption by our heavenly Father is our only hope. You cannot seek your own adoption but you can start praying right now if it pleases the heavenly Father to adopt you into His family. At the end of Ephesians 1:5, it says "adoption of children by Jesus Christ to Himself according to the good pleasure of His will." Jesus Christ is the one adopting the elect to Himself according to God's good pleasure. The idea of "good pleasure," means that God is at liberty to choose who He decides to adopt and no one dares have the audacity to question Him and His motive. I am a spiritual orphan and I have been humbly adopted by God through Christ and I don't know about you! Would you want to be adopted right now?

Elects are Heirs of Salvation

Now those, whom it pleases Him to adopt, are also given an inheritance to possess. When someone is about to die, long before their death, they may most often designate an heir to inherit their earthly and material possessions. The heir is anyone who they handpicked to receive the inheritance. The heir is most often a trusted family member or friend but it does not have to be. The key word here is "election." The living person designates their heir while they are alive and the heir may never know that they are the heir.

The concept of an inheritance is so vitally important to the doctrine of salvation yet it is widely ignored. I am amazed at how much the bible talks about heirs and inheritance and yet millions of people simply don't get it. This humble teaching is all over the bible yet millions of people are completely and totally blinded to the truth of the gospel. The idea that you can do some deed or work to earn yourself a place in heaven is the most widely taught teaching and yet, that teaching is foreign to the bible. Have you seen an heir who works to earn their inheritance? If you find one then please let me know.

That is why it is called an inheritance, because you don't earn or deserve it. When you work, you earn wages but when you inherit you do absolutely nothing. Believe it or not, people fight and kill one another because of inheritance. If a very wealthy person died and left, say, ten children to succeed him, and designates one of them to inherit his assets, there will be a war over inheritance and yet only the person with the assets chooses his heir and the rest have no part in the inheritance. Yes, people actually pull out knives, guns, or go to court, and kill over inheritance. An heir is designated or elected by the person who owned the assets and an inheritance is never to be taken by force or coercion.

Unfortunately, millions believe that they deserve an inheritance and will do anything to get it. But what is really an inheritance as it relates to salvation? When we talk of inheriting salvation, some have concluded that it means having salvation passed down from the parents to children and here is one such opinion: No.Salvation is not inherited at all.If it could be inherited Jesus' death would be in vain. Ephesians 2:8 is clear:"For by grace you have been saved through faith. And this is not your own doing; it is the gift of God..."Salvation is God's work from beginning to end.We cannot inherit salvation from our parents or from Godly people we may know.They can help us to come to know Christ by teaching us about Him, but no one can save himself or another person. Christ alone brings salvation to lost people.

In 1 Corinthians 4:14 Paul refers to the Corinthian believers as his "children" because he has invested much time in them as a spiritual parent/pastor to them. However, to push the analogy, he did not birth them. Pastors, Bible Fellowship leaders, small group leaders, one-to-one disciplers function, to a large extent, like surrogate spiritual parents to those younger in the faith. We did not birth any of the children we teach, but we are given great responsibility in teaching them.[208]

So someone raised a very interesting objection, that salvation is not inherited in terms of getting it passed down from some earthly person to another and they are very correct in that regard but completely missed the point on what the bible means by inheriting salvation. You will never become saved just because your father was a pastor, then he died and you inherited their salvation. Never in a million years is there any remote possibility of such an occurrence. Salvation is never transferable from one human being to another; that is not the concept of inheritance that is taught in the bible. Inheritance, in the context of this writing, is: "the

208
https://enoughfortoday.org/2011/06/16/is-salvation-inherited/

share which an individual will have in that eternal
blessedness."[209]

Even salvation in the bible is clearly regarded as an
inheritance, not from man but from God, and here is an
example: Are they not all ministering spirits, sent out
to *provide* service for the sake of those who
will inherit salvation? Hebrew 1:14.This verse is speaking of
angels who are ministering spirits to those who will inherit
salvation. So salvation is clearly a gift from God and not a
work that we can perform to earn it. Here is another verse
about inheriting the kingdom of God: "Then the King will say
to those on His right, 'Come, you who are blessed of My
Father, inherit the kingdom prepared for you from the
foundation of the world," Matthew 25:34. Ephesians 1:4 says
that you were elected by God from the foundation of the
world and this verse says that the kingdom also is an
inheritance that was prepared for you from the foundation of
the world.

Kingdom is used in this passage as a synonym for
salvation. You can also see that the biblical concept of an
inheritance is synonymous with election. These are all
actions taken by God from the foundation of the world.
God's actions and initiatives make the elect heirs of salvation
and here is what God says: "so that being justified by His
grace we would be made heirs [a]according to *the* hope of
eternal life," Titus 3:7. So according to this verse, the elect are
justified or made righteous by God. The text also says that,
"we would be made heirs," and to be made heirs means that
there is an inheritance in store for the heir and that
inheritance is "the hope of eternal life." So hope is a very
powerful force in the life of the elect that keeps us grounded

---

[209]   https://biblehub.com/thayers/2817.htm

in a world that is riddled with trouble and chaos. But this hope transcends this life and beyond.

Hope Beyond this Life and the Grave

Let's go back once more to the earthly human inheritance analogy: So, let's say that you inherited life insurance proceeds – land, houses, and money from your parents who passed on and over time, you sold the house, land and the life insurance proceeds, spent the money and completely run dry. You have depleted your inheritance but not so with the inheritance that God grants to you. This inheritance cannot be depleted and it is eternal and everlasting in nature. Wouldn't you want such an inheritance that fades not away? Real hope has to transcend the grave and any hope that ends in the grave is no hope at all. Real inheritance has to transcend this life and any inheritance that ends in this life is no inheritance at all.

Here is what Peter said about an incorruptible inheritance: *according to the foreknowledge of God the Father, by the sanctifying work of the Spirit, to obey Jesus Christ and be sprinkled with His blood: May grace and peace be multiplied to you.*

Blessed be the God and Father of our Lord Jesus Christ, who according to His great mercy has caused us to be born again to a living hope through the resurrection of Jesus Christ from the dead, to obtain an inheritance which is imperishable, undefiled, and will not fade away, reserved in heaven for you, 1 Peter 1:2-4.

These sets of verses begin by saying that God has caused us to be born again. This is another text that rules out any iota of human effort in our salvation. This also ties in perfectly with election in that God has done all the work in getting us saved. We are born again to a living hope, not a dead hope. A hope that is alive and vibrant and that hope is obtained through the resurrection of Jesus Christ. This is the hope beyond this life. The resurrection of the dead is central to our faith and hope, without which, there is no salvation. The entire Christian faith hangs on the doctrine of the resurrection. There will be no Christianity without the resurrection of Jesus Christ.

The apostle Paul made this forceful argument: what was the goal of his labor if the dead do not rise? He fought a wild beast for what purpose if the dead do not rise? He was shipwrecked on a missionary journey to Rome for what purpose if the dead do not rise? He was in and out of jail for what purpose if the dead do not rise? He was beaten and left for dead for the sake of the gospel, and why did he do all that if the dead do not rise? Here is what Paul concluded: *If from human motives I fought with wild beasts at Ephesus, what good is it to me? If the dead are not raised, LET'S EAT AND DRINK, FOR TOMORROW WE DIE,* 1 Corinthians 15:32. Paul is basically saying that, if the dead do not rise then let's just stop this church ministry and do something else with our time. Let's just have a good old party because we just have one life to live. Let's just eat and drink for tomorrow we die. Practically speaking, if the dead are not raised then Christ was not raised, and if Christ was not raised then we have believed in vain and we will die with our sins. Again, here is Paul: *14 And if Christ be not risen, then is our preaching vain, and your faith is also vain.*

15 Yea, and we are found false witnesses of God; because we have testified of God that he raised up Christ: whom he raised not up, if so be that the dead rise not.

16 For if the dead rise not, then is not Christ raised:

¹⁷ And if Christ be not raised, your faith is vain; ye are yet in your sins.

¹⁸ Then they also which are fallen asleep in Christ are perished.

¹⁹ If in this life only we have hope in Christ, we are of all men most miserable, 1 Corinthians 15:14-19.

Our faith and hope is solely dependent on the fact that the dead do indeed rise. Life will lack meaning and purpose if our hope is limited to this life alone. That is why almost anyone who commits or is thinking about committing suicide also has a faulty belief about the resurrection. Read more on this in my other book, titled: "Fending off Suicidal Thoughts," available on Amazon and other book retailers. If anyone believes that life ends at the grave, then that is a recipe for hopelessness. There is even more lasting hope when someone believes that there is life beyond the grave and that life is in Christ Jesus. Believing that the human soul is temporal is part of the problem. The human soul is not temporal but eternal.

The soul does not cease to exist at the moment of physical death but continues on into eternity, either in heaven or in hell. This is the only hope for humanity and this is the only hope for you. Now, back to the quote in 1 Peter above which reads," *to obtain an inheritance which is imperishable, undefiled, and will not fade away, reserved in heaven for you,*"1 Peter 2:4. This verse clearly makes a contrast between an earthly and a heavenly inheritance. The earthly inheritance is perishable, the heavenly is imperishable; the earthly inheritance is defiled and heavenly is undefiled; the earthly inheritance fades away and the heavenly does not fade away; and they both have different locations; the earthly inheritance is located on earth and you will not take it with you when you die but the heavenly inheritance is located in heaven and is yours for all eternity. Which will you pick?

This is the power of hope and this has been tested and tried. This kind of hope will sustain you when you feel like giving up on life. This kind of hope will sustain you when you feel like quitting and giving up on life. This hope will sustain you when you are ashamed of your sex life. This hope will sustain you when you have low self-esteem. This kind of hope will sustain you when you are dealing with addiction of any kind. This hope will set you free from the penalty, power and presence of sin. This hope will help you to enjoy sex as was intended by the creator. This hope will not fail you. This kind of hope will sustain you when you feel fearful, lonely, alone, stressed, anxious, depressed, and even downright suicidal.

Here are a few assurances of hope that God is giving you today: "For I know the plans I have for you," Declares the Lord, Plans to prosper you and not to harm you, Plans to give you a hope and a future," Jeremiah 29:11.It does not matter where you have been or what you have done, God has a plan and a purpose for your life. God is able and willing to make all things new. He is able and willing to give a brand new beginning. Christ is our only hope. Christ in you the hope of glory. If Christ is in you then you are heaven bound when you die physically and that is hopeful and good news. Enjoy sex now to the fullest as you are getting ready to attend the heavenly wedding ceremony. In the meantime, be ready for the groom who will soon return at any moment for His bride to consummate the marriage.

Conclusion

Sex is by far the most enjoyable and pleasurable thing on the planet with the potential to become self-destructive. Sex is exhilarating, animating, thrilling, and full of excitement. Sex is full of passion but must also be restrained for the good of those involved and for society as a whole. Why are humans unable to tame or control their sexual desires? This is a sobering question! Love is often used and understood to be synonymous with sex. You may often hear things like, "I am making love," to mean "I am having sex," but are they the same? These are questions to think and ponder! And where did sex really come from? What is the origin of sex?

The origin of sex is a function of the creation of man. Without humans on the planet sex, as to mean sexual intercourse, would not be possible. Mankind did not suddenly appear upon the earth as some would have us believe but there is an intelligent designer behind the origin and creation of mankind and hence, the origin of sex. There is pleasure in sex but that is not its primary purpose. Sex was made for man and not man for sex. Man's underlying purpose in life is not sex yet it has dominated man's existence.

The primary purposes for sex by the creator of it are: procreation, companionship and lastly, pleasure. Yet pleasure is widely believed to be the primary purpose of sex. As a result, all kinds of sexually deviant behaviors have come about. The level of confusion about the meaning of sex, love and marriage is mind boggling and as a result, all kinds of STDs have entered the human population. Everyone has their own idea as to the meaning of sex, love and marriage. Everything is up for debate; the meaning of love is up for debate, the meaning of sex is up for debate and the meaning of marriage is also up for debate. And as a result STDs are up to the roof.

All forms of STDs imaginable have entered the human population and the full effects and consequences are unknown but millions of people are dead and continue to die. We have concluded that bestiality is the source of most, if not all STDs in the human population. This is a very serious sexually deviant behavior that has brought every kind of illness imaginable into the human population. Having sexual intercourse with an animal is a sin against God, morally depraved, and illegal in most jurisdictions. The human being becomes one flesh with an animal. All kinds of STDs, from AIDS to gonorrhea, are all linked to bestiality.

And to make matters worse, many cancers in the human population are as a result of STDs. People think and breathe sex and that is mostly what is on people's minds.And so marriages have all kinds of problems because of sexually deviant behaviors. Marriages also reflect the union between Christ and the church and how Christ will soon come back someday to take home His bride, the church. The meaning of marriage is also constantly being redefined and debated, and we conclude that only the creator of mankind has the unquestionable authority to define marriage. Mankind did not make themselves and lacks any moral authority to make such a definition. The redefinition of marriage has driven people into all kinds of sexually deviant and addictive behaviors.

Sexual addiction has left a lot of destruction in its path. This is one of the most destructive parts of sex. The sex industry is one of if not the largest on the planet and the demand for more sex is driving the growth. Lives are being ruined and cut short all because of sexual addictions. These have increased the probability of sex as a commodity. Sex has been used as a commodity to generate income. The human body has been devalued and sold for commercial purposes. The body was created and designed to bring glory to God and not for sexual immorality. Sexual addiction has also led to other sexually deviant behaviors like rape, incest and more.

The situation looks pretty bleak. Is there really any hope for mankind? Sex has saturated the entire culture to a point where everything is about sex. And millions are losing their lives or paying a very high price for poor sex decisions. Is there any hope? The good news is that there is hope available. Every sex act that deviates from God's plan is a sin. God has carefully laid out His plan for sex in His book, the bible,and any deviation from that is called a transgression of the law. Sin is the breaking of the law or the transgression of the law.

The only solution is for man to acknowledge and admit that they are sinners and have transgressed or broken God's law. And with God's help, they can turn from sin to God. Marriage has to be between a man and a woman in a heterosexual, monogamous, God-ordained marital relationship. Sexual sin is not a joke and not to be played with. It will burn both you and your clothes. When faced with sexual temptation, flee and run for your dear life. Sexual sin will eat you alive. Sex is indeed very enjoyable and pleasurable but only to be truly enjoyed in the context of a God-ordained heterosexual, monogamous, marital union. Enjoy the ride, have fun, and enjoy sexual intercourse to the fullest.

Appendix A

Advice to Parents of Middle & High Schoolers

1) Talk about Sex to your Children

As early as it is age appropriate, talk to your children about sex. As far as STDs are concerned, it is very appropriate to engage children of both sexes but girls need special attention. They can get pregnant and that may derail their entire future. They may attempt an abortion that may end their life. Boys may end up with some deadly STD, like AIDS. If you don't talk to them, somebody else will and you won't like the result. They have their friends, teachers and the internet. Be proactive about this!

2) Lead by Example

As important as talking may be, children may likely follow what you do rather than what you say. Let your lifestyle do most of the talking. If your children watch you having multiple sex partners then you will lose any credibility to talk to them about sex. If your kids watch you do drugs then they are likely to do drugs. Don't do what you don't want your children to do. It is that simple!

3) Talk to your Children about Vaping, Drugs, Marijuana, Cigarettes and Alcohol

Middle and High School kids are developing at a very fast and rapid pace and as such, are also dealing with rapidly changing emotions. Most middle and High school kids lack any sense of purpose and direction. They are confused about a lot of things, including handling changing emotions, like, fear, anxiety, depression and suicidal ideation are going through the roof during this stage of their lives. Be there to provide guidance and direction. I understand that most schools have guidance counselors on staff but the parents should be the primary guidance counselor. I wrote two other books titled: "Fending off Suicidal Thoughts," and "Handling Changing Emotions," available on Amazon and wherever books are sold. These are good resources for some of these issues.

4) Pray for your Children

Assuming that you are a follower of Jesus Christ, then I exhort you to pray daily for your children. Raising and parenting teenagers is the most humbling and challenging event in the life of a parent. If you hardly pray in your life then wait until your children are teenagers and see what happens. You will be stretched to the limit, and sometimes asking yourself questions like: "Where did I go wrong?" Here is how Job handled praying for his children: *When the days of feasting had completed their cycle, Job would send word to them and consecrate them, getting up early in the morning and offering burnt offerings according to the number of them all; for Job said, "Perhaps my sons have sinned and cursed God in their hearts." Job did so continually,*

Job 1:5.This text said that Job did so continually, which means that we too should pray continually for our children. Job got up early each morning to intercede for his children, just in case they have gone places or did things that were not pleasing to God. Job said that perhaps his sons and daughters have sinned and cursed God in their hearts and so he continually interceded on their behalf. Now,do not cease to go on your knees daily and regularly to pray for your children.

5) Talk with Your Children about Pregnancy &Abortion

Explain abortion as the result of having sexual intercourse. Sex is not for pleasure and it is not a game. If you have sexual intercourse then there is likelihood that you will get pregnant. If you get pregnant then you have a person living inside of you, and not some lifeless tissue but a real person, with a heartbeat and a DNA. Teenage pregnancy leaves your child with several consequences: 1) economic; 2)sociological; 3)theological;4)academic.

First, economic consequences of sex and pregnancy: Talk with your child, male or female child about the economic impact of sex and pregnancy; ask them questions like: who will raise the child? Who will take care of the child while you finish school? You may have to move out and pay for your apartment, but you have no skills to get a Job so who will pay for your apartment? How will you support yourself financially? Do not be an enabler and normalize their bad decisions. Let them take responsibility for their actions and that may be better for them long term.

If you are having a son then you may ask something like: How would you feel if some dude got your sister pregnant? Are you ready to become a dad? Are you ready and able to take care of a wife and children? Second, sociological impact; Bringing a child into the world is a major responsibility. If you bring up children in poverty then there is a strong likelihood for generational poverty to be perpetuated. Thirdly; theological; sex outside of marriage is fornication and it is a sin against God that needs to be settled. Lastly, academic: Dropping out of school or college may leave your child in perpetual poverty. Is all the sex really worth it? Wait for a few years and enjoy healthy and lasting sex. No need to be in a hurry! All the sex that they will ever need is waiting for them if only they are ready to wait!

6)Get Involved and Know Your Child's Friends

Do all that you can to know who your child hangs out with. The kind of friends that they make may determine where they end up in life. Friends may sometimes have more influence on your child than you, and so it makes a lot of sense to know who they are. They are talking on the phone until 3AM, every single day and so you better know them. If all your child's friends smoke marijuana or weed and your child hangs out with them 24/7 then they too must likely do what they do. Here is a quote: [33] Do not be misled: "Bad company corrupts good character."[a] [34] Come back to your senses as you ought, and stop sinning; for there are some who are ignorant of God—I say this to your shame, 1 Corinthians 15:33-34. Your child may tell you something like this: "My friends don't influence me," really? Who are they kidding?

It is very unlikely that your child will constantly hang out with people and not do what they do. The only reason that a child makes some other child their friend is that they believe in who they are and in what they do. So parents, get involved and know your child's friends. You may have heard the saying, "show me your friends and I will tell who you are."Here is how Solomon puts it: *The one who walks with the wise becomes wise, but a companion of fools will suffer harm*, Proverbs 13:20.Warn your children to choose their friends wisely because their future may well depend on it.

7) Invest in their Spiritual Life

Buy your child a bible and encourage them to read it daily. Of-course they may only be inclined to follow your advice if the bible is a priority in your own life. A child's mental state is one of the biggest determinants for their success academically and life in general. You may often hear them say things like, "I don't know my purpose," "I am depressed," "I am lost," "I am confused". These kinds of statements come from kids in middle and high school, sometimes college and beyond. They are dealing with low self esteem and low self-worth and a host of emotional issues. They may sleep in their room for days and never talk to their parents, only come out to eat and sleep.

8) Give Your Children only what is needed:

God only gives us what is needed to sustain life and not what we want. Because, we will never be satisfied with our wants. Wants will destroy us. A child who is given everything that they want may hardly succeed in life. Show a child how to catch a fish and not always give them a fish to eat. Help them succeed but not be an enabler. Remember that they are on loan from God to you and your job is to prepare them to be released into the world. I have seen countless cases where parents are doing everything for a child who is in their late twenties and early thirties. That is not love but destruction. They will never walk until they crawl. Stop catching them! Sometimes, if you let them fall, they will get up !

9) Listen to Your Children!

Listen to their concerns and what is on their mind. Build trust with them so that they can share their hurts and accomplishments with you. You may not always agree with them but listen to them.

10) Be Your Kid's Life Coach!

Allow them to talk to you about anything! Talk to girls about what to say or how to respond when boys approach them for sex. Remember that this is totally new territory for them. Think about a girl being approached by a boy for the very first time. She was never coached on how to respond to such advances. She is just thrown out there to figure things out for herself. It is like throwing a wolf in the midst of lions! It will be eaten alive! Remember that most boys have only one thing on their mind! Sex! And they will destroy any girl that will succumb to their advances. Talk about owning and operating a car, getting a driver's license, opening a bank account. A lot of parents don't even know how to check the oil level in their car and so their kids are in trouble. Lastly, point their hearts to Jesus, let them excel in academics, preserve sex for marriage and enjoy a full life.

Advice to Middle and High Schoolers Concerning Sex and Life

1) Children, Obey Your Parents in all things Lawful

Parents are the first authority figures in your life. Just in case you didn't know, you were created to be under authority.

The sooner you know and believe this, the easier your life will be. I know that you may believe that you are now in high school and you are free to do as you please. Not quite! You will be under authority all your life and your parents are the first in a series of such authority figures. If you don't obey your parents, you will not obey your teachers. You will not obey the police on the highway; you may passively obey your boss on your first job only because you want your check. You may not obey the government and end up dead or in jail soon. It all begins with obeying your parents. I also understand that you cannot truly obey your parents until you have been given a transformed and regenerated heart. Sin is keeping you from obedience. Please, ask God to give you a new heart and new abilities so that you can truly obey God, your parents, your teachers, and all other authority figures who will come your way. Enjoy life to the fullest.

Here is what God said: *Children, obey your parents in the Lord, for this is right, "Honor your father and mother," "(this is the first commandment with promise; that it may go well with you and you may live long in the land,"* Ephesians 6:1-3. *Children, obey your parents in everything, for this pleases the Lord*, Colossians 3:20. If you are disobeying your parents, it is because you are,first and foremost, disobeying God. Unless you are in good standing with God, you can not be in good standing with anyone else, and all will not go well with you, and whatever you do, you will not prosper.

2) Never Talk Back or Argue with your Parents

Talking back and arguing with your parents is a very risky business. Talk with them in a calm tone of voice, not argumentative. In Ephesians 6:1-3, *you are commanded to honor your parents*. The word "honor" carries the idea of reverence and fear of your parents. They are not your pal,and you will exchange words with them back and forth.

They are your mom and dad. Give them the reverence and honor they are due. Obeying your parents is so important to God that disobedience is punishable by the death penalty.

Here is what God said about this: If a man has a stubborn and rebellious son who will not obey the voice of his father or the voice of his mother, and, though they discipline him, he will not listen to them, then his father and his mother shall take hold of him and bring him out to the elders of his city at the gate of the place where he lives, and they shall say to the elders of his city, "This our son is stubborn and rebellious; he will not obey our voice; he is a glutton and a drunkard." Then all the men of the city shall stone him to death with stones. So you shall purge the evil from your midst, and all Israel shall hear, and fear, Deuteronomy 21:18-21. The death penalty was instituted by God as a remedy for disobedience to parents. Disobedience is sin and it spreads like cancer. The disobedient person must be killed for sin not to spread and instill fear on the rest not to walk in disobedience.

3) Do not think that you know more than your Parents

You may become a medical doctor, lawyer but your parents never finished 12th grade. Or you are 15 and in high school, your parents are three times your age and you think that you know more than them. This is also sin and pride. Stop it before it destroys you.

4) Respect your Teachers

Arguing with your teacher in class may make you look cool in-front of your friends but not in-front of God and your parents. It is actually a disgrace to your parents and to God to disrespect your teachers. Remember that someday you may come back to that teacher to write your college admissions recommendation and they will remember and never lie about your character.

5) Abstain from Sex before Marriage

I understand that this goes against culture. You don't have to follow culture. You don't have to follow what everyone else is doing. You can be alone and be right. Yes you may be ridiculed for not having a boy or girlfriend but follow God and not the crowd. In Daniel 6:10-24, Daniel was a teenage Israelite who was captured and taken to Babylon; he stood alone obeying God and disobeying the King. You will always win by obeying God even when you are alone. Your body is not for sexual immorality but to be enjoyed in a healthy marital union.

6) Avoid Flirting

Avoid any actions that may lead to sex. Be careful how you talk to people of the opposite gender because everything is taken to mean sex. Do not say something in a text or email that you are unable to say in person. Avoid dressing that makes the opposite sex uncomfortable or drawn to you for sex.Dress to cover your body and not to expose it and attract the opposite gender for sex.

Avoid flirting with your eyes, glances, lips, walks, dances, fingers, breasts, backsides, Facebook posts, Tiktok posts and any social media posts. Boys and men most likely lack self control, so girls and women help them by dressing not to entice them but helping them to remain sober sexually. Some women and girls also struggle with self control, so boys and men help them by not enticing them with your empty flattering words that will destroy them.

7) Know your Gender and Sex

398

High and Middle school students are in a period of great confusion and uncertainty. You may be questioning who you are as a person. Don't be confused about your identity. You did not create yourself and you lack the capacity and authority to determine your identity. Your identity was set at birth. It is like a car that is manufactured by Mercedes Benz and suddenly decides that it wants to be called Ford. You can decide to be called a Ford but that will never make you a Ford.

The manufacturer sets and determines the identity and it is unalterable and unchangeable. Likewise God made mankind and set in stone his or her identity. This is pretty simple: If you are in Middle or High school and you undress in the rest-room and you look in-between your thighs, if you find something sticking out then you are a male but if you find nothing sticking out but a hole from where you urinate, then you are a female.

It is that simple and cannot be altered until death and not even a sex change will alter your internal organs that are intricately shaped by the creator. Your internal organs that determine your sex cannot be altered through surgery. It is very important that you are secure in your identity else this may lead to an unstable emotional state, struggles with self-esteem, and other emotional issues. Here is what God said about you: I will give thanks to Thee, for I am fearfully and wonderfully made; Wonderful are Thy works, And my soul knows it very well, Psalms 139:14. God says that you are fearfully and wonderfully made. Wow, let that sink into your soul! Do you truly believe that? God made you in His image and likeness. You are precious in His sight and let no one tell you otherwise. You have a choice to believe God or to believe Satan, who is the god of this world.

8) Know Your Purpose

Knowing your purpose is the single most important thing in your life. Know why you are on earth and where you go from here when it is all over.

9) Pursue your Purpose

Make it your life's mission to pursue your purpose while you have time.

10) Know your Creator

You might think that you are young and have plenty of time in your hands! People die at one and others die at one hundred. Learn to number your days. Here is what God said: *Remember your creator in the days of your youth, before the days of trouble come and years approach when you will say, "I find no pleasure in them,"* Ecclesiastes 12:1. Another text says: *How can a young man keep his life pure? By living according to your word,* Psalms 119:9. *Put God first and see what He will do with your life,* paraphrase of Matthew 6:33. Put God first and enjoy life to the fullest.

Premarital Counseling

Apart from your relationship with Jesus Christ, marriage is the second most important decision that you will ever make. How you will live the rest of your life will largely depend on the person who you select or choose as your lifelong partner. Your life on earth may be very miserable if you chose the wrong partner. Imagine that you live for sixty years and spend twenty years with the wrong person! That is one third of your life wasted! Sadly, more than fifty percent of all marriages end-up in divorce.

Premarital counseling helps both potential partners to sit down with a third party like:a pastor, marriage therapist, or someone with similar capacity to provide guidance and discernment. This counseling may help uncover things that both of you are blindsided about. Such counseling may even reveal that the differences between the potential couples are just too much to be reconciled. This is the moment of truth to determine if this is a match made in heaven or in hell. The marriage may be called off after such counseling. Several areas of guidance are probed during such counseling sessions. The topics discussed below are only to serve as a guide and never to be taken as an exhaustive list of items since each case is unique and different:

1) **Reason to get Married**

The reason to get married to that person is like the foundation of a house or a building. Everything depends on it for the marriage to succeed. One partner may be genuine and the other may have hidden and unrevealed motives. If you are not really sure as to why you are getting married to that person then back out immediately. It is like a building that is not sitting on a sure or secured foundation that may soon collapse with the wind, tornado, or hurricane. Likewise a marriage that is established for hidden or unknown reasons will soon crumble.

People get married for all kinds of reasons: Here are some of the reasons why people may get married; economic security, protection, being provided for, sex, to get immigration documents, love (erotic), and the reasons are endless. This is very difficult because you may never know what is in your potential partner's heart. They may conceal their true reason to marry and make you think only about the love (erotic) part. Marriage is way bigger than love (erotic). Look at your potential partner in the face and ask them plainly: "Why do you want to get married to me?" And listen for clues in their response if you find it to be genuine! This is not a game for it is your life! You cannot afford to make a mistake!

2) Never have sex with your potential partner before making a decision to marry

Having sex with your potential marriage partner impairs your judgment and decision making capabilities. Once you are emotionally attached to that person, you become blind and incapable of seeing anything wrong with that person. You start thinking with your vagina or your penis as opposed to using your brain or heart. Avoid any sexual intercourse so that you may be able to think clearly about the other person. Any sex at this point is also fornication and a sin against God.

Make decisions based on facts, not emotions. A person is not a car that needs to be test driven before making a buying decision. Families and friends may see things about your potential partner and warn you but you are unable to see what they are seeing because you are standing inside and they are standing outside. You are inside and too emotionally involved to see any potential faults about the other person. Stand outside and from a distance so that you may be able to see clearly before you move inside. Avoid years of future regrets. This is not a game. Avoid sexual immorality.

3) **Compatible Belief System** Is your belief system compatible with that of your potential spouse? A unified belief system will lay the foundation for the proper functioning of the marriage. How do you raise children with a divided belief system? How do you serve and worship your creator if you do not believe the same thing about your creator? A healthy marriage will depend on a unified belief system. You cannot be married to someone and you wake up one Sunday to go and worship Jesus Christ and your spouse wakes up on a Friday, and goes to the Mosque to worship Allah, or if you are Baptist and they are a Jehovah witness.

There must be a unity in belief for a well functioning marriage to happen. You may mostly have cases where someone claims to follow Jesus Christ and meet someone who does not. Now they are emotionally glued to each other and confused on what to do. Now the one who claims to follow Jesus Christ may say something like this: "Well, I know that they are not a Christian but I will evangelize to them and maybe God will save them." Really! Disaster in the making!*How can two walk together unless they are agreed?* Amos 3:3.

There is no guarantee that your partner's belief system will change down the road. Be forewarned! You cannot change anyone's beliefs; only God, by His mercy, can do that. So don't presume because you have no clue on what God will do. Having divided belief systems is like having two captains on a ship! If one says the ship should go north and the other concludes that the ship should proceed south then the ship is stuck and sinks in the middle of the Atlantic ocean and so will your marriage with divided beliefs.

4) **Money in Marriage**

Money is one of the leading reasons why many marriages end in divorce. Money problems can arise from many angles. Find out if your potential spouse is a saver or a spender. This can be a source of conflict in a marriage. One likes to spend money foolishly and the other likes to think about the future and save for rainy days. Does your spouse agree to a joint bank account or do they prefer their own bank account? Money issues will reveal a lot of things about the marriage.

Ask your potential spouse if they would like to discuss major spending decisions with you. Will your spouse agree to paying all the bills for the household just in case one of you becomes disabled or unemployed? Will you argue over who is paying what bill? Will you undertake hidden investments not discussed or known to your spouse, here or anywhere in the world? The bottom-line is that money issues are trust issues.

You cannot simply get married to someone who you don't trust. You say that you are married but are living completely separate lives. If you can't even trust your potential spouse to use your ATM card then you should not get married to that person. These are signs of bigger problems to come. Do you plan to hide any money matters from your potential spouse? If you do then you simply do not trust them and should not get married to them at all. You cannot plan to get married and also live separate lives. This is not compatible with a real marriage. Discuss money expectations! Who is responsible for what! Who pays what bill and when? Make no assumption but ask questions and demand direct answers. Any sign of evasion or not giving a direct response to questions is a red flag.

5)Marriage and Income

Income should not be a determining factor to get married to someone unless income security was the reason to get married. Income is no doubt important. If a marriage is primarily based on income then it may not last because money is never going to be enough. Nonetheless, be open to discuss your income and potential income. Ask questions like: How much money do you make? Ask about their spending habits. Ask about your potential spouse's outstanding debt obligations! Know their borrowing habits because their debts become yours.

Now, as crazy as this may sound, know your potential spouse's driving history from the DMV, credit history (score), and criminal history. I know that some might say that this is going too far and you may be correct but we are talking about someone with whom you plan to spend the rest of your life with. You need to know them well. Some one's credit history is somewhat of an indication of their character and trust. Someone with good credit also means that they can be trusted with money and many other things.

No bank will ever loan you money to buy a house or car without first running your credit and background check. Banks don't know you and they sure don't trust you either.

Isn't your potential spouse more important than a house or car? A person is more important than a car or a house. The banks must know something that we don't. The FBI will never hire anyone as an agent without running a background check, credit history, driving record and even interviewing all their family, friends and co-workers from middle school and all your neighbors at any address that they had ever used. In countries where there is no credit system, investigate your potential spouse's background by sending people to investigate their past. How do you know if you are getting married to a serial killer or rapist? That is why you don't begin by having sexual intercourse.

6) **Family Planning**

Ask your potential partner the question, "Do you want to have children?" Know this ahead of time! People assume that when people get married in heterosexual marriages that one of the main goals is to have children. You may be surprised to hear that your potential partner responds to your question about having children by saying, "No I don't want to have children!" There is no point getting married if there is disagreement on the question of procreation. These issues are discovered during premarital counseling so as to avoid disappointment and embarrassment later.

7) **Faith and Belief**

If you are a follower of Jesus Christ and are grounded in your faith and belief then it becomes very important that you only marry someone who shares your faith and belief. It would be very different if you were not a follower of Jesus Christ. You cannot be a follower of Jesus Christ and marry a non-follower thinking that you will help convert them to your faith. That is why premarital sex will cloud your judgment on these matters and you end up paying a hefty price years later. Hear what God says about getting married to unbelievers: Do not be unequally yoked together with unbelievers. For what fellowship has righteousness with lawlessness? And what communion has light with darkness? 2 Corinthians 6:14. Thinking that you may convert an unbeliever through marriage is wishful thinking.

8) **Blood Test**

Ask your potential spouse if they are willing to do a blood test, especially if you are of a child bearing age and you intend to have children. Test blood for the sickle cell gene. This may complicate the bearing of children. This may impact your decision to get married or not. Test for STDs also and it may save your life. You will not want to get married to someone who has tested positive for HIV/AIDS or some other deadly STDs, would you?. If your potential partner refuses to do a blood test then you may be wise to call off the marriage. That is why premarital sex is dangerous and irresponsible. Your life is worth more than sex, don't you think?

9) **Share Common Interests**

Try to find out what common interest do you have with your potential spouse? What will you potentially enjoy doing together on a daily basis? Do you enjoy praying together on a consistent basis? Do you enjoy regular bible studies together? Do you enjoy singing together? Do you enjoy dancing together? Do you enjoy traveling together? What common interests do you share? I will hope that your interest is your common salvation and out of that flows praying, and doing bible studies together. You may have heard the saying: "A family that prays together stays together."

10) Handling In-laws

Handling in-laws is an area of potential conflict. Does your potential spouse enjoy family gatherings or are they a loner? If you love people and love your family dearly but your potential spouse does not care about family then know what you are getting yourself into. Imagine that your potential spouse does not want your mom, dad, family and friends to call or visit you! That is a living hell! Never be rude to your in-laws if ever you intend to have a happy marriage. Be hospitable to your in-laws if you intend to have a happy marriage.Never insult your in-laws, especially mother, father, brother, and sister-in-law. That may potentially end your marriage. Those are your own children's grandparents that you are insulting. Think about that!

11) Conflict Resolution

Discuss in advance how you will handle and resolve conflicts. Will you need a third party intervention or will you be able to handle it on your own? Make it a rule never to go to bed angry. It may be easier to follow this if you are both followers of Jesus Christ. Resolve disputes on the same day. Tomorrow is a new day. Here is what Paul said: *Be angry but do not sin; do not let the sun set on your anger*, Ephesians 4:26. Decide in advance who will be called to resolve conflicts when and if unable to reach a resolution.

12) Infidelity in Marriage

This is probably the leading cause of divorce anywhere in the world. Discuss fidelity with one another. Discuss in advance if your potential spouse intends to be faithful to you. Look them in the eye and ask, "Will you be faithful to me and to your God?I need to know this now."

13) **Career Choice and Educational Level**

Discuss career choice and educational level with your potential spouse to be sure that you are comfortable. Your potential spouse may make a good income as an airline pilot but they are never home. Are you ready and willing to live with that? Or they may be an ER nurse who always works overnight, how would you feel about that? Your spouse is a medical doctor, lawyer or pharmacist and you have a high school diploma, will there be conflict because of the gap in education level?Don't expect your spouse to be educated to your level after you are married. That may be a potential source of conflict.

Other Premarital Questions to Consider and Ponder

14) How would you feel being betrayed with infidelity?

15) How important is your belief in God?

16) How important is the bible to you?

17) What are your ideas about who should do household chores?

18) What are your ideas about who should pay the rent, mortgage and utilities etc.?

19) Is going out to night clubs and partying important to you?

20) Will you be satisfied with having sex only with your spouse or is it ok to try others also?

21) What are your ideas about who should clean, cook, wash dishes, take out trash and do laundry?

22) How do you feel about having a joint bank account or separate?

23) Do you trust your potential partner?

24) Do you love your potential partner unconditionally?

25) Have you ever caught your potential partner in a lie about simple things?

26) How would you feel if your potential partner does not share your faith?

27 How would you feel if you do not attend the same Church or faith?

28) Are you ready to cut all contacts including sexual ties with past relationships?

29) Are you comfortable listing your spouse as beneficiary to your life insurance policy?

30) How do you feel about drinking any intoxicating drink if your spouse does not?

31) How do you feel about smoking cigarettes, weed, marijuana or whatever if your spouse does not?

32) How do you feel about taking any controlled substances?

33) How do you plan to handle conflicts?

34) What are some things that irritate you?

35) How would you handle your spouse if they are a perfectionist and you are not?

36) Do you like to plan and do everything on time?

37) Do you like to procrastinate?

38) Are you very organized and neat?

39) Are you very disorganized?

40) Do you experience snoring while sleeping? (Sounds crazy but it may be a point of irritation for some)

41) Do you prefer public or private school for your children?

42) What is your idea about disciplining children?

43) Is your spouse dependable?

44) Can you count on them when really in need?

45) Can they put your needs above theirs?

Put Jesus Christ at the center and enjoy the ride. Enjoy life to the fullest with Jesus!

Marital Counseling

Now you made the decision, and are in a marriage and if things are going well for your marriage then we praise God but for many others things may not be going so well. What went wrong and where do we go from here? There isn't much to say if your marriage is going pretty well with no major issues but a lot of marriages are in trouble and I really mean deep trouble.

Images from counseling site. [210]

Couples do not go to talk to a third party unless they are in serious trouble. They must have exhausted all available resources before the decision is made to go and talk to a

---

[210]

https://anchorlighttherapy.com/33-premarital-counseling-questions-from-a-couples-therapist/

third party. To be honest and frank, the state of marriages is not good. There are some good marriages but on the overall, things look pretty bleak. And so if your marriage is in trouble, never think for a moment that you are alone because that is furthest from the truth. Here are some stats on the state of marriages: *Marriage and divorce are both common experiences for adults, although both can be challenging. About 90% of people in Western cultures marry by age 50. In the United States, about 50% of married couples divorce, the sixth-highest divorce rate in the world. Subsequent marriages have an even higher divorce rate: 60% of second marriages end in divorce, and 73% of all third marriages end in divorce.*[211]

This is the state of marriages in America and if you are married today then there is a 50 percent chance that your marriage will end in divorce. And that chance is even greater for second and third marriages. Here are some more stats on marriages: *The average age for couples going through their first divorce is 30 years old. Couples are more or less likely to get divorced based on several factors. Couples married between the ages of 20-25 are 60% likely to get a divorce. Those who wait until they are older than 25 to get married are 24% less likely to get divorced. Those with strong religious beliefs are 14% less likely to get a divorce. The higher attainment of education someone has, the lower their risk of divorce is. According to a U.S. Census Bureau survey, the top three reasons for divorces are*

[211]

https://worldpopulationreview.com/state-rankings/divorce-rate-by-state

incompatibility (43%), infidelity (28%), and money issues (22%)[212].

Interestingly, this secular survey gives evidence to back what this book is all about. The survey finds out that, "those with strong religious beliefs are 14% less likely to get a divorce." This secular study only validates and makes the case for the thesis of this book. They carefully used the phrase, "strong religious beliefs," to set apart those who are less likely to divorce. This group sets themselves apart from the rest. The divorce rate in the churches is not much different from that of the general population because most church members do not have any core convictions about their beliefs.

Another survey found out that only about 2% of people who say that they are born-again are committed to a consistent daily bible study and prayer. Most are merely church goers and not followers of Jesus Christ. Only those with strong doctrinal convictions would hardly contemplate divorce. And no one would gain any doctrinal conviction without spending a lot of time in the bible and in constant prayer. And for most, the church is a social gathering place on a Sunday morning, so it is then no surprise as to the state of marriages today. Imagine what happens in most marriages! Two sinful, selfish, egoistic human beings are merged together and are made to cohabit together. It will be a miracle if they last more than three years together. Each person is there for their own

---

212

https://worldpopulationreview.com/state-rankings/divorce-rate-by-state

interest and gain. It is like trying to mix oil and water. Even those that manage to hang in there without any strong faith may have other reasons for hanging in there. That is also why some with no strong belief may hang in there until that last child turns 18 and goes to college, then all fall apart. They stayed together this long because of the children and once they are done then the marriage falls apart; not true for all but for most. So what are some reasons why marriages struggle?

1) Lacking strong beliefs and doctrinal convictions

People may have a lot of knowledge but very little doctrinal conviction.

2) Infidelity

Infidelity is often listed as the top reason for most marital problems but underneath all of that is a faulty belief about sex and marriage. Lacking the spirit of God and doctrinal conviction.

3) Money

Money is also listed as probably the second source of marital problems. Love of money and greed are at the root. Constantly arguing over money will definitely bring a marriage to its knees. If there is no love of money and greed then this will hardly be an issue. This love of money is no doubt quoted as the root of all kinds of evil. It is impossible to love money and God. You must give up one for your marriage to strive.

When couples are considering marriage counseling then that means that they are unable to resolve the differences on their own. They may not even be talking with each other. They may be sleeping in separate rooms in the same house and may have been doing that for a few years. One of them may have moved out of the house and lived elsewhere.There may have been repeated calls to the police to intervene. There may be physical hostility towards each other. The home has become a hostile environment and the children are caught in-between.

Things may have been said to each other that can simply not be withdrawn. Insults have been thrown at each other that everything seems hopeless. There may have been no sexual intercourse between them for a while, sometimes a few years. There is not even the desire for that.This is where the partners are vulnerable to infidelity, adultery. There may even be a restraining order in place to keep the partners apart and to prevent further violence. The marriage counselor has to determine the state of the marriage. Is there any hope? Are the differences reconcilable? Depending on the context and situation, the counselor may talk with each partner separately and then talk with them together.

During those separate sessions you may often hear each party accusing the other of being the one causing all the problems.The counselor may play more of a listening role than a fixing role.Of course, behavior that is detrimental should not be ignored. One goal is to get them talking to one another, point where each went wrong, let each accept responsibility for their actions and point them to a new direction. Admission of wrong is key to changing any behavior for the better. Forgiveness of the wrong of the other party is also a very powerful tool in moving forward. If one party refuses to forgive the other party then there is no reconciliation. You cannot hold onto the wrong of your partner and also want to stay in the marriage. They are mutually exclusive! If they admit wrong doing then forgive them and you may still find a place in your heart to forgive even if they refuse to admit wrong doing.Here are some probing questions that may be asked!

4) Do you want to stay together?

5) Do you love (agape) your other half?

6) What do you like most about them?

7) Do you trust them?

8) Can you give the marriage another chance?

9) Are you seeing anyone else? Do you expect to?

10) How did you get here?

11) What do you expect from your partner?

12) Where do you see your marriage years from now?

13) What changes do you expect from your spouse?

14) Will you accept their forgiveness?

15) Do you have difficulty letting off the wrong that they did?

16) Are you very angry and bitter?

17) Are you ready to accept God's forgiveness for you?

18) Are you ready to extend that same forgiveness to your partner?

At the end of the individual session, the couple is brought in for a joint session. This may be the first time that they are sitting together in over a year, maybe two years. So it may be a little tense. They are seated next to each other and looking each other in the eyes. At this point they both have given indications that they want to work things out and save the marriage. So at this point the counselor may ask them to look at each other and take turns in saying, "I have forgiven you," and wait for an audible response from the other party in accepting your offer of forgiveness.

Once forgiveness has been offered and accepted by both then it is hoped that reconciliation has been achieved. The counselor may ask the couple to stand and hug each other. The counselor may encourage the couple to be part of a bible believing church and be involved in regular bible study and prayer so that they may grow together in their faith. And if reconciliation is not achieved then divorce is probably the only next viable option.

Divorce Counseling

Now that you have tried everything to save your marriage and it did not work or the abuse was so bad that you were completely exhausted and just could not take it anymore, and either you or both of you could not reconcile your differences,then divorce is the only option left. This is a pretty painful experience to be avoided if possible. Divorce rips families apart, including children, and lives are sometimes altered beyond repair.

Or maybe one of you has already contacted a divorce attorney but you have not yet signed the retainer agreement as you are weighing your options. The house that both of you bought years ago is about to be sold or foreclosed upon and all your joint bank accounts have essentially been closed. The children have now been taken to live with their maternal grandmother while things are being sorted out. There are all kinds of emotions going through both of your minds.

There are feelings of rejection, abandonment, fear, anxiety, worthlessness, low self-esteem, depression and downright suicidal ideation being bombarded through both of your minds at a rapid pace. The result is that one or both of you are suffering from high blood pressure, chest pain and sudden cardiac problems because of the heightened levels of rapidly changing emotions. This is the real world and this is the situation for millions of people around the world on a daily basis. There are rarely winners and losers in most divorce cases except for the attorneys involved raking in millions of dollars.

So going through a divorce, especially in cases where you never truly saw it coming, hurts a whole lot. Maybe you thought that you were in a really good marriage and invested a lot into the marriage then suddenly, you caught your spouse in the act of infidelity. Your entire world is turned upside down. So life has basically come to an end, so it seems. So going through this kind of divorce is like receiving the news of the sudden death of a loved one, because divorce is actually death. As you may well know from reading my other books, death is a separation of two entities.

When someone dies physically, it simply means that the soul or spirit has separated from the body. When people die spiritually, it simply means that they are separated from God though yet physically alive. When someone dies eternally then it simply means that they are separated from God eternally or for all eternity. So divorce is death or sudden death as it is the separation of two people. And so if love was really involved then one or both parties will experience the four stages of grief: (1) Denial: Once the news breaks, that your spouse was caught pants down in an affair, your first reaction is denial and total disbelief.

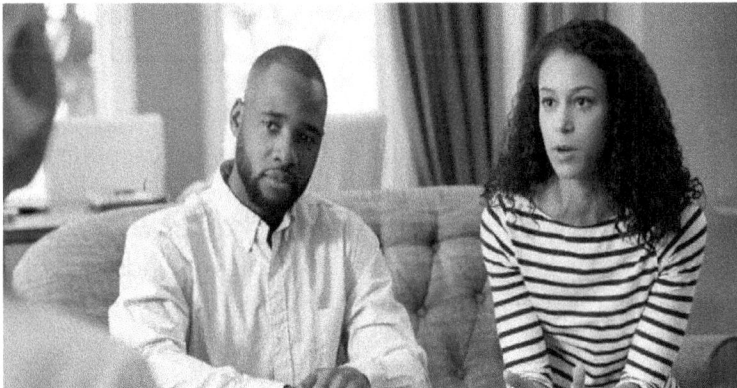

Your next reaction is (2) Bargaining: You may be bargaining with God that if this is not true then you will do better in your marriage. (3) Despair: Now all the facts and evidence are out and they are indisputable that your spouse whom you love dearly has fallen over into the arms of someone else. Then lastly, (4) Acceptance & Recovery: You are slowly coming to terms with reality and trying to pick up the pieces to move forward to see if the marriage is salvageable or not.

At the root of most if not all divorce cases is the foundation upon which the marriage was standing. Even a house or a building with a faulty foundation may take years to finally crumble when tested through the storms. So is a marriage built on a shaky foundation. It may appear to stand for a while but it will eventually crumble. A marriage must be built on the rock and any marriage that is built on sand cannot take root because it is built on the sand and when the storms of life come upon it then it will crumble because it is standing on sand.

Have you ever built a house on sand as the foundation? What happens when the storms come upon it standing on the sand? It will crumble and great will be its fall! A marriage that is not built on Christ is like a house that is built on a sandy foundation. It is not stable and always shifting with the wind or storm. Very unreliable, and not dependable.

I am sure you don't want to spend your vacation in any house built on sandy foundations by the beach prone to hurricanes, would you? So is a marriage built on a sandy foundation. Here is what Jesus said about two kinds of foundations: [24] *"Therefore, everyone who hears these words of Mine, and ₐacts on them, will be like a wise man who built his house on the rock.* [25] *And the rain fell and the ᵇfloods came, and the winds blew and slammed against that house; and yet it did not fall, for it had been founded on the rock. ²⁶ And everyone who hears these words of Mine, and does not ʿɡact on them, will be like a foolish man who built his house on the sand. ²⁷ And the rain fell and the ɡfloods came, and the winds blew and slammed against that house; and it fell—and its collapse was great."* Matthew 7:24-27.

Christ is the foundation upon which you should build your marriage. And He is not only the foundation upon which the entire building rests, but is also the Chief cornerstone of the building. Here is a definition of a chief or head cornerstone: *A chief or head cornerstone is placed above two walls to maintain them together and avoid the building from falling apart.* [213] Below is an image of a chief or head corner stone that holds the building together.

Interestingly, Jesus Christ is identified as the chief cornerstone upon which the church is built. If you are in Christ then your marriage is built on the cornerstone. Here is what is said of Christ as the cornerstone: *¹⁹ Now, therefore, you are no longer strangers and foreigners, but fellow citizens with the saints and members of the household of God, ²⁰ having been built on the foundation of the apostles and prophets, Jesus Christ Himself being the chief cornerstone, ²¹ in whom the whole building, being fitted together, grows into a holy temple in the Lord, ²² in whom*

213

https://www.google.com/search?q=what+is+a+chief+cornerstone+ in+architecture&oq=what+is+a+chief+corner&aqs=chrome.2.0i512j 69i57j0i512j0i10i22i30j0i22i30j0i15i22i30j0i22i30l4.18273j0j4&sour ceid=chrome&ie=UTF-8#imgrc=m1HZhhh4g9HYfM

you also are being built together for a dwelling place of God in the Spirit, Ephesians 2:19-22.

Image of a Chief or Head Corner Stone in a building

So if you build your marriage on any other foundation then it will be unsustainable or if it is not resting on the chief cornerstone then it will soon come to ruin.

So what does God think about Divorce?

Any divorce hurts the heart of God but especially that of a God ordained marriage. You may have heard me use the term "God ordained marriage" very often but is there really a God ordained marriage? That is a fair question! Some have argued that every marriage is ordained by God but is that really the case? Listen to this profound statement: *⁵and said, 'FOR THIS REASON A MAN SHALL LEAVE HIS FATHER AND HIS MOTHER AND BE JOINED TO HIS WIFE, AND THE TWO SHALL BECOME ONE FLESH'? ⁶So they are no longer two, but one flesh.*

Therefore, what God has joined together, no person is to separate," Matthew 19:5-6. So in this text, Jesus made an exposition of Genesis 2:24 and expounded that the two shall become one flesh and because they are one flesh, they cannot be separated. This is a mystery to the human mind. Now if they are truly joined then they are no longer two but one. They have a unified purpose to serve God. Their individual plans have perished because they are no longer two. Then God made this very profound statement: "what God has joined together, let no man separate." This is very profound in the context of divorce. But what about the exception clause?

Marriage Exception Clause

Jesus had an interaction with the Pharisee concerning divorce and here is what some Pharisees asked Jesus: *Some Pharisees came to [b]Jesus, testing Him and [c]asking, "Is it lawful for a man to [d]divorce his wife for any reason at all?,* Matthew 19:3. A lot has been made of the exception clause as grounds for divorce but a lot has also been ignored. There is the question that was raised by the Pharisee and this is very important to note. The purpose of the question was to test Him (Jesus) and not to seek the truth.

Their intention has never been to seek the truth but to trip Jesus in order to have Him arrested and killed. They were not seeking to know anything about divorce but only to test Him. They could have asked the question like this if they were sincere: "Is it lawful for anyone to divorce their spouse for any reason at all?"

They instead asked the question using,"man," implying that only men can seek a divorce for any reason. And taking their question at face value and the subsequent response by Jesus would mean that a woman cannot divorce for sexual immorality but a man can.

The Pharisees were probably reading into what Moses said about divorce and here it is: *"When a man takes a wife and marries her, and it happens, if she finds no favor in his eyes because he has found some indecency in her, that he writes her a certificate of divorce, puts it in her hand, and [a]sends her away from his house,* Deuteronomy 24:1. So Moses was saying that a man could divorce his wife because he has found some indecency in her. So the intent of the Pharisee was to tempt Jesus. The Greek word that is translated in Matthew 19:3 as testing is "Peirazo," and this word could also be translated as *tempt, test, to solicit to sin, the tempter*[214] This same Greek word could be translated into English as a test.

This word should be translated in Matthew 19:3 as "tempt," not a test. The King James Version is one of a few translations that got it right. A test has the best of intentions to reveal your character but a temptation is intended to cause the one being tempted to sin or stumble. So the intentions of the Pharisees were to trip Jesus as they asked Him, "*Is it lawful for a man to divorce his wife for any reason at all?*" If Jesus had said no then the Pharisees would have used that to accuse Him of not following that law of Moses. That would have been enough evidence to incite the population against Jesus since the population revered Moses. But Jesus, knowing their thoughts, did not give them the response that they were expecting but instead used the

---

[214]   https://biblehub.com/thayers/3985.htm

question to expound on the permanency of marriage. Jesus expounded on the permanency of marriage by quoting Genesis 1:27 and 2:24 in Matthew 19:4-6.

Then the Pharisees returned with a rebuttal by asking this question: *They said to Him, "Why, then, did Moses command to* GIVE HER A CERTIFICATE OF DIVORCE AND SEND HER AWAY?" Matthew 19:7.This is a fair question! You say that there is no divorce but Moses allowed for divorce! They are basically asking the question, Is He contradicting Moses? and He will respond by saying, not at all! Here is what He said: He said to them, *"Because of your hardness of heart Moses permitted you to [a]divorce your wives; but from the beginning it has not been this way,* Matthew 19:8. Moses allowed for divorce to accommodate the people but it was not God's plan and desire. Just as the Israelites wanted a King like all the other nations and God gave them Saul but that does not mean that God approved of it but because of the hardness of their hearts, God gave them Saul and so it is with divorce.

Divorce was allowed because of sin. Jesus was speaking to a mixed audience: the Pharisees and His disciples! They both heard the same message but ended up with different conclusions. The Pharisees heard that you can divorce for sexual immorality and His disciples heard that you cannot divorce at all based on their response and here it is: *The disciples said to Him, "If the relationship of the man with his wife is like this, it is better not to marry."*Matthew 19:10. His disciples clearly understood marriage to be permanent but the Pharisees did not. That was what they (Pharisees) wanted to hear and that is what they got. They got the answer that they wanted and remained in their sins. This exception only appeared as a response to the Pharisees question. Paul wrote a lengthy thesis on marriage in 1

Corinthians 7 and not once did he mention sexual immorality as a divorce exception and why is that? No other New Testament author mentioned any exception to divorce. The exception clause was only introduced as a response by Jesus to the Pharisees, whose goal was to tempt and trap Jesus. He responded by keeping them in their blindness.

Marriage in a God ordained union is joined by God. For marriage to be joined by God, there must be evidence that the two are indeed one flesh. God Himself must be present in both of their lives. The spirit of God must be active and present in both of their lives, for without which, God did not join them together. Think about this philosophically! How can a being with lesser power undo what a being with much greater power has joined? How can man separate what God has joined?

If that were possible then man would be incharge, not God. How do you rip apart one flesh? Even the secular evidence supports this thesis! This divorce rate among couples with a devout faith is very low and near impossibility. But if it happens then it breaks God's heart. God hates divorce, Malachi 2:16. Divorce is a very complex matter and every context may be different and may God grant you wisdom as you seek His guidance. This section is not able to look at every possible nuance in the matter of divorce. Some questions to consider and ponder as you may be contemplating divorce:

1) If your spouse wants to work things out are you willing to reconsider?

2) Is the reason for the divorce adultery?

3) Do you have any doubts if your spouse genuinely cares about you?

4) Does your spouse get along well with your side of the family?

5) Are you willing and ready to admit to any wrongs done to your spouse?

6) Can you name at least one or more things that you have done that your spouse doesn't like?

7) Do you readily admit you are wrong about anything?

8) Do you have difficulty admitting that you are wrong about anything?

9) Do you readily take responsibility for your actions?

10) Do you find it very difficult to say that you are sorry to your spouse?

11) Do you readily accept forgiveness from your spouse?

12) Do you often cut your spouse off when they are talking?

13) Are you a good listener?

14) Do you often interject before your spouse finishes talking?

15) What activities do you do together?

16) Does your spouse often tell you where they are going and when they will return?

17) Does your spouse value and respect your opinion in decision making?

18) Is your spouse dismissive of your opinion in decision making?

19) Is there mutual consultation in family decision making?

20) How do you handle disagreements in decision making?

21) Do you ridicule your spouse in front of others, including close family?

22) Do you discuss your spouse's sexual performance with anyone outside your bedroom?

23) Is your spouse part of you?

24) Do you put your interest above your spouse's?

25) Do you find it difficult to forgive anyone who has hurt you with their words or actions?

26) Are you willing to forgive your spouse even if you are proceeding with the divorce?

27) Will you accept forgiveness from your spouse?

28) Are you ready and willing to accept God's forgiveness?

29) Are you willing to commit to praying with your spouse daily?

30) Are you willing to commit to a weekly bible study with your spouse?

31) Are you ready to ask Jesus Christ to take control of your heart?

32) Will you commit to be part of a bible believing church and grow in your faith?

If God has changed your heart then enjoy the ride in your new found faith. My prayer is that you remain married and grow stronger together. But maybe you have already filed for divorce and you are finally divorced or you and your spouse have a change of heart or you are thinking about marrying someone else but you are a little confused.

Appendix F

Re-Marital Counseling

So now you may be divorced and contemplating remarriage, but you may be a little skeptical and confused. Getting remarried is a very emotional place to be especially to a new person whom you know little or nothing about. All the old emotions are rushing through your heart and you want to be sure that you are doing the right thing. You surely should have every reason to be worried because history is not in your favor. Second and third marriages fail at a much higher rate. About 60% of second marriages fail and over 70% of third marriages fail.

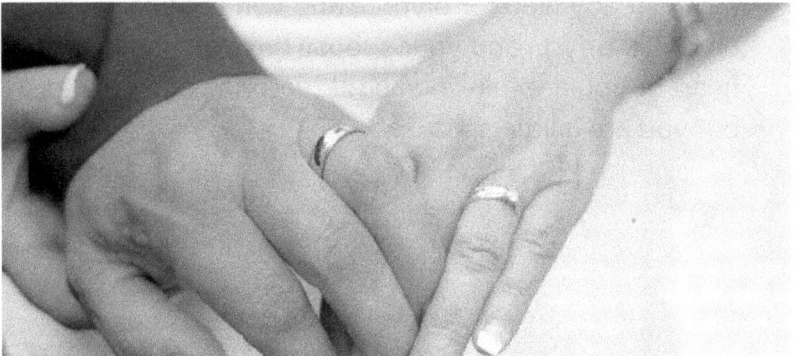

You may be filled with fear, guilt, shame and anxiety from the previous marriage and saying to yourself, is it worth the trouble? Going through a divorce is traumatic enough but plunging into another marriage may be even more traumatic. There is societal shame from being a divorcee and getting remarried may even compound the problem.

It may not be a wise idea to rush right into a new marriage after just ending another. It may make sense to take some time to reflect on yourself and to know yourself a little deeper. Ask questions like what is driving you to rush into another marriage and sometimes, even rushing into dating. Are you truly secure in your own skin? Do you feel incomplete without another human being of the opposite sex in your life? The simple truth is that no human being can make you adequate or complete. This longing may be an indication of some much deeper emotional and spiritual problems. Our completeness and adequacies are in Christ alone and no human being has the ability to make us complete and adequate. You may never attain true completeness and happiness if you are seeking that from another person with a sinful nature like yours. Feel complete alone and God will bring someone into your life at the appropriate time.

So, some may question if remarriage after a divorce is even a possibility! Depending on your views on marriage, divorce then remarried will all be affected. If someone holds very strong views that marriage is permanent then they may also frown at divorce and remarriage. I believe that the bible teaches that there is no divorce in a God ordained heterosexual monogamous marriage. Now if there is no divorce then there will be no need for remarriage because no one divorced. This may not apply to you if you are not in a God ordained marriage, which is the case for most people. No one can obey God's law unless God's spirit is living inside of them. Your relationship with Jesus and your beliefs about marriage and divorce will definitely affect your views about remarriage.

After just separating from a very difficult and abusive marriage, many may hurriedly run into another relationship or marriage after not being completely healed from the first. Piling wounds of hurt over wounds of hurt. Some just feel empty, alone and lonely. Rushing into another relationship to heal these emotional wounds may prove to be catastrophic after all. So search into the deaths of your soul to truly know what is underneath your decision to get remarried so quickly?

For some, it is a struggle with loneliness! You see, being alone and being lonely are completely different! Being alone means lacking physical companionship with another human being. A dog has earned the title of "man's best friend," but you are still alone when you are with your dog in bed or wherever. But being lonely is an indication of the spiritual condition of your heart. If you are feeling empty and void of purpose then that may be an indication of the emotional and spiritual condition of your heart.

So getting into another marriage may temporarily remedy your problem of aloneness but may hardly provide any lasting remedy to the more deeper and important problem of loneliness. (Consult my other book titled "Fending off Suicidal Thoughts" on the difference between aloneness and loneliness). If you are really feeling empty and lonely then ask God to help you and He is ready. But on the question of remarriage, what does the bible say about that?

Remarriage in the Bible

The bible has quite a lot to say about remarriage. Here is how Paul began this chapter:1 *Now concerning the things about which you wrote, it is good for a man [a]not to touch a woman,*[2] But because of sexual immoralities, each man is to have his own wife, and each woman is to have her own husband 1 Corinthians 7:1-2. Paul began this chapter admonishing his readers to abstain from all sexual contact and then he goes on to say that because of sexual immorality, get married.

Paul goes on to argue in the chapter that marriage is good but singleness with contentment is better so that the person can give full devotion to God without distraction. Here is Paul's admonition on marriage and divorce: *¹⁰ But to the married I give instructions, not I, but the Lord, that the wife is not to leave her husband ¹¹ (but if she does leave, she must remain unmarried, or else be reconciled to her husband), and that the husband is not to ⁽ⁱ⁾divorce his wife,* 1 Corinthians 7:10-11.

This is Paul expounding on what Jesus said in Matthew 19 and 5, that there is no exception for divorce, else Paul would have said so. Here is Paul's final admonition on the issue of remarriage: *³⁹ A wife is bound as long as her husband lives; but if her husband ⁽ʷ⁾dies, she is free to be married to whom she wishes, only in the Lord. ⁴⁰ But in my opinion she is ⁽ˣ⁾happier if she remains as she is; and I think that I also have the Spirit of God,* 1 Corinthians 7:39-40.

Paul makes the final argument here that there is no room for divorce if either spouse is alive. But only death will release either spouse from the marriage. In case of remarriage, they can only marry "in the lord," meaning, marrying another follower of Christ. No one, not even Paul, would expect these commands to apply to non-Christians. Once both of you are followers of Christ then you are bound by these commands.

If you are facing a remarriage decision and you are a Christian, first pray that God would open your eyes and heart to His truths. These are extremely tough decisions needing long periods of prayer and fasting. You will need plenty of wisdom to be at peace with your decision. Here are some question to ponder if you are considering remarriage:

1) Is reconciliation with your former spouse a possibility?

2) How do you feel about being alone? Does being married make you complete?

3)What was it that attracted you to your former spouse?

4) What is attracting you to a new potential spouse?

5) What lessons have you learned from your divorce?

6) How have you grown through your divorce process?

7) How important is faith and belief to you?

8) How important is the faith and belief of your potential spouse?

9)Is it okay if your potential spouse believes differently from you about Jesus Christ?

10) What mistakes do you plan not to make if you were to remarry?

11) How do you plan to embrace the children of your potential spouse?

12) What will you do if the children of your potential spouse do not respect you as their parent?

13) How will you handle disobedience from children who are not biologically yours?

14) How will you handle your spouse's ex-spouse coming over to see their children?

15)How will you blend your children and your spouse's children, if any?

16) How would the character of your new spouse be different from your former spouse?17) Were you really connected spiritually to your former spouse?

18) Will you be connected spiritually to your present spouse?

19) How will you be connected spiritually to your new spouse?

20) Do you have any non-negotiables in the character of a new spouse?

21) What is the foundation of your marital union?

22) How long would you date someone before considering marriage?

23) Do you need to have sex with them before considering marriage?

24) Can you date someone without having sex?

25) If both of you own houses from prior marriages, would you sell yours or keep it?

26) Will you be fully devoted to God and to your spouse?

27) Will you keep separate bank accounts?

28) What common interests do you have with your potential spouse?

29) What do you dislike about your potential spouse?

30) Do you have a common faith and salvation?

Settle the issue of your faith and salvation before venturing into such an adventure.Have fun and enjoy the ride!Make Christ the Lord of your life and enjoy life to the fullest.

About the Author

Waltere Asili Koti is the author of several books, including, "Fending off Suicidal thoughts," "You are Elected," "Understanding and Overcoming your Emotional Issues," "Understanding and Overcoming your Emotions," and recently, "The Power of Sex."

Waltere earned his master of divinity degree (MDiv) in theology from Capital Bible Seminary in Lanham Maryland and was completing his doctor of theology (ThD) degree from Faith Theological Seminary in Baltimore Maryland. He also completed several years of clinical pastoral education and practical training at several hospitals, including, the VA Medical Center in Hampton VA, Washington Adventist Hospital in Takoma Park MD and Washington County Hospital in Hagerstown MD. He is *a* board certified clinical chaplain and a board certified pastoral counselor. He worked as a clinical chaplain at Washington Adventist Hospital in Takoma Park, MD.

He has counseled thousands dealing with all kinds of spiritual and emotional issues, like aloneness, loneliness, fear, anxiety, depression, sexual addictions, addictions in general, marital issues and even suicidal ideation.

He lives in the Baltimore area with his wife and family.

Reviews Request

We are very grateful that you have purchased a copy of this book and have labored tirelessly to read it. We hope and pray that you have gained valuable and life transforming insight. If this book has touched and impacted your life in any way, then we will appreciate it, if you will be so kind to let others know, by leaving a review for us on Amazon, Barnes & Nobles, Goodreads, Google.

If you were looking for somewhere to eat and you found two restaurants, one with zero reviews and the other has fifty five stars reviews, where would you go to eat? Your review is very important to us.

Thank you very much for taking the time to leave a review.

www.ingramcontent.com/pod-product-compliance
Lightning Source LLC
Chambersburg PA
CBHW062111020426
42335CB00013B/926